The Comic Irishman

The Comic Irishman

Maureen Waters

Department of English
Queens College, New York

State University of New York Press   ALBANY

For my mother and father, who told the stories,
and for David, who encouraged me to write them down

Published by
State University of New York Press, Albany
©1984 State University of New York

All rights reserved

Printed in the United States of America

No part of this book may be used or reproduced
in any manner whatsoever without written permission
except in the case of brief quotations embodied in
critical articles and reviews.

For information, address State University of New York
Press, State University Plaza, Albany, N.Y., 12246

Library of Congress Cataloging in Publication Data

Waters, Maureen, 1939—
    The Comic Irishman.

    Includes index.
    1. Irish wit and humor—History and criticism.
2. English literature—Irish authors—History and
criticism. 3. Comic, The, in literature. 4. Satire,
English—Irish authors—History and criticism. 5. Irish
in literature. 6. National characteristics, Irish, in
literature. I. Title.
PR8815.W37 1984   820'.9'352039162   83-4888
ISBN 0-87395-766-0
ISBN 0-87395-767-9 (pbk.)

Contents

Acknowledgments

Part I: The Folk

Introduction   *1*
1. The Rustic Clown or Fool   *9*
2. The Rogue   *28*
3. The Stage Irishman   *41*
4. The Comic Hero   *58*

Part II: The Masque of Satire

Introduction   *84*
5. James Joyce and Buck Mulligan   *95*
6. Samuel Beckett's Murphy   *110*
7. Flann O'Brien and Mad Sweeny   *123*
8. Patrick Kavanagh and Tarry Flynn   *137*
9. The Paycocks of Sean O'Casey   *149*
10. A Borstal Boy   *161*
    Conclusion   *173*
    Notes   *181*
    Bibliography   *195*
    Index   *202*

Acknowledgments

I WISH to thank the staff of the National Library, Dublin, and the Folklore Department of University College, Dublin, for their kind assistance. I am especially grateful to Thomas Flanagan and to Agnes Waters for reading the manuscript and offering advice.

Research for this book was supported by a Research Grant from the City University of New York.

I wish to acknowledge the following for (their generous) permission to quote from unpublished material: Colin Smythe; The Rare Book and Manuscript Library, Columbia University; Department of Manuscripts, National Library of Ireland; The Head of the Department of Irish Folklore, University College, Dublin; The Henry W. and Albert A. Berg Collection, The New York Public Library, Astor, Lenox and Tilden Foundations. Thanks are also due *Éire-Ireland* for permission to republish a portion of my article, "No Divarshin': Samuel Lover's *Handy Andy*."

I

The Folk

Introduction

Because comedy necessarily mirrors the culture from which it springs, this study draws upon history and folklore as well as fiction and drama. Part I traces the development of the comic character from Handy Andy, a rustic clown or *omadhawn*, to Synge's playboy, an authentic hero. It concentrates on nineteenth century rural Ireland, a world rich in tradition but economically impoverished, where life in fairly isolated areas encouraged strong religious and communal ties. To writers of the time, many of them Anglo-Irish and Dublin born, the old-fashioned country people appeared more and more a race apart. From a distance their speech and customs began to seem amusing. "Paddy" was made sport of because of his ignorance, his whiskey drinking, his interest in pigs. And so the Irish peasant appeared on stage and in fiction as a comic character, whose incorrigible ways and talent for "blarney" became the basic ingredients of farce.

There is considerable variation in the qualities eventually associated with the nineteenth century comic Irishman, but one feature remained constant: he spoke with a *brogue*, that is, the Irish English[1] dialect attributed to the country people. The term is from the Irish word *bróg*, meaning shoe. Hence a person with a "brogue" sounded as if he had a shoe in his mouth; his speech was regarded as clumsy and unclear. The differences between Irish English and standard English were largely due to the influence of native idiom and syntax as well as to the fact that for many country people, English was a second language, imperfectly understood.

For centuries much humor has been generated by the peculiarities of Irish English. There is nothing surprising in this because deviation from the standard, whether it be in matters of language or behavior is a subject for humor the world over. In

Ireland, however, the question of language has a political edge to it because of the destruction of Irish cultural institutions through English conquest and colonization.

Native language and culture flourished until the latter part of the sixteenth century despite numerous invasions and the power of the Old English earls (that is, the descendants of the Norman invaders of the twelfth century) in Leinster and Munster. The Irish chiefs still retained their lands in the North and the West while the Old English tolerated local customs, when they did not actually adopt them, despite such legal prohibitions as the Statutes of Kilkenny in 1367. During Elizabeth's reign, however, the Gaelic[2] order was eroded through a long period of military campaigns that gradually devasted the country, killing off thousands.

Records kept by the Elizabethans bristle with contempt for Irish personal and domestic habits, for their long hair, their fondness for cattle raiding and their quarrelsome temperament. Only their *uisque beatha* (whiskey) was universally admired. Punitive measures were taken against the brehons, a hereditary class of jurists, and the poets, who were regarded as incendiaries, responsible for much of the military ardor of the ruling class.[3] Commentators agreed that in order to subdue the population, it would be necessary to make them as much like the English peasants as possible by forcibly introducing English law, customs, and language.

Historians generally cite the collapse of the Ulster rebellion in 1601 and the subsequent exile of the Gaelic chiefs as the death blow to Irish hopes for political and cultural autonomy. The people were left starving with much of their land confiscated by English settlers, protected by English garrisons and English law. The bardic tradition which depended on the patronage of the Gaelic aristocrats also broke down. The classical language fell into disuse as did the ancient and complicated art of poetic composition. English hegemony was further strengthened by the Cromwellian invasion in which approximately two-fifths of the population perished while thousands more were deported to Barbados or driven west into Connacht. War erupted again in 1689 when the Irish supported the Stuart cause and were again badly defeated. In the aftermath of the Williamite Wars, the penal laws were formulated to check further rebellion. The result was to impoverish the remaining Irish population and make it extremely difficult for an effective leadership to reemerge.

After the devastating wars of the sixteenth and seventeenth

centuries, Irish became the language of the poor and illiterate. The monasteries had been ransacked during the Reformation, and the monks who had been teachers and scribes had been disbanded. Music and poetry and tales from the early sagas were still preserved, however, in the oral tradition, and continued to be circulated in manuscript form until the late nineteenth century, the heritage of that "Hidden Ireland", which has been partially illuminated by Daniel Corkery. That Ireland, which contemporary historians like W. E. H. Lecky ignored, was regarded as vastly inferior by the settlers who became the new Anglo-Irish or Ascendancy class. The novelist Maria Edgeworth observed that the brogue was a "great and shameful defect, but it does not render the English language absolutely unintelligible." Even ministers of the established Anglican Church, to whom the people were forced to pay tithes, refused to learn Irish.

By the time the penal laws began to ease up at the close of the eighteenth century and a small middle class began to emerge, it was clear to the Irish themselves that if they were to prosper they had to learn English. The Irish language was more and more regarded as a handicap because of its association with a culture widely regarded as morally and culturally inferior to the Anglo-Saxon. This attitude grew more pronounced during the nineteenth century when many English historians were committed to ethnic or racial interpretations of history.

The Irish were placed in a paradoxical position. They were a people with a highly cultivated pleasure in the spoken word, which is reflected both in the oral tradition and in the nature of the language itself. According to the poet and critic Seán Lucy, there is a close interrelationship between Irish speech and the flexed stressed line, the so-called *amhrán* rhythm of Irish music and poetry. The language of the native speaker is "musically organized" and is "highly and subtly accented," the "musical phrases" being made up of a number of well-defined stresses linked by well-controlled "runs" of unaccented syllables. Lucy proposes that Irish speech is generally in what Gerard Manley Hopkins called "sprung rhythm."[4] Despite the high value placed on the art of language, many of the people had come to regard Irish as an inferior instrument, but their efforts to speak English resulted in the brogue, which was grounds for further humiliation.

During the nineteenth century two additional factors contributed to the decline in the number of Irish speakers. The first of these was the Great Famine, which decimated the rural population between 1847 and 1851. The second factor was the national school system, in which, according to Douglas Hyde, "teachers who knew no Irish were appointed for students who knew no English." The children in some district wore sticks, suspended from their necks, on which notches were carved to indicate any lapse into Irish, for which punishment was duly meted out. Parents were apparently so eager for their children to acquire English that they raised no objection.

When the Gaelic League was founded by Douglas Hyde in 1893 as part of the revival of Irish culture, many of the people steadfastly refused to learn or relearn the language. My father, who grew up in Sligo in Yeats country, remembers local apprehension that Irish might put a *curwhibble* or "twist" on the tongue, preventing one from speaking English "properly." The language movement came not from the people themselves, though it used their dialects and did not attempt to revive the classical language; it was Dublin based, the efforts of an educated class who were not themselves native speakers. Today, Irish is the official language of the country, taught in the schools, printed in the newspapers, but the number of native speakers has dwindled to approximately 30,000, despite government subsidies to the *Gaeltacht* or Irish speaking regions. One observer summed up the problem this way:

> Deep down, Irish is bound up in our feelings with that world
> of things "native, narrow, old peasant and poor" which we have
> been struggling desperately to get out of. We feel that a "native
> Irish" mentality and way of life betoken insecurity, insularity,
> intellectual impotence and lack of status in contemporary
> circumstances.[5]

Disparagement of the "native Irish mentality" is broadly evident in the fools and clowns which appeared in the early nineteenth century. Subsequent figures, however, reflected changing and more complex attitudes toward the old Gaelic culture, which eroded as the Irish language was displaced by English. Chapter 1 focuses on the *omadhawn* or rustic clown, best exemplified by Handy Andy in Samuel Lover's novel of the same name, which was first published in serial form in 1837. The *omadhawn* bears some resemblance to that creation of Yiddish folk culture, the *schlemiel*. Each is a born loser, a naïf, foolish in the ways of the world and easily duped by a faithless wife or cunning competitor. Each, because of an inexhaustible faith or optimism, manages to survive the vagaries of Fortune. The schlemiel, poor in material goods, is rich in imagination, which becomes his defense against reality; Handy Andy relies on sheer physical exuberance. To further clarify this type, chapter 1 also discusses comic characters created by Somerville and Ross and by Lady Gregory.

While the *omadhawn* amused Irish as well as English audiences well into the twentieth century, he was gradually superseded by the witty rogue or "broth of a bhoy" who could talk his way out of any predicament.

The rogue was a popular figure in Irish ballads and folktales of the nineteenth century. He was typically an outlaw, a highwayman, one who lived on the fringes of the community. In a particularly oppressive period in Irish history, the rogue was audacious, eloquent, clever at outwitting formidable opponents. Much of the humor associated with him had a decided tinge of the macabre, which focused on details of public execution, mutilation and deformity. In contrast to the volumes of broad and sentimental "Irish Humor" exported to England and America during this period, the comic songs and tales of the peasant or the Dublin tenement dweller were ferociously mocking and far more vital. Some of the qualities of the rogue, notably his wit and boldness, came to be associated with the Irish comic character. Chapter 2 describes some representative rogue tales, taken from folklore and from the penny press, before concentrating on Phelim O'Toole, a wonderfully comic rogue created by William Carleton (1794–1869).

In contrast to *Handy Andy*, a far more complex view of the peasant world emerges from the work of Carleton, who grew up on a small farm in Ulster. It was Carleton's intention to provide an accurate account of what remained of the older Gaelic civilization before it vanished entirely: "I found them a class unknown in literature, unknown by their landlords, and unknown by those in whose hands much of their destiny was placed."[6] Carleton's fiction weaves back and forth between scenes of terror and degradation and scenes of wildly extravagant farce. His novels and short stories constitute the most compelling and vivid literature written in Ireland during this period.

Carleton's peasants are poor and their experience is narrowly circumscribed, but they enjoy a rich community and family life, secured by faith and tradition. While there are certainly fools among his characters, he produced not only a distinctive rogue type but a comic hero, Denis O'Shaughnessy, whose career in many ways anticipates Synge's playboy and will be discussed in relation to him.

Chapter 3 is concerned with the stage Irishman, typically a merry, whiskey drinking, pugnacious clown. The most significant figures of this type were created by Dion Boucicault (1820-1890), whose influence stretches as far as Samuel Beckett. Boucicault's characters reinforced the widely accepted image of the Irishman as a lazy, fun loving devil-may-care personality, the very antithesis of Victorian respectability. They were popular with Irish, English and American audiences and were admired by critics as discriminating as Henry James and George Bernard Shaw, particularly when played by Boucicault, himself, an accomplished actor. Myles-na-Coppaleen is clearly a relative of Handy Andy, but there are important distinctions which reveal the influence of the rogue. Myles lives outside the law, poaching salmon, distilling whiskey, refusing to work as a laborer or a servant. He is adventurous, even heroic, in a highly melodramatic way and, like Phelim O'Toole, has a flattering tongue and an innate cunning that allow him to wiggle his way out of many a compromising situation.

With *The Playboy of the Western World*, the country bumpkin becomes the actual hero of the play. He is the one folk figure who becomes fully autonomous. All the others are limited or defined by traditional values even when they are outlaws like Boucicault's rouges. Christy Mahon begins as the community scapegoat like Handy Andy, but he has enough courage and imagination to break free of that role and to become his own man. His extraordinary growth in stature is reflected in his increasing facility with words. Much of the joking about Andy has to do with his awkward speech, his blundering with the English language. The same kind of humor operates in Carleton, though it is more sophisticated and more truly amusing because of the superior abilities of his comic figures. It is their vast conceit that we laugh at as well as the extravagance of their imaginations. Christy also talks with a brogue but by sheer creative energy transforms his language into poetry, quite powerful enough to win that fierce woman, Pegeen Mike, and to convince the community of his own prowess. It is hardly a coincidence that *The Playboy* was written on the eve of revolution in Ireland, in fact, during the land wars in Mayo that won the small farmer ownership of the fields he tilled.

It is instructive to compare Irish comedy to the pattern of the Menandrine tradition or New Comedy, which influenced Moliere and Jonson and is still popular today. In this tradition the hero is embattled with some authority figure and must successfully overthrow that figure before he can win the girl of his choice. The comedy depends on a reversal of the classical oedipal situation; the social order is represented by the *senex* (father figure) with whom the hero comes to terms when he gratifies his desire.[7]

Now all of the comic figures discussed in Part 1 must deal with authority whether they are sons, or servants or outlaws. But authority in Ireland, particularly as it was embodied in the father or the priest or the owner of the Big House, was seldom a laughing matter. There was an enormous gap between those in power and those who were powerless. Even in the nineteenth century the landlord could turn a tenant out of his home or raise the rent at whim; there was no recourse before the law. The priest who represented the eternal power of the Church, and was frequently the only educated man in the community, was feared and respected. Ireland was traditionally a patriarchal society, and those fathers who owned their own land enjoyed unusual authority. The son who was selected as heir, and he was not necessarily the eldest, had to wait in patient celibacy until the father was willing to give up mastery of the house with title to the farm. The daughters were also affected. If no dowry had been accumulated for them, and usually only one daughter might expect such a dowry, they had to choose between emigration and servitude in some one else's home. In nineteenth century Ireland few young people could afford to marry solely for love. Survival depended on economic considerations. Marriages were arranged through careful bargaining to assure that each partner was offering equal value in property or money.

This social pattern helped to determine the peculiar rhythms of Irish comedy. Neither Handy Andy nor Denis O'Shaughnessy comes into his own until his father has died. Only then do they marry and become reconciled to their respective communities. Neither of them has a serious quarrel with the world in which he finds himself, and so their final reconciliation does not result in a "deliverance from moral bondage"; Andy and Denis will simply perpetuate the social order. The oddity of Irish comedy is that *senex* and hero may have close bonds of mutual sympathy, while the heroine is a peripheral figure. This fact is even more clear in the case of Boucicault's rogues. Ostensibly outlaws, they have considerable contempt for civil law and are quite skillful in avoiding or manipulating most forms of authority. But they are putty in the hands of the priest. And so they remain *boys*, mischievous, amiable boys, never men.

With Synge we have the first real stirrings of revolution, and it is *The Playboy*, interestingly enough, that is closest to the classic comic pattern. But even here, the force of Irish social customs is felt. Christy Mahon is the true comic hero who directly confronts his own tyrannical father and quite literally overturns him and so wins autonomy, freedom, manhood. However, the father is not simply a *senex* figure. Half mad, drunken, furious though he is, he is also heroic. Once Christy breaks his stranglehold, he is free to become more like his father, unconventional, visionary, a threat to the conservative community which is then left behind. The true *senex* figures are Michael Dougherty and the priest, who is anxious to expel "that young gaffer who'd capsize the stars." Once Christy leaves, they resume control, and there is no question that their world is sterile and embittered. At this point the play is shifting into the tragic spectrum. There is no reconciliation between man and woman, between the new vision of society and the old. Christy Mahon goes forth as a vital revolutionary spirit, but the woman he has loved remains behind.

1. The Rustic Clown or Fool

I N AN unpublished essay, "Laughter in Ireland," Lady Gregory discusses the Irish love of satire and mordant humor, offering as an example this description of a man who used to be in the Ballinasloe lunatic asylum:

> . . . that was not very mad, just a little mad and he used to
> be raking about the gate, and there was a clock over the
> gate; and one day the doctor was going out and he took the
> watch out and looked up and said to himself: "That clock is not
> right." "If it was right it wouldn't be here" said the man
> that was raking.[1]

She proposes that the broadly comic fiction and drama of the nineteenth century were created in response to an English audience which demanded "Handy Andy, the butt, the blunderer, the inferior, who to them symbolized Ireland, whose mistakes would make them feel comfortably superior, over which they could comfortably laugh."[2]

Handy Andy by Samuel Lover originally appeared in *The Bentley Miscellany* edited by Charles Dickens in 1837. It was one of the first Irish comic novels and also one of the first to employ folk materials.[3] Episodic in structure, the novel draws freely on fantasy, farce and romance, ranging in tone from the sentimental to the macabre, and includes many delightful tales like the legend of Tom Connor's cat who demanded shoes. The focal figure is Andy Rooney, who best represents the simple rustic clown popular in fiction and drama of the early nineteenth century.

The novel is set against the background of rural Ireland in the years prior to the famine. It is a turbulent and colorful world in which many of the customs and privileges of the eighteenth century landed gentry still prevail. Lover offers us a view of an emerging middle class: lawyers, apothecaries, tavern keepers, surgeons and the like, a rowdy group caught up in a round of social and political activity which has little to do with the lives of the great majority.

In these scenes Lover, who was Anglo-Irish and Dublin born, often displays a genuine understanding of the rural people. The figure of Andy Rooney does, however, present a problem. It is difficult to understand how an imaginative writer could have produced such a predictable clown. Lover seems to have become trapped by his own efforts to vindicate the Irish peasant by divesting him of "the vice and coarseness which has been so repugnant to English sympathy, and doing something to abate one of the prejudices" against his country.[4]

The key phrase here is "English sympathy," for Irish writers during this period, as Lady Gregory realized, were inordinately sensitive to English opinion, and not only because their earnings depended on it. They felt defensive because of ethnocentric theories that relegated the Irish to the lower rungs of the evolutionary ladder. The Anglo-Saxons tended to regard themselves as a superior species, uniquely fitted for Empire building, while the Celts, along with the colored people of the Empire, were regarded as innately inferior, childish, lazy, unreliable, treacherous, etc., etc. Irish poverty was widely regarded as the result of racial character and moral degeneracy.[5] The script is a sadly familiar one. As a result, even so gifted a writer as William Carleton, describing famine conditions in *The Black Prophet*, pauses in midnarrative to observe that, while the starving populace occasionally stole food, they were normally law abiding. During the nineteenth century, however, the Irish were quick to produce opposing myths. They romanticized the Gaelic tradition as Lady Morgan did in the *The Wild Irish Girl*, or they presented the peasant as broadly farcical as Samuel Lover did in *Handy Andy*.[6]

Andy is an *omadhawn*, that is, a simpleton, a figure of humor which is fairly primitive as it depends on the revelation of his ignorance or ineptitude. Poor and illiterate, Andy is unaccustomed to the ways of the gentry who employ him. He doesn't understand how the postal system works or how to serve dinner or to use any mechanical device, so he is taken advantage of as the butt of Fortune or "he who gets slapped." Virtually guileless, Andy is incapable of hitting back or improving his lot, but because he is sturdy and good humored, he never becomes a mere victim, and despite his personal confusion, events tend to work out well for those around him. Thus he is linked to the traditional figure of the Fool who was considered lucky, who drew the blows of Fortune which otherwise might have landed on more normal heads. Enid Welsford has pointed out that "the genius of the Fool is manifested by his power of deluding us into the belief that he can draw the sting of pain; by his power of surrounding us with an atmosphere of make-believe in which nothing is serious, nothing is solid, nothing has abiding consequences. . . ."[7]

Unlike the comic figures who follow him, Boucicault's rogues or O'Casey's paycocks, for example, Andy has little talent for blarney, for smoothing his way with a few well chosen words. He speaks with a brogue that is, itself, considered comic and further amuses his audience with bulls, or, more typically, blunders, stock features of the stage Irishman of the nineteenth century. These terms, which tend to overlap in meaning, require some explanation. The *blunder* grows out of the confusion of the Gaelic speaker who doesn't fully grasp the meaning of English words. For example, inquiring about the sex of a new born infant, Andy wants to know if his friend, Dick Dawson, is now "an uncle or an aunt."

The point of the *bull*, as has often been said, is its pregnancy; it is a metaphorical statement stressing apparent connections which are not real. Bulls were commonly attributed to English speakers in Elizabethan times. During the last decade of the seventeenth century with the publication of "Teagueland Jests or Bog Witticisms," the bull became associated with the Irish who had recently suffered defeat at the Battle of Boyne and, since they were no longer a military threat, they became fresh targets for comic assault. Ironically enough, it was a fellow countryman, George Farquhar, who put the bull-making Irishman on the stage in *The Twin Rivals* in 1702. Thereafter, dialogue attributed to the Irish in popular plays, such as Richard Howard's *The Committee*, was revised to conform to the growing stereotype.[8] By the nineteenth century, bulls were included in sketches of Irish life to illustrate a "laughable confusion of thought":

> Well Mick . . . "I've heard some queer stories about your doings lately." "Och, don't believe thim, surr," replied Mick. "Sure half the lies tould about me by the naybours isn't thrue."

Two Irishmen, fancying they knew each other, crossed the street to shake hands. On discovering their error, the following dialogue ensued: "I beg your pardon," cried the one. "O don't mention it," said the other. "It's a mutual mistake; you see I thought it was you and you thought it was me, and after all, it was neither of us."[9]

Andy's background, like his manner of speech, is exploited for its quaintness and local color much like Catfish Row in *Porgy and Bess*. Squalor is made to seem comic as the peasants are clearly thriving in their thatched hovels, impervious to ill health and ill temper, the women virtuous and the men sturdy, if stupid. Andy's mother and cousin Oonah dress in tatters and subsist on potatoes. The mother is a cantankerous old lady who has long despaired of her son ever amounting to anything; the cousin, simplicity herself, is there to provide a little romantic interest. Their possessions are as scanty as their clothes, and they share their living quarters with their few chickens and, of course, the pig. Much is made of that pig as an intimate of Andy Rooney's, for it was during this period in history that the pig became emblematic of Irish stubbornness and squalor. Irish peasants were caricatured, particularly in the pages of *Punch*, as pig-like,[10] and the pig was soon associated with the stage Irishman to produce a few laughs. William Carleton, the most gifted of the nineteenth century Irish writers, reversed the process in a remarkable story, "Phil Purcel, the Pig Driver," in which the wily Irish pig, accustomed to being coaxed in Latin or Gaelic, eludes his English pursuers.

As a Dublin born Anglo-Irishman, Lover would naturally see the peasant from a distance as an outsider, even though as a child he had spent time in the countryside. Today it is generally recognized that humor may be a defensive reaction against members of a minority group or a group considered socially inferior. Hugh Duncan, for example, in *Language and Literature in Society* concludes: "When we laugh together, we close ranks, so to speak, in the face of something that threatens the solidarity of the group."[11] Andy's clumsy peasant qualities are precisely those with which the cultivated Irishman would not want to be associated. Andy is being judged exclusively by what he lacks, by his inability to measure up to the standards of the upper classes. His characterization shows little if any understanding of the Gaelic culture which enriches the lives of

Carleton's people. There is no evidence that he even speaks Gaelic though there is much joking about his lack of English and his mispronunciation of that language.

There is yet another element which helps to explain Andy's popularity with English audiences. The nineteenth century was a time of turmoil when the landlords, many of whom resided in England, felt threatened by a rapidly growing and impoverished peasant class from which they extracted exorbitant rents. The uprising of 1798 was a recent memory, and the so-called ribbon societies were active in the countryside mutilating livestock and committing other outrages against the landlords and their representatives. Andy provided comic relief. He was the Step 'N Fetch It of his time, a foolish, amusing sort of fellow, quite harmless after all. He is untrustworthy, not because he is dishonest, but because he is not too bright. Fit only for the most menial kind of work, he readily accepts his role as a servant and, because he has a thick hide, he doesn't mind an occasional thrashing.

As the story progresses, however, the *omadhawn* begins to act the part of the traditional comic hero, an uneasy transformation, which Synge was to handle much more deftly in *The Playboy of the Western World*. Questioning the injustice and the blows that have been his lot, he states what are obviously the author's sentiments as hardship makes him bolder: "The law is a dainty lady; she takes people by the hand who can afford gloves, but people with brown fists must keep their distance."[12]

The truth of this observation is borne out at the finish with the melodramatic discovery that he is the long lost son of an eccentric aristocrat. He is rapidly spirited away to England (where else can his rough edges be honed down?) and eventually marries the woman of his choice after performing several astonishing feats to settle the exigencies of the plot. Thus the fool is redeemed, restored to his rightful heritage, and declared his own master. There is even a concluding feast at which Andy Rooney, the newly determined Catholic aristocrat, and Edward O'Connor, the descendant of an upper class Protestant family, sit down to dinner together. To cement the possibility of peaceful coexistence, both their wives soon find themselves in a "delicate situation," and both manage to give birth in the last chapter.

The novel ends on this note of conciliation with Andy smiling, though with better reason than before. Despite the fact that he has changed his motley for the robes of an English peer, however, the servile, foolish Andy is still there underneath his new dignities. Still the butt of humor, at dinner he manages to swallow the paper frill along with the main course. Thus Samuel Lover, despite his acknowledged sympathy for his fellow countrymen, helped to popularize the image of the Irish peasant as a childish, blundering clown. The persistence of that image effectively undermines the political solution advocated by the plot. After all, how could a simpleton be trusted to govern himself?

It is interesting to compare Samuel Lover's concept of the *omadhawn* with the figure which appears in folklore. Like Handy Andy who, when he is told to throw a pitcher out the window, throws both pitcher and water, the folk fool creates havoc by too literal a response. He is amusing because of this tendency, never because of his peasant manners, which are presented realistically rather than caricatured. Although in many stories he is simply the butt of a joke, the folk fool often has a certain cunning that demands respect; he may also resort to thievery or crude tricks to gain the upper hand. Like Handy Andy, he lacks a sense of irony and the marvelous verbal imagination of the schlemiel. Nor does he seem to be on such familiar terms with his creator. His struggles are centered on this world where he is clearly at a disadvantage, but his resiliency and energy and frequently his sheer stupidity enable him not only to survive but to outmaneuver a stronger or more clever opponent.

In "Shan an Omadhan and His Master," for example, Shan is employed by a brutal farmer who has severely injured his two brothers. By responding to the exact verbal commands of his employer (literally "casting a sheep's eye") with little regard to his intention or the dictates of common sense, Shan forces him to make ample restitution, so anxious is he to avoid further disaster. [13]

A distinction should be made between such figures and the visionary fool who plays an important role in Yeats's plays and also appears in some of Lady Gregory's works as, for example, *The Full Moon.* Of the visionary fool, Lady Gregory comments: "the pity for him is mingled with some awe, for who knows what windows may have been opened to those who are under the moon's spell, who do not give in to our limitations, are not 'bound by reason to the wheel' ". [14] *Visions and Beliefs in the West of Ireland* contains several tales of the Fool of Forth (the Amadán-na-Briona), a creature from the other world whose touch meant death or madness and who was deemed a "fool" because he apparently selected his victims by chance. As one witness put it: "I suppose the reason of the Amadán being wicked is he not having his wits, he strikes out at all he meets."[15]

Visionary or simple rustic clown, the folk fool does the unexpected, a fact which makes the countryman wary of him and makes it less likely that he will be treated as a mere scapegoat.

Before turning to Lady Gregory's comedies, I would like to consider the "Irish R.M." stories of Somerville and Ross in which there appears a far more cunning kind of clown. He may well blunder in speech, but he is innately inventive and skillful in protecting his own interests. Although he has a well defined position in the lower social ranks, within those ranks he maneuvers with considerable freedom. He belongs, in fact, to the ancient company of tricky servants. Like Phormio and Pseudolus, he often contrives to turn the tables on his alleged masters.

Somerville and Ross (pen names of Edith Somerville and Violet Martin) were residents, respectively, of the South and West of Ireland where their families had enjoyed positions of influence and wealth for hundreds of years. Their stories, which appeared in three collections between 1899 and 1915,[16] grew out of personal experience at a time when the power of the old Ascendancy class was on the wane. The point upon which their comedy turns is that Irish and Anglo-Irish cultures are wholly antithetical, and it is the Anglo-Irishman who must bend.

The character of Major Yeates, the R.M. or Resident Magistrate, provides these stories with an important unifying element since it is from his perspective that the comedy develops. Civil, modest and good natured, Yeates is spokesman for a legal system represented as equally benevolent. He is, however, continually frustrated by Gaels of every description, by the climate, the animals, the landscape, the physical stubborn quality of Ireland, itself. Moreover, Yeates discovers soon after his arrival at Shreelane, in the Southwest near Cork, that there is a mysterious dynamism at work, an energy, a palpable resistance to reason. The method which he attempts to apply is everywhere undermined by a mode of life that is distinctly alien. This is not to suggest that Yeates is doctrinaire in his thinking; he is generally tolerant and even humorous but, in the main, consistent in his behavior and attitudes and so becomes a perfect foil to the unpredictable countryman.

In his *Study of Celtic Literature* (1867), Matthew Arnold put an authoritative gloss on qualities attributed to Saxon and Celt[17] during the nineteenth century. Although his intention — the establishment of a Chair of Celtic Studies at Oxford — was both magnanimous and successful, one result was the perpetuation of a stereotype which had an adverse effect on the Home Rule movement. On the one hand he postulated a balanced, rational Saxon with a genius for government and material prosperity; and on the other, an emotional, sensual Celt, wanting in "sanity and steadfastness," quick to rebel against the "depotism of fact." Such qualities were said to account for the failure of the latter to reach any "material civilization sound and satisfying and not out at elbows; poor, slovenly and half-barbarous." He wrote at length of the Celt's love of beauty, his spirituality and "penetrating melancholy." He pronounced the Celtic sensibility with its "nervous exaltation" to be "feminine" in quality and remarked on the "extravagance and exaggeration of the sentimental Celtic nature" before concluding that the Celt lacked "a promising political temperament."[18]

The "Irish R.M." stories may be read as a comic exposition of Arnold's thesis because the duality that he argues for is basic to the authors' conception of character. One difference worth emphasizing, however, is that Yeates, who bears the burden of reason and steadfastness, is Anglo-Irish and consequently more resilient than the merely English stereotype would allow.

Violet Powell has commented on the fact that "Great-Uncle McCarthy," the opening story in *Some Experiences of An Irish R.M.*, offers a paradigm of the relationship between Yeates and the country people.[19] The dominant image in the story is the large old dilapidated house rented by Yeates, which he tries to make over according to his own standards. The house is drafty, damp and riddled with vermin. But the most disquieting element is the mysterious shuffling at night along the upper floors, a "pervading subpresence," which Yeates is encouraged to believe is the ghost of his landlord's great-uncle McCarthy. He eventually discovers that he is the unwitting host of some elderly McCarthys who, with the aid of the housekeeper, have made themselves comfortable in the attic, helping themselves to Yeates's food and whiskey. The McCarthys, comic tattered ghosts of a once powerful clan, never concede any wrongdoing. They insist that the rights of kinship have precedence over any legal contract.

Yeates's struggle with that house and its inhabitants is the first stage of a continuing effort to domesticate and civilize, to bring order and harmony and cleanliness to the province of Shreelane. The local people resist by adhering to tribal rituals and loyalties which are inscrutable to the R.M. Wakened one night, he goes out into the garden where a dead crow falls at his feet. An odd enough circumstance, rendered all the more peculiar by the fact that the crow has been dead for some time. In Shreelane, however, a fact is not easily or necessarily linked to a definable cause.

In "Great-Uncle McCarthy," as in many of the stories that follow, Yeates is the butt of the joke. He is frequently duped by local people who know much more about a given situation than he does. They connive and collaborate all the while covering their tracks by a pretense of ignorance or ineptitude or superstitious fear. While they obviously reflect nineteenth century stereotypes of the Irish, to a certain extent they use these stereotypes to advantage, enjoying the game while profiting from Yeates's inability to check them even when he guesses the truth.

Through Yeates's eyes the Irish often appear vigorous and imaginative, but they are also unreliable, highly emotional, manipulative, verbally very clever clowns. They seem eager to please, but are, in fact, intractable and impervious to change. As a result, the Anglo-Irishman must suffer his property to deteriorate, must be prepared for discomfort and delay, and the continual intrusion of the "personal element" in all details of life. The perspective of Somerville and Ross is not completely one-sided, however. The vagaries of the pleasure loving Irish are to some extent balanced by those of the Anglo-Irish gentry who seem to have an infinite capacity for discomfort and boredom, much of it endured in the name of sport or social obligation. Yeates and his English wife, Philippa, are discreet, polite, conventional people, more fitted to accept than to alter circumstances. It often seems that the clash of cultures provides the only real excitement in their lives.

These cultural differences are best illustrated in the matter of law. As Resident Magistrate, Yeates attempts to render judgments on the basis of an objective examination of the evidence. The local people, on the other hand, openly flout the law when they cannot bend it to their own interests. Giving testimony in court is looked upon as an opportunity to demonstrate their powers of rhetoric and flair for the dramatic. This is vividly demonstrated in "The Waters of

Strife" when the mother of a man accused of murder is called as a witness. She pretends great ignorance and humility, trembling before the lawyers with their "big rocks of English," sobbing into her handkerchief, but nonetheless quick to offer a bribe. On the stand she proves her mettle: "Bat Callaghan's mother had nothing to fear from the inquiry. She was by turns deaf, imbecile, garrulously candid, and furiously abusive of the principal witness."[20] The case ends with the complete certainty that the accused is guilty, but the law is rendered helpless by the tactics of witnesses like Mrs. Callaghan. Justice is finally achieved when the guilty man dies of fright, imagining he is pursued by the ghost of his victim. It is notable that in this story, as in so much nineteenth century fiction, the Irish are regarded as primarily "superstitious" rather than "religious."

The circumvention of the law is also an important theme in "The Holy Island" and "Oweneen the Sprat." In these stories humor is generated by the legendary capacity of the Irish for hard liquor and linked to Yeates's futile efforts to establish order in the place of anarchy.

In "The Holy Island" a ship is wrecked off the coast of Shreelane and barrels of rum are washed ashore. The local people regard the whole thing as a great "spree," drinking up as much of it as they can get their hands on, despite Yeates's attempt to save the cargo. Some of the more enterprising make off with a sizable quantity of liquor, which is then concealed on the "holy island." Subsequent disturbances on that island are attributed to supernatural causes, and there is considerable rumor about the potency of the "holy water" to be had there. Before the police can investigate, however, the rum has been happily sent on to Cork attached to the bishop's funeral train.

In "Oweneen the Sprat" Yeates is threatened with a suit by a local character who fell, while drunk, in the path of his carriage. Although uninjured, Owen Twohig pretends to be crippled for life, and terrible tales of his sufferings and obscure threats of vengence trickle back to Yeates's household, to be related with pleasurable hysteria by the Irish servants.

Yeates resists the growing pressure to capitulate, but his determination crumbles once he meets Mrs. Twohig, the mother of "Oweneen," and is forced to listen to an interminable account of the "hard life," that is, the unmerited suffering of her "little orphans" for the last thirty years.[21] The details are strangely garbled, palpably false and delivered in a medley of words in which English has undergone a transformation of both sound and meaning. Not even Yeates's disgust at the squalor of her home, with its implication of idleness and poor management, frees him from her spell, from the unswerving righteousness of her manner, her apparent conviction that Oweneen will be "under clutches" ("on crutches") for the rest of his life. Conceding defeat, he offers her money and flees.

Yeates's dilemma is resolved just as he is about to abandon all efforts at a legal solution. He sets out laden with gifts, prepared to offer personal restitution when he surprises a group of men enjoying a bowling game. In hot pursuit of a ball, Oweneen runs straight into the arms of Yeates. Thus the duplicity is exposed, but the result is laughter. What better jest than to bring suit against a magistrate, to force him into a position from which neither the law nor his superior social advantage can extricate him?

In these stories the Irish continue to be judged purely in terms of establishment norms, and there is not the slightest hint that there might be any flaw in a legal structure which is inappropriate to and out of sympathy with local interests. The poverty of the Irish is typically linked to their unsteadiness of character, their indifference to material needs, to authority, to practical forms of organization. John Kelleher has pointed out that many of these so-called Celtic qualities, exphasized by Matthew Arnold and other Victorians like Somerville and Ross, were taken as virtues by the writers of the Revival.[22]

The "Celtic imagination" is treated with some ambivalence by Somerville and Ross who enjoy a laugh even at their own expense but tend to see the Irish countryman as primarily manipulative and weak in moral judgment. This is evident in "Lisheen Races, Second-Hand" even though the butt of the joke turns out to be an Englishmen, Leigh Kelway, who is gathering material for a novel. The plot moves quickly through a series of mishaps which leave Kelway more and more gloomy, but which certainly afford him opportunity to study his subject at close hand. He is marooned for hours in a public house crammed with men drinking together after the races, where the "bread tasted of mice, the butter of turf-smoke, the tea of brown paper." The high points of the races are provided by Slipper who, in many respects, is a throwback to the simple clown. Dressed in ill fitting and oddly assorted garments, he is invariably drunk, self-effacing, unreliable. His humor reveals an "ex-

ulting pessimism" and a taste for extravagant detail, but the climax
of the story, in which one of the riders is thrown, is a comic version
of a near fatal injury suffered by Violet Martin:

> . . ."before ye could say 'shnipes,' the mare was standing on her
> two ears beyond in th' other field! . . . she stood that way till she
> reconnoithered what side would Driscoll fall an' she turned about
> then and rolled on him as cosy as if he was meadow grass!"
> Slipper stopped short; the people in the doorway groaned
> appreciatively; Mary Kate murmured: "The Lord save us!"
> "The blood was dhruv out through his nose and ears," con-
> tinued Slipper, with a voice that indicated the cream of the
> narration "and you'd hear his bones crackin' on the ground!
> You'd have pitied the poor boy."
> "Good heavens!" said Leigh Kelway, sitting up very straight in
> his chair.
> "Was he hurt, Slipper?" asked Flurry casually.
> "Hurt is it?" echoed Slipper in high scorn; 'killed on the spot!'[23]

The unfortunate rider eventually turns up "with a face like a red-hot
potato tied up in a bandage."

In his classic essay, *On the Study of Celtic Literature*, Matthew
Arnold suggested that the imagination and energy of the Celt be
viewed as complements to the genius of Saxon and Norman and that
a fruitful culture would emerge once these elements were properly
understood. Somerville and Ross, speaking out of personal and
historic circumstances, took a skeptical view. In their stories wily
Irish clowns seem bent on pulling down every outpost of civilization.
In the face of their contempt for English government and their
adherence to a more primitive, but always more inspired, way of
life, Yeates's system of reason and moral order is doomed to failure.
The best he can do is maintain an ironic distance while bending to
the inevitable. His decision is no doubt related to the fact that
Somerville and Ross witnessed the collapse of their own familiar,
privileged world. With the establishment of the Irish Free State in
1921, Edith Somerville (Violet Martin died in 1915) became a
displaced person, forced to sell her family estate because of debt.

There is certainly a class consciousness and a racist consciousness at work in Somerville and Ross, and they undoubtedly
contributed to the stereotype of the Irish countryman as a tricky
clown, which has currency even today. It should be acknowledged,

however, that their faults are outweighed by the merit of their best stories. On the whole their characters have wit and vitality, and the dialogue attributed to their country people, despite some stage Irishisms, is better and more accurate than that of most comic writers who preceded them. Like their contemporaries, John Synge and Augusta Gregory, they listened avidly and recorded local speech, and they made some attempt to learn Irish. In many instances their dialogue ("That one has a tongue that'd clip a hedge"; "I had to put the height of the house of curses to it before Mary would believe me")[24] is an exact replica of this recorded speech. Rejecting the sentimental comedy of the previous era, Somerville and Ross wrote with a biting humor and satire which reflects their kinship with Jonathan Swift, Maria Edgeworth and John Synge.

Somerville and Ross have that firm grasp of detail and economy of plot essential to good satire. Their precisely polished prose is distinguished by metaphor which is often original and zany in character. Even their hunting stories, which seem tedious today, are redeemed by flashes of wit. Few writers are so successful in recording the distinctive qualities of dogs, horses, animals of all kinds.

In many stories, such as "Oweneen the Sprat," "Poisson D'Avril" and "The House of Fahy," animals, objects, even the physical landscape take on an eccentric character of their own. The effect is to suggest the uncertainty of life in a way that is peculiarly modern because of its fusion of the comic and the grotesque. In the first story, for example, Yeates imagines the bicycle on which he travels a mountain road being transformed into "an opinionated and semi-paralyzed wheelbarrow."[25] In "Poisson D'Avril" he takes a slow and difficult trip by a train which makes unscheduled stops to allow the crew to enjoy a card game. Yeates has the additional burden of an enormous salmon which has been promised for a wedding feast:

> We had about fifteen miles to go, and we banged and bucketed over it in what was, I should imagine, record time. The carriage felt as if it were galloping on four wooden legs, my teeth chattered in my head, and the salmon slowly churned its way forth from its newspaper, and moved along the netting with dreadful stealth.[26]

"The House of Fahy" begins with a voyage aboard a dingy yacht where Yeates has a premonition of the comic disaster which looms ahead: ". . . resting on the sea's rim, a purple bank of clouds lay awaiting the descent of the sun, as seductively and as malevolently as a damp bed at a hotel awaits a traveller." The night which finally envelops them is as "black as the inside of a cow."[27]

Somerville and Ross underscore the limitations of human resources in the face of a reality which is faintly sinister but clearly absurd. In their work as a whole, however, the theme of the absurd — that unsettling and inexplicable "sub-presence" — is most consistently and forcibly linked with the Irish country people against whom the Sisyphean Yeates may persist but never prevail.

In the one-act plays of Lady Gregory the Irishman again appears as a simple rustic clown or fool. Her work nonetheless reflects a growing and sympathetic interest in the native culture and a conviction that it would provide a rich source of inspiration for poets, playwrights, and novelists, the new breed of writers who together would create the Revival. She, herself, was an avid collector of folklore, who grounded her plays on careful observation of the traditions and customs in her native Galway. While one may discern the influence of Matthew Arnold on her work, like other writers of the Revival, she tended to transform the characteristics that he attributed to the Celt into strengths. Her country people, enclosed in the isolated little world of Cloon, may be judged on their own merits rather than by their failure to measure up to an Anglo-Saxon or Anglo-Irish norm. At her best Lady Gregory, like Joyce, Yeats, Synge, and O'Casey, used the particular elements of Irish culture to develop themes of universal interest.

In drawing up their plans for the Abbey Theatre, Lady Gregory and W.B. Yeats vehemently rejected the stage Irish tradition: "We will show that Ireland is not the home of buffoonery and of easy sentiment as it has been represented, but the home of an ancient idealism."[28] It soon became evident, however, that the lyric theatre envisaged by Yeats would not prove financially successful, and so his early plays frequently shared the bill with a popular farce written out of expediency by Lady Gregory. With her customary modesty, she praised Yeats's work, offering this explanation:

> But the listeners, and this especially when they are lovers of
> verse, have to give so close an attention to the lines, even when
> given their proper value and rhythm as by our players, that ear and
> mind crave ease and unbending, and so comedies were needed to
> give this rest. That is why I began writing them, and it is still my

pride when one is thought worthy to be given in the one evening with the poetic work.[29]

Elizabeth Coxhead has pointed out that Lady Gregory flourished as a playwright between 1902 and 1912, that is, when she was between fifty and sixty years of age.[30] She tells us herself that she began casually enough "by writing bits of dialogue, when wanted."[31] She helped to extend the range of Irish English, traditionally considered appropriate only to comedy, by rewriting the epic tales in Kiltartan dialect. The fact that she had mastered Irish, also in middle age, gave her direct access to the folklore and a common language with the *seanachie* or story teller, which Samuel Lover had lacked despite his interest in the subject. This knowledge of folklore is an integral part of her plays, entering into the very life of her characters, not simply stitched into the narrative as is often the case in *Handy Andy*.

While Lady Gregory accurately noted the Irish love of satire and mordant humor, she seems to have underestimated the purely comic element in the oral tradition: "I find in our Irish country people . . . the underlying melancholy, the tragic dignity, the poetic imagination I find in the Gaelic writers, old and new. And these songs of sadness are the ones most cared for."[32] However, there are literally thousands of funny stories, *grinn-scealta*, in the archives at University College, Dublin, and some story tellers specialized in them. Among the ten most popular types are tales about numskulls, of which she and Samuel Lover offered very different accounts.

Like Samuel Lover and Somerville and Ross, Lady Gregory approached Gaelic culture from a distance; she was, after all, a member of the Anglo-Irish landed gentry. Her bias is mainly that of the Romantic; her people lack the toughness and the realism, the diversity of interest and passion evident in a writer like William Carleton, who was born into the peasant world he described. One can even complain that there is a certain childishness in the people of Cloon; they are so very gullible and superstitious, so extremely fanciful in their beliefs, so lacking in concrete knowledge. This quality is most evident in the lesser plays, such as *The Full Moon* and *The Jackdaw*, and it irritates the way jokes about Irish drinking continue to irritate. In her best work it is merely one aspect of human folly which provokes laughter in the same way as Argan does in *Le Malade Imaginaire*.

Spreading the News, Hyacinth Halvey and *The Workhouse*

Ward are tightly constructed in the manner of Moliere, whose work she translated for the Abbey Theatre. They have little in common with the musical melodramas of the Victorian Age, with their roistering physical energy and blunt humor. Instead, Lady Gregory focused on qualities which she had observed as peculiar to the temperament of the Irish countryman, notably his capacity for "fantasy and imagination." I am certainly not the first to point out that these qualities have distinguished Irish satire from the middle ages. Vivian Mercier has argued that the best Anglo-Irish satire, including that of Jonathan Swift, has drawn upon or been otherwise influenced by Irish material.[33] This is also true of Lady Gregory's plays which, though modest, continue to be produced. Her efforts to catch the authentic Irish note have been well documented in her dairies, her volumes of folklore, plays, and various other publications which record the accomplishments of the Revival.

When we first meet the inhabitants of Cloon, we begin, as in all farce, by laughing at the foolishness of the clowns. But we eventually see our own tendencies, exaggerated perhaps, but certainly recognizable. Thus our laughter is not that of superiority but of complicity. Her country people are no doubt related to Handy Andy and to the inhabitants of Shreelane in their naiveté, superstition, and ignorance of the larger world. They are an emotional, excitable people, inclined to be morose and stubborn and easily at odds with their neighbors. They are creatures of whimsy, whose folly is attributable to their lack of connectedness with tangible things. Curious and obsessive, they exist in a world unto themselves, outside the interdependent relationship with the gentry which distinguishes the traditional peasant. Many of them, of course, are shop keepers, postmen, policemen, the usual inhabitants of a small country town.

Lady Gregory has described the Irish countryman's love of conversation which provided him with news, entertainment, drama — substance for the imagination in rural areas with few books and few sources of amusement for adults. She notes that the people would say, "There is no man able to read books who can tell a story out of the mouth." The highest compliments were paid to those who were articulate and could relate a good story; thus it was great praise to say of someone: "She could keep you talking until morning," or "You wouldn't be tired of listening to him."[34] While it was earlier a common assumption that the peasant who couldn't speak English fluently — typified by Handy Andy — was mentally and linguistically defective, Lady Gregory proposes that the problem is precisely the reverse. She satirizes the countryman's love of talk, his tendency to lose himself entirely in the play of imagination. The dialect of Cloon is marked by Gaelic rhythms and inflections and is intended to be amusing because of its variation from English; however, it is also rich in wit and imagery and unexpected associations.

Cloon is a fairly static community, and comedy is generated by the effort of its people to create drama out of the nonevents of their lives. The force of public opinion and established custom functions as a monolithic backdrop against which the smallest ripple of deviant behavior is exposed to scrutiny.

In *Spreading the News*, which is based on a folktale, we meet a group of foolish busybodies who, because they have little better to do, exaggerate a piece of misinformation into a full scale tragedy of murder and adultery. No one comes forth with the least modicum of common sense or reason to put a stop to the gossip — there's too much pleasure in it. When the "dead" man appears on the scene, the people simply assume he's a ghost. At the finish the alleged murderer and his victim are taken off to jail together until the "real" corpse can be located. The human capacity for self-delusion, for choosing fiction over reality and sound over sense is a familiar comic theme the world over.

There are threats of violence in Cloon, but anger is almost invariably discharged in verbal tirade; there is none of the brutal horseplay, the laugh at the expense of injury or humiliation which erupts in *Handy Andy*. There is, however, a similar sense of fate at work. In Cloon the *expected* tends to occur, providing an unusual kind of irony. In *Spreading the News* Bartley Fallon complains that he is always being victimized, and the absurd round of events in which he is hopelessly entangled only confirms his judgment. In *Hyacinth Halvey* the central figure cannot escape being held up as a model of moral conduct although he steals a sheep and robs a church in a desperate effort to avoid the role being thrust upon him. His crimes are simply attributed to a local ne'er-do-well, who cannot escape his reputation either.

In *Hyacinth Halvey* Lady Gregory very skillfully and ironically exposes the petty crimes committed by the citizens despite the rigid moral code to which they all subscribe. The typical offender is James Quirke, a butcher who sells his highly suspect meat only to strangers. Mrs. Delane, the postmistress, who keeps an observant eye on local affairs, is sympathetic: "Indeed, you always treat the neighbors very decent, Mr. Quirke, not asking them to buy from you." He admits to the questionable aspects of his trade only under threat of fine and imprisonment. Normally, it is no easy thing to pin down a citizen of Cloon to the exact truth of any particular event, and while cheating a neighbor is not tolerated, a much more lenient view is taken of offenses against outsiders or the authorities, excepting always the priest.

There is a decidedly morbid quality in the local temperament. The people are petulant with minor grievances, and their imagination is most readily stirred by misfortune. Like Mrs. Delane, they are quick to predict worse and worse calamities with every evidence of pleasure, which seems to derive from the confirmation of their own sense of themselves as victims of history. They have survived, but they are poor, ignorant, gullible, full of prejudice and suspicion, which they can endure or transcend only by their capacity for self-dramatization.

In a footnote to her plays, Lady Gregory quotes an old Irish proverb: "It is better to be quarrelling than to be lonesome."[35] This becomes the theme of The Workhouse Ward in which two old men, Michael Miskell and Mike McInerney, quarrel to pass the time. Each is highly skilled at hurling invective, at deriding the character, the appearance and the past life of the other. They have evidently quarreled all their lives, each striving to gain the upper hand and to offer the most violent denunciations:

McInerney. . . . You're as tricky as a fish in the full tide.
Miskell. Tricky is it! Oh, my curse and the curse of four and twenty men upon you!
McInerney. That the worm may chew you from skin to marrow bone![36]

Their skill at invective is reminiscent of early Irish satire which will be discussed in the second part of this book. The intent seems always to cap the previous insult, to come as close as possible to the verge of physical or emotional violence and the annihilation of the friendship. Each is testing the imagination and fury of the other in a combat of wit which is mutually exhilarating.

As a consequence of their quarreling, they have become closely identified and mutually dependent like an old husband and wife; they will not part even when the opportunity for a better life is offered one of them. As Miskell concedes: "All that I am craving is the talk." And the talk is full of zest and energy. Disabled in body, reduced to the misery of the workhouse, the two old men are nonetheless alive in imagination. The continual pricking and jabbing of verbal combat provides drama and a way of enduring the harsh poverty of their lives.

The relationship of these two old men seems to me to foreshadow that of Estragon and Vladimir in *Waiting for Godot.* In Beckett's play the two old tramps, also impotent, without a future, with little tangible connection to ordinary reality also talk to pass the time, to give structure and meaning to life. They have come to the end of an uncertain journey, and so they wait in poverty and physical pain, defending themselves against isolation and dispair with the quintessentially Irish belief that "it is conversation that keeps away death."[37]

As Lady Gregory has suggested, the Irish clown was primarily the creation of Anglo-Irish and English writers.[38] Although the clown shares some of the features of the folk fool, the humor which he generates is largely based on cultural differences. In the early nineteenth century he is a blundering, often hot tempered but benevolent buffoon, ignorant of the modern world and incapable of speaking English properly. A second type, brought to perfection by Somerville and Ross, is the cunning clown who seems bent on dissolving the foundations of Anglo-Saxon civilization. In the work of Lady Gregory the clowns are imaginative though often foolish creatures who have little interest in the practical concerns of this world. Gaelic culture is thereby imbued with romantic qualities, but there is an accurate perception of the value of the spoken word. In succeeding chapters I will elaborate upon the process by which the comic Irishman, originally portrayed as incapable of rational speech, became a wit of considerable renown.

2. The Rogue

THE FIGURE of the outlaw or the dispossessed, the man who is hunted and betrayed, is one of the great archetypes of Irish literature. He appears in many guises as hero and anti-hero, as rogue, artist and buffoon. As a tragic figure he is most brilliantly realized by Joyce in Stephen Dedalus; as a comic figure, in Synge's playboy. The rogue is probably the earliest embodiment in the English language of those themes of alienation and resistance which characterize modern literature in Ireland.

During the eighteenth and early nineteenth centuries, the rogue was a popular subject of ballad and tale, and these provided material for William Carleton, Samuel Lover, Charles Lever, Dion Boucicault and Mrs. S. C. Hall, among others. The rogue literature of England and the continent, with the exception of *Gil Blas*, which Carleton discovered at an early age, apparently had little impact.

I would like to offer here a brief account of the history and contents of representative rogue tales, including material circulated in the penny press and in the oral tradition. These stories have many variants, and often no clear distinction can be made between folklore and the tales to be found in such chapbooks as *Rogues and Rapparees* (1799), a famous account of outlaw life by J. Cosgrave, which went through at least ten editions in Ireland and America.[1] One medium fed the other if only because the chapbooks were often the only books available in the hedge schools.

The outlaw depicted in the penny press was frequently a highwayman or *rapparee* a term which referred originally to the Gaelic aristocrat whose lands were confiscated after the wars of the mid and late seventeenth century. The historian William Lecky tells us that

in a country where the clan spirit was intensely strong, and where
the new landlords were separated from their tenants by race, by
religion and by custom, these fallen and impoverished chiefs
naturally found themselves at the head of the discontented classes;
and again after the Revolution, they and their followers . . .
waged a kind of guerrilla war of depredations upon their
successors.[2]

After the early years of the eighteenth century, however, this kind of
warfare seems to have ceased, and the term *rapparee* merged with
rogue to refer to a robber or highwayman.

During this period English roads also swarmed with
highwaymen, but they rarely received the kind of sympathy afforded
them in Ireland. Because of the oppressiveness of a colonial government, particularly evident in the penal codes which impoverished
the Catholic majority and barred them from the benefit of religion
or education, the "man on the run" was often protected by his countrymen. Lecky cites the case of Teige Finagan, an outlaw, wounded
and then pursued by soldiers through village after village in Kerry,
who escaped because no citizen would lay a hand on him.[3]

Largely because of native hostility toward English law and
because of their association with the dispossessed chieftains of the
seventeenth century, rogue and *rapparee* were transformed by
legend into daring Robin Hood figures who harrassed landlords and
English settlers. Many were undoubtedly cruel, but the more
popular figures had redeeming qualities and were not perceived to
be ordinary criminals. Many were said to adhere to a code of honor
and to have a fondness for music and poetry. While they robbed un-
wary travellers, they treated them courteously, particularly women,
and they were generous to the poor. Unlike the classic picaresque
tale, these stories offer little in the way of social criticism, and they
contain little satire or conscious irony. Some of the robbers are pictured as "gentle and unoffending" until poverty or the harsh laws
against Catholics force them into a life of crime, but in the main
such stories are told for the pleasure in sensational detail and in the
boldness and cunning of the outlaw. J. Cosgrave occasionally
moralizes ("nothing is more commendable in youth than industry"),
but that tendency is overridden by the excitement of the tale of
"drinking, whoring, gaming and playing the devil in every shape;

night and day." One of the best know outlaws was Redmond O'Hanlon, whose career epitomizes those qualities associated with rogue and *rapparee:*[4] "Though he was so notorious a plunderer, he was naturally of a very generous disposition, frequently giving a share of what he got from the rich to relieve the poor." Hanlon clearly enjoyed danger, giving up a general pardon for the life of the road. He was an artful imposter who could impersonate an officer or an ordinary soldier, and his history contains innumerable escapades in which he eluded pursuers by disguise or other trickery and by his superior strength and athletic ability. Like many another highwayman, he was betrayed by a woman and condemned to death: "his body ordered to be cut up in quarters and to be hung in different places as a terror to others; notwithstanding which he gave three surprising jumps in court, to show his activity, tho' so heavily laden with irons."[5] He escaped once more to be finally trapped by a foster brother, who for the sake of the large reward, had his own wife lure O'Hanlon into bed and there shot him to death in 1681.

Similar to O'Hanlon is Captain Power, "a genteel robber," who was never violent "unless opposed." He too was betrayed by a woman (a common theme in the rogue stories), who like the gal in "Brennan on the Moor" soaked his pistols in water. At the place of his execution he "gave a very kind caution to all young men, desiring them to shun the company of lewd women. . . . 'By women (said he) was I enticed to continue in sin and by a woman was I at last betrayed, tho' she pretended to be my friend,' which speech melted the spectators into tears."[6] John MacPherson, also betrayed by women, is said to have played "a fine tune of his own composing" on the bagpipes as he approached the gallows. The importance of dying well by providing an appropriate tune or making an eloquent speech — a fundamental tenet of Irish patriotism — is another theme woven into these stories. Cahier na Cappul, for example, a noted horse thief, was executed in 1735 after a trial that lasted twelve hours, so forcefully did he argue for his life. He also attempted to confuse the court by speaking only in Gaelic, a ruse followed by many an enterprising Irishman, including the late Brendan Behan.

Rogue tales often reflect the savage humor and the emphasis on cruelty, particularly mutilation, to be found in the oral tradition. A chilling example comes from "The Life of Richard Balf," a "common" criminal, who ended up on the "three legged tree" in

Stephen's Green. He was introduced to crime by his parents, who "got more by begging and cheating than by fair dealing; and at length by thieving and robbing, made a shift to obtain the favour of a hempen necklace, which eased them of their care."[7] Young Richard was their executioner, for which deed he was pardoned, but unable to earn a livelihood, returned to the Dublin underworld with the aforementioned results.

In *The Irish Sketch Book* William Thackeray describes how he spent a rainy night in Galway reading the *Life and Adventures of James Freney* (c. 1750), which was to have a direct bearing on *The Luck of Barry Lyndon*, the best known portrait of an Irish rogue. In fashioning Lyndon's portrait, Thackeray retained the sense of adventurous melodrama that is characteristic of the rogue tale circulated in the chapbooks of the eighteenth and early nineteenth centuries. Lyndon's career is launched by a duel over a woman which ends in the apparent death of his rival. He flees the country, first joining the army and then escaping that hardship to become an accomplished gambler, welcome in the great salons of Europe. Thackeray speaks of James Freney's "sporting bearing in the face of danger" and of his marvelous escapes, observing that "it is impossible not to admire his serenity, his dexterity, that dashing impetuosity in the moment of action."[8] These qualities are most evident in the character of Thackeray's adventurer as a young man when his courage and naiveté as well as his sentimental attachment to his family and native land make him a fairly sympathetic figure. Lyndon, is, however, far more ambitious than Captain Freney and increasingly unscrupulous and cruel in his efforts to achieve wealth and position. At the height of his fortune he marries into the British aristocracy and enjoys a life of extravagance and luxury. Although he does not realize it, he always remains an outsider, a parvenu, mocked by the better educated and more discerning members of the upper classes. Thackeray treats his rogue satirically, exposing his ignorance and the preposterous nature of his claims through a number of intersecting perspectives.

In "The Irish Hero" Robert Colby observes that *Barry Lyndon* was intended as a corrective to the broadly humorous characterizations of Charles Lever's *Harry Lorrequer* and Samuel Lover's *Handy Andy*. Thackeray apparently intended to establish a more realistic view of Irish life and character as well as of the military exploits which Lever described as so many jolly picnics.[9] In contrast to both

Harry Lorrequer and Handy Andy, Barry Lyndon's candor is confined to the reader. He is extremely manipulative, and while he starts his career by a romantic duel over a woman, he ends by abusing one unmercifully, threatening her with physical violence, and actually driving her son and heir to his death. He does not merely embellish the truth but offers elaborate fabrications to support his claims to wealth, nobility and an adventurous past. In these fabrications he often appears to delude himself, to actually believe he is the magnificent gentleman he pretends to be. It is clear that Thackeray, who visited Ireland in 1842, found the claims of the dispossessed Gaelic aristocrats very hollow indeed, and so the names of Lyndon's reputed ancestors (Roaring Harry Barry) and their possessions (Ballybarry) are made to seem ludicrous. More important, Lyndon has no conception of the constructive potential of great wealth. Through folly and ignorance, he wastes all the money extorted from his wife, acquires enormous debts and eventually dies in prison a confirmed alcoholic. The mature Lyndon is less interesting than the young rogue because the former is a stereotypical embodiment of the worst excesses attributed to the eighteenth century Irish squire.

In Ireland, on the other hand, the roguish adventurer was often seen as a heroic figure, and the very certainty of his downfall made him more appealing. He was a man determined to make the most of a short life, and his position as an outsider, generally free of domestic concerns or religious scruples gave him a decided advantage. Furthermore, while the chivalric code was treated mockingly in *Barry Lyndon*, it was associated by the Irish with their lost leaders. Thus embued with romance, the rogue held out the possibility of change, of rescue, of driving out the English settlers. He embodied the spirit of resistance against the new order.

These outlaw tales provided material for highly melodramatic fiction such as William Carleton's *Red Count O'Hanlon*, Charles Lever's *The Confessions of Con Cregan*, and Mrs. S.C. Hall's "The Rapparee" in which James Freney is turned into a Byronic hero. Nineteenth-century fiction and drama in fact contained innumerable romatic outlaws, whose influence has not yet entirely faded away. It was, however, the comical rogue who came to the forefront to provide a prototype for Synge's playboy and the paycocks of Sean O'Casey. This "broth of a bhoy" is a curious amalgam of qualities attributed to the legendary outlaw and the anti-heroic and humorous qualities of other rogue figures to be found in folklore.

The most celebrated, though certainly the most unconventional, rogue of this kind is Finn MacCool,[10] whose exploits are preserved in manuscript and in the oral tradition and who emerges in the twentieth century as the sleeping giant of *Finnegans Wake*. He is a complex and infinitely variable figure. Adventuresome, generous and brave in early Middle Irish tales, he could also be shrewd and trecherous as in the story of Diarmuid and Gráinne. In the oral tradition he is often confused with Brian Boru, and he is at times described as a man of ordinary size, at times as a giant. While the Ulster cycle in which Cúchulainn appears is based on the principles of an ordered society, Finn early assumes a role outside the tribe as a hunter and warrior; men join his *fianna* (warrior band) by choice once they have passed certain tests of skill. Finn, himself, is a seer and a poet, whose magic powers reside in his thumb.

David Krause has argued that a comic Finn, a deprecated father figure, may be found as early as the eighth century.[11] In the so-called *bruidhean* tales (about an enchanted dwelling) dating from the tenth century, Finn is humiliated by supernatural powers and subjected to physical and verbal abuse which is at times clearly humorous in effect. Such tales as *Bruidhean Chaorthainn* (The Rowan-tree Dwelling), in which the heroes are captured when their buttocks become fastened to the seats of their chairs, were popular in the oral tradition in the Irish language; however, purely comic portrayals of Finn are more common in English. During the nineteenth century he is represented as a rogue or prankster who indulges in outrageous tricks.[12]

The most widely circulated tale of this kind is related by William Carleton as "A Legend of Knockmany."[13] Here Finn is a very evasive character who spins one tale after another to conceal his fear of a rival giant, Cucullin (this may be a confused reference to Cúchulainn). He stops working on the Giant's Causeway purportedly because of a "very warm and sudden fit of affection for his wife, poor woman," actually to avoid Cucullin, who follows him home anyway, but not before he and his wife have arranged a plan to outwit and destroy this terrifying figure who keeps a flattened thunderbolt in his pocket. We are told that despite his own great strength and the magical thumb from which he sucks wisdom and logic, he is saved primarily through the cleverness of his wife who disguises him as a child and then tricks Cucullin into placing his own magical finger into the mouth of Finn. He immediately bites it off, destroying the source of Cucullin's strength and finally Cucullin, himself.

In this story two men are clearly rendered impotent and foolish by the strategems of a woman; the relevant point is the willingness of Finn to adopt an anti-heroic posture out of expediency. This is a controversial issue, but it seems likely that the increasingly comic character of Finn is related to the disastrous fortunes of the Irish, who lost battle after battle from the sixteenth century onward and had to resort to trickery to outwit an enemy they could not subdue by force of arms.[14]

A similar theme may be found in other kinds of tales in which rogues appear. These are also tricksters, but decidedly down to earth, often cruel, though not criminal. They are on intimate terms with the peasant world, which in this case provides the standard of behavior that is violated. Rather than subscribing to any Christian ethic, they seem to reflect the substratum of pagan sentiment which survived in Ireland into modern times.

One widely recorded example is "Little Fairly,"[15] the tale of a little man who outwits and finally destroys his younger, bigger brother. The brothers are paired with mothers of corresponding size; both of whom are wives to a prosperous farmer. Disinherited by his dying father, Little Fairly turns everything to his advantage in the long run. He tricks somebody into purchasing the hide of the one cow which he owns, and which his brother killed, for a great deal of money. He then tricks his brother into foolishly killing all his own cows. The story emphasizes Fairly's shrewdness as well as his willingness to resort to the most brutal tactics in order to rid himself of a powerful enemy. He tricks a passerby so that the latter is drowned in his place. And when his mother is accidentally killed, he doesn't hesitate to play a trick with her corpse to acquire more money, a fact which is regarded as one more example of his "cuteness." In the end Little Fairly persuades his brother that a local bog is the entrance to a kind of fairy world, and that oaf jumps in leaving our hero free and prosperous.

The macabre strain in Irish folklore is certainly apparent in this story in which a gullible passerby as well as a troublesome brother are tricked into killing themselves, and humor is generated by the "drowning" of a corpse.

A more comical rogue appears in "The Three Wishes" by William Carleton, another literary version of a folktale.[16] The central character, Billy Dawson, a lazy but clever ne'er-do-well, repeatedly outwits the devil, who supplies him with money, which he consumes as conspicuously as possible. For all his deprivation and quarreling with an equally cantankerous and drunken wife, he can be quite amusing and droll, particularly in his contest with the devil. Like so many folk figures, he is able to outmaneuver a much more powerful antagonist by his cleverness and lack of scruples. He is quite willing to resort to cruelty in order to gain an advantage, whether it be against a neighbor or the devil himself. At one point he takes a pair of red-hot tongs and pulls on the devil's nose, which stretches like a "piece of warm wax" until it extends through the chimney and five feet above the roof of the house.

This tale, unlike "Little Fairly," has a moral tone, but it tends to be submerged by the storyteller's pleasure in the cunning and malicious humor of the rogue. Like the fools, Billy is a resilient figure. Whenever he reaches the point of absolute destitution, he invariably tricks the devil into a new contract and a fresh supply of money. He never despairs, nor worries about the future and the debt that the devil intends to collect in the usual way.

When Billy Dawson finally expires, he discovers that the gates of both heaven and hell are closed against him. Putting his nose defiantly through the bars of the devil's stronghold, he finds it gripped by a familiar pair of red-hot tongs; whereupon it begins to burn as a result of all the hard liquor Dawson consumed in his lifetime. He ends up as a "will-o'-the-wisp," haunting the bogs and quaqmires in order "to cool his nose" and characteristically leading the unthinking and tipsy traveler astray.

In "Phelim O'Toole's Courtship" by William Carleton, one of the best comic stories of the nineteenth century, there is a fully delineated rogue. The story is of interest because of its merit and because its humor is truly Irish and thus different in certain respects from that of Samuel Lover, Lady Gregory and Dion Boucicault, whose comic rogues were to win him unprecedented success in Ireland, England, and America.

There is, first of all, little that is sentimental or whimsical or romantic in the character of Phelim O'Toole. And the wit which distinguishes the story is sharply satiric. Phelim is an imposter of a special order, a notorious liar, well known for his trickery and petty thievery, a man frequently called to give false testimony for friends with legal difficulties.

There was no such hand in the county as Phelim at an alibi. Just give him the outline — a few leading particulars of the fact — and he would work wonders. . . .

> Phelim, on other occasions, when summoned as evidence
> against his well-wishers or brother Ribbonmen, usually forgot his
> English, and gave his testimony by an interpreter. Nothing could
> equal his ignorance and want of common capacity during these trials.
> His face was as free from every visible trace of meaning as if he had
> been born an idiot. No block was ever more impenetrable. . . .[17]

His testimony on behalf of the prosecution usually so damages the
validity of a case that it has to be dropped. Far from putting people
on their guard against him, however, he is applauded by the community for circumventing a legal system which is alien to local
customs and to the local sense of justice.

Phelim's very appearance signifies his role as a witty rogue. As a
result of small pox, one eye is closed in a perpetual wink, and his
face resembles the "rough side of a cullender, or, as he was often
told in raillery, 'You might grate potatoes on it.' " He is dressed in
tatters and wears a cap of rabbit skin with the ears protruding over
his forehead. His physical vitality and his affinity with the animal
world, with appetite rather than reason, is underscored. Carleton
does not smooth away the rough edges; his character is physically
ugly, full of contradictions and utterly lacking in any code of ethics.
He is self-seeking and self-indulgent, but never an out and out
villain. The priest and the school master disapprove, but the women
think him "comely," and the villagers generally enjoy his outrageous
antics, his defiance of law and order and respectability. Acting out
the impulses which they suppress or conceal, he clearly represents
the spirit of anarchism.

A significant difference between *omadhawn* and rogue is that
the latter makes more conscious use of his verbal skill, upon which
he depends even more than on trickery to accomplish his ends.
Phelim uses the Irish English dialect with great fluency and
dramatic effect. He has a fine sense of his own powers to seize upon
the weaknesses of others and manipulate them to his advantage. Phelim could be said to have the real blarney;[18] his speech is a
necromancer's art, creating illusions in others, bewitching and
betraying them, making each of the women whom he courts believe
that she is the eminently desirable one. The language is comical
because of its deviation from standard English. As in much Irish
writing from Samuel Lover to Sean O'Casey, humor is generated by
blunders or malapropisms: "You blarnied and palavered me, you

villain, till you gained my infections." But one is struck primarily by
the energy and wit of the Irish English idiom, by its taste for
metaphor and alliteration, its pronounced rhythms and inflections:
"There won't be sich a lovin' husband, bedad, in Europe. It's I
that'll wax you; an' butther you up like a new pair o' brogues. . . ."

This last expression reveals a more complex kind of humor than
was previously associated with the comic Irishman. There is a teasing irony imbedded in the central metaphor. The woman whom
Phelim is addressing is "well seasoned," that is, an older woman who
has already been so "flattered" and "butthered" up that she has
given Phelim her money.[19] The comparison between the woman and
the shoes (which will be broken in and well used), is typical of the
kind of ludicrous details yoked together in an Irish conceit. There is
also a tendency, as in the expression the "well seasoned" woman (a
double pun) to state the opposite of what is meant and then to exaggerate or to understate the descriptive modifier.

Sometimes these two elements of Irish humor are joined in a
single grotesque metaphor. For example, speculating on how young
Phelim's thievery might prosper had he only a pocket in his trousers,
the narrator observes ironically: "virtues which circumstances
supressed in his heart might have flourished like cauliflowers."

One of the major themes in the story and one which, as we have
seen, interested Lady Gregory, is the human predilection for self-
delusion, for avoiding unpleasant realities at all cost. The theme is
first introduced in Carleton's satirical account of Phelim's early life
as the son of indulgent parents who refuse to see any flaws in him
despite ominous signs. After years of childlessness, they regard his
birth as a miracle, naming Phelim after the saint to whom they
made a pilgrimage in hope of children. Phelim is regarded as a "rare
beauty," a prodigy of the first order, and his father is particularly
pleased to have an heir to his "snug estate of half an acre." The
discrepancy between the viewpoint of the O'Tooles and that of the
reader is a major source of amusement.

Even as a child, Phelim is a remarkable specimen. Carleton
tells us that

> for the first ten years of his life Phelim could not be said to owe
> his tailor much . . . he might be seen every Sunday morning, or on
> some important festival, issuing from his father's mansion, with a
> piece of old cloth tied about him from the middle to the knees,

leaving a pair of legs visible, that were mottled over with characters which would, if found on an Egyptian pillar, put an antiquary to the necessity of constructing a new alphabet to decipher them. This, or the inverted breches, with his father's flannel waistcoat, or an old coat that swept the ground at least two feet behind him, constituted his state dress (1038).

There is a good deal of excellent visual description in "Phelim O'Toole's Courtship," which typically emphasizes the incongruous or the fantastic. It is not enough to say that Phelim has dirty legs; the spots must take on the character of Egyptian hieroglyphics. His "state dress," like a monarch's train must sweep the ground "at least two feet" behind him. His poverty is thus comically transformed to suggest his essential nature, that powerful narcissism and self-confidence that is in no way hindered by material reality. Comparison is pushed beyond the limits of logic or of ordinary expression; yet remains consistent with the original ironic conceit: Phelim as heir to a "snug estate of half an acre."

Phelim early manifests a talent for mischief and a taste for hard liquor. The neighbors begin to hint at the "probability of his dying something in the shape of a perpendicular death" (an airy metaphor for hanging), but his parents are as indulgent as ever. When Phelim is stricken by small pox, they give up all efforts to "thwart him" and find even his disfigurement appealing:

> "Doesn't he become the pock-marks well, the crathur?" said the mother.
> "Become!" said the father; "but doesn't the droop in his eye set him off all to pieces!" (1042)

As he grows to manhood, Phelim manages to avoid the physical labor that is the foundation of peasant life. Instead he becomes a formidable fighter, sportsman and bon vivant, gradually corrupting his own father, who likes nothing better than to go drinking with Phelim. Master of ceremonies at every kind of social occasion, Phelim is much in demand as a dancer who can perform a hornpipe on the top of a five gallon keg, snuff a candle with both heels and never lose the beat. He is an active Ribbonman, although he lacks real political conviction. He is fundamentally an outlaw figure, bold, reckless, unpredictable.

Despite his notoriety (Carleton is telling us — because of it), Phelim is attractive to women. They enjoy his impudent, flattering ways and prove even more capable of self-delusion than their men, even when it is discovered that he has proposed to three of them at the same time. Despite his extravagant professions of love, it should be noted that Phelim never attempts to seduce any of the women involved; his tactics are mainly verbal ones, and the humor is never bawdy or even risqué. This is generally true of Irish comedy in the nineteenth century, which placed the erotic in a romantic light.

Phelim comes courting in a borrowed suit with the bottle of whiskey that is essential to negotiation. The few articles possessed by each party are discussed with as much pomp and solemnity as though a vast estate were involved. One of the interesting aspects of this story, as in much of Carleton's fiction, is his account of folk customs, which are rendered in considerable detail down to the eggshells with which all parties toast one another in the absence of glasses. For the most part Carleton's peasants are a volatile and imaginative people with strong appetites and strong passions. They make do with very little and still manage to be merry and hospitable and to observe the fundamental rites of courtship, marriage, birth and death with considerable ceremony.

Phelim's amorous career is nipped in full bloom when he is unceremoniously tossed in jail, tricked by Fool Art, whom he has underestimated and abused. Art is another *omadhawn* who has turned his simplicity into a formidable asset. He is full of guile and cunning, but manages to keep a low profile and so defeats the vainglorious Phelim O'Toole. Poor Phelim, left to molder in solitary confinement, begins to see himself as another "martyr for ould Ireland."

The end of the story is, of course, ironic as Phelim becomes a victim of his own delusions, unable to acknowledge the truth so long obscured by a great flurry of lies. A propensity for self-delusion, also notable in the portrait of Barry Lyndon, is not usually a feature of the rogue as far as I can determine. It is, however, a universal comic quality and one that is stressed in Irish fictional characters in the nineteenth and twentieth centuries. With them talk is often evasion, a clever maneuvering around what Matthew Arnold termed the "despotism of fact."

While the clown is the butt of Fortune, the rogue may be seen as a gambler upon whom Fortune often smiles. The figures who appear in the plays of Lover, Synge, Boucicault and O'Casey share many of the qualities of the rogue. They tend to be outsiders, articulate and flamboyant, who live by their wits and avoid the drudgery of the average man. They flourish because they break through the conventional boundaries or the usual domestic ties. Unlike the peasant who subordinates himself to family, community or some higher authority, the rogue is characterized by self-interest and by a desire for freedom and autonomy. He rarely worries about tomorrow or where the next meal is coming from.

The rogue is often pitted against an adversary whom he defeats by shrewdness or boldness, rarely by direct assault; violence is diffused by humor. Entertaining, high spirited, and flirtatious, he is nonetheless unlikely to form an alliance with a woman. The roguish heroes of Lover and Boucicault prove themselves masters of disguise and as adventurous as any of the legendary highwaymen. They share some of the romantic and chivalric qualities attributed to the latter, but as they are ostensibly peasants, they have no pretense to poetry or learning. They provide much of the energy of the plot, often taking command or offering a solution when the conventional hero begins to falter. While the most appealing Irish rogues are comic figures, the nineteenth century literature in which they appear — with the important exception of William Carleton's fiction — has little of the earthy and macabre humor of folklore.

3. The Stage Irishman

The Stage Irishman habitually bears the general name of Pat, Paddy or Teague. He has an atrocious Irish brogue, perpetual jokes, blunders and bulls in speaking and never fails to utter, by way of Hibernian seasoning, some wild screech or oath of Gaelic origin at every third word: he has an unsurpassable gift of blarney and cadges for tips and free drinks. His hair is of a fiery red: he is rosy-cheeked, massive, and whiskey loving. His face is one of simian bestiality with an expression of diabolical archness. . . . In his right hand he brandishes a stout blackthorn, or a sprig of shillelagh, and threatens to belabour therewith the daring person who will tread on the tails of his coat.[1]

SINCE the Elizabethans the Irishman has been a stock figure on the stage, intended to amuse insofar as his customs and speech deviated from the English norm. As increasing numbers of Irish immigrants made their way to London, their presence was reflected in dramatic characters which varied in conception and were drawn from many different levels of society. There were military and professional men, fortune hunters, sailors, tradesmen, beggars, and bawds. And these appeared in a sympathetic or a hostile light according to the state of English-Irish relations at the time. Irish playwrights, actors, and actresses flourished during the eighteenth century, for example, a period of relative calm when Dublin rivaled London as a center for the performing arts. Among the memorable characters created in this era were Callaghan O'Brallaghan in Charles Macklin's *Love a la Mode* (1760), Lucius O'Trigger in *The Rivals*, and Lt. O'Connor in *St. Patrick's Day* by Richard Sheridan (1775). With the nineteenth century, however, comedy began to focus on a stereotype of the peasant, which became a staple of music hall entertainment and melodrama.

In *The Stage Irishman*, a study of theatre from the sixteenth through the eighteenth century, George Duggan cites an important precedent in the work of John O'Keefe, who, he believes, established a vogue for the comical peasant. O'Keefe, born in Dublin, created fairly life-like characters such as Thady MacBrogue, a vigorous serving man in *The She-Gallant* (1764) and Felix, a devil-may-care wanderer in *Wicklow Gold Mines* (1794). His plays offered pipers and a host of other entertaining Irish characters as well as authentic music by Carolan. Duggan argues that subsequent writers drew upon this precedent, but lacking O'Keefe's ability, produced a crude clown, the type, in fact, so vividly described by Maurice Bourgeois,[2] as stated above.

There is, as yet, no comprehensive study of nineteenth century Irish drama, but even a brief survey suggests that Duggan and Bourgeois exaggerate the crudeness of the stereotype. The typical peasant tends to be, as a character in *The Irish Engagement* (1848) by W. Watts puts it: "full of fun, humor and impudence." That "fun," as in this same play, can degenerate into mere buffoonery. Whiskey drinking and fighting are expected to draw a big laugh, and there is invariably some joking about Irish ignorance, but I have found few characters who approximate Bourgeois's definition.[3]

Among those who shaped popular conceptions about the Irish in the nineteenth century was Tyrone Power, the founder of a well known family of actors. Power was himself a writer of farce and melodrama which exploited those peculiarities associated with the "rollicking" type of stage Irishman. The hero of his farce *Paddy Carey* (1833) is an amorous and adventurous fellow who brandishes his blackthorn at the bailiffs who come to confiscate the property of the woman he loves. His speech is animated, but he has little of the wit to be found in the comic characters (aside from Handy Andy) of Samuel Lover or Dion Boucicault; instead the dialogue contains the usual blunders and malapropisms ("the first man that ever perspired for my hand . . ."). On the whole this is a rather stilted but good humored play in which a happy resolution is brought about through the agency of the comic Irishman.

Another common plot turns upon the ancient device of the underling disguised as his superior. In *The Irish Tutor* by R. Butler, Earl of Glengall (1846), *The Irish Doctor* by G. Wood (1844) and *The Irish Engagement*, for example, the audience is invited to laugh at the blundering incapacity of the "Oirish oaf" pretending to be an aristocrat or a professional man. The Irishman, however, brings cunning and gusto to the role and, like Xanthias in *The Frogs,* usually manages to get in a few strokes on his own behalf or to somehow turn the joke to his advantage.

Many plays produced in England, Ireland, and America during this period made similar use of the Irishman, while the Irish locale provided a colorful, entertaining, and even exotic background with its "romantic" ruins. It was, after all, the heyday of melodrama when audiences expected fast moving plots, sensational rescue scenes, recognizable heroes and villains, pretty and virtuous women, as well as songs and dances, jokes and buffoonery to enliven the performance. The Irish background and character types were fitted to conventional formulas.

When Edmund Falconer's *Eileen Oge* appeared in 1871, the program noted that it was "a drama illustrative of Irish character and the romance of life in the land of the shamrock." The hero is Patrick O'Donnel, a man of honor, religious and chivalrous toward women, who is accused of forgery and exiled to a penal settlement. He submits to the law without a struggle even though he is taken from his sweetheart on their wedding day. His comic foil is Brian O'Farrel, a roguish fellow who, interestingly enough, speaks with a more obvious brogue than the "heroic" O'Donnel. The play is full of clichés about virtuous Irish girls and the "impetuous Irish nature," and it incorporates scenes of singing and dancing, whiskey drinking, and at least one brawl.

In *The Green Bushes* (1845) by John Buckstone there is a stage Irishman who comes close to Bourgeois's description. Wild Murtogh is a comical villain who appears in rough dress flourishing a shillelagh and threatening to do violence to anyone "who'll tread on the tail" of his coat. This play follows the pattern of classic and renaissance drama in that the tragic action involves only the Irish gentry (indistinguishable from their English counterparts), while the peasants provide entertainment by dancing and singing and talking with a brogue. Murtogh, like his predecessor, Malvolio in *Twelfth Night,* hopes to get on in the world by knavery, but remains an outsider because of his crudeness and his drinking habits. Murtogh has little wit; he is comic by virtue of his pretensions and his "wild Irish" mannerisms. The locale of this melodrama shifts back and forth between Ireland and America during the 1740's; the implications are clear enough: both countries are perceived as exotic to the

English eye, and both are exploited for their value as entertainment. Wild Murtogh has a curious parallel in the woman Miami, who is of Indian blood and comes, of course, to a tragic end much like Cora in *The Last of the Mohicans.*

It has often been suggested[4] that the Englishman sees the Irishman as a kind of anti-self upon whom he projects repressed instincts and desires or in whom he sees tendencies that he fears in himself. Thus throughout the nineeenth century British travellers complained about the dirt, the ignorance, the laziness, the incompetence of the Irish in contrast to Saxon thrift, industry, and discipline. John Bull was male, aggressive, authoritative: Eire was feminine, weak, romantic, and impulsive. A corollary myth, evident in many nineteenth century melodramas, was that of the Irishman as a laughing boy in relation to the sober, judicious English man. One explicit example is *The Irish Attorney* (1840) by Bayle Bernard in which Pierce O'Hara, dressed in scarlet and green, appears as yet another blustering, hard drinking, hard riding Irishman addicted to dueling and pretty women (surely a Victorian equivalent of the American cowboy). He is a thoroughly exaggerated, unreal figure who resolves all problems happily and resolutely through his unconventional approach to the law. He is contrasted with the Englishman Jacob Wylie, dressed in black, sober, conventional, short sighted, overly concerned with money, who is eventually shown the error of his ways.

Pierce O'Hara clearly derives from the eighteenth century, from Callaghan O'Brallaghan and Lucius O'Trigger, but Samuel Lover's Rory O'More is a new type of comic character. Based on the novel by the same name *Rory O'More* appeared in 1838; it contains — as far as I can determine — the original dramatic prototype of the Irish peasant who is hero rather than villain but as crafty, impudent, and witty as Billy Dawson or Phelim O'Toole. Rory is a man of unswerving integrity, a quality no doubt intended by Lover to offset contemporary stereotypes of the peasant as "vicious." He is a romantic figure, who despite his humble origins, is very much the center of the drama with many of the trappings of the traditional hero. In the manner of the legendary highwayman, he is chivalrous toward women, courageous, and eminently skillful at outwitting and outmaneuvering his opponents. He joins the nominal hero, De Lacy, a gentleman patriot, in bringing about the resolution of the plot by rescuing two women and dispatching the villains of the piece. And it is he rather than De Lacy who is united with the heroine, a pretty colleen, at the conclusion. I should mention in this regard that Rory, in the tradition both of the rogue and the stage Irishman of the eighteenth century, is an amorous fellow whose flattery women find difficult to resist. The stereotype of the amorous Irishman may have grown out of tales about the "lewde libertye" of the Irish circulated among Elizabethans who were scandalized that the natives might commonly sleep together in the nude. (In *A View of the Present State of Ireland* Edmund Spenser warned that Irish women might be concealing bastards as well as knives under their mantles.)

Lover's rogue also retains qualities associated with the *omadhawn*. The comedy depends to some extent on his ignorance, his blundering with English and confusion over French. He repeatedly uses the term "vagabones," for example, and "portmantle" for "portmanteau." He also comes up with an occasional bull:

> Rory: Faith, I'd be very glad to see you; but how can I see you in the dark? — barrin I was a cat.

On the whole, however, though his brogue is intended to amuse, he is skillful with language and fond of playing or punning in a farcical, Groucho Marx sort of way.

> *De Lacy.* Were you long under an arrest?
> *Rory.* Devil a rest I had at all. . . .

Lover works several stories about drinking and about pigs into the plot, stock features of Irish comedy in the late eighteenth and the nineteenth centuries. In these stories Rory makes himself the butt of the joke though his aim is typically to evade and confuse his questioner by taking refuge in a stereotype:

> *Col. Thunder.* But how came you into the street at an unlawful hour?
> *Rory.* That's what I'm coming to, your honour — as I was saying, I got dhrowsy, and fell asleep — till I was woke with a ruction.
> *Col. Thunder.* What's that?
> *Rory.* A skirmmage, your honour.
> *Col. Thunder.* A fight you mean.
> *Rory.* Yis, a little innocent sort of a fight, with sticks and chairs, and the like: but I had nothin' to do with it, your honour;

and so them that was in it, seein' I wasn't amusin' myself, got
displeased with my company, and at last they gave me a hint
to lave the place.(2.1.)

In fact, Rory is thrown out bodily. So Samuel Lover has it both
ways: exploiting the conventions of Irish character and background
and at the same time challenging English and Anglo-Irish assump-
tions about the peasant.

Rory is distinguished from Handy Andy not only by his heroic
qualities but by his playfulness and foxiness. In fact, he tells an
amusing tale about a fox at the climax of which Rory gains the advantage and escapes from his captors. He is a conscious entertainer,
a good teller of tales, always ready with an explanation, plausible or
implausible, and while the singing is left to the women in this play,
he does manage to dance a jig in the first act.

Rory is a consistently amusing and optimistic character who,
far from being the butt of Fortune, acts effectively to ward off
disaster. He succeeds in accomplishing all he sets out to do by virtue
of his wit and physical courage and strength. He is genial, faithful in
meeting obligations, respectful but never self-effacing toward the
gentry. At one point the nominal hero, De Lacy, in a reversal of the
traditional pattern even offers his life to save Rory, who has a con-
fidence and, in fact, an authority which evolves out of his obvious
merit.

Rory O'More represents one end of the spectrum of broad
humor which characterized the stage Irishman during this period.
At the other extreme was the crude buffoon, the fighting Irishman
such as Wild Murtogh, who was much less popular because he was
much less amusing. More important, Rory O'More offered a model
for Dion Boucicault,[5] who was to dominate the Irish stage in the late
nineteenth century and whose influence is still felt today.

Born in Dublin in 1820, Boucicault was associated with the
theatre for some fifty years as an accomplished actor and director as
well as a prolific playwright who was admired for his stagecraft in
Europe and America. He wrote or adapted at least 150 plays and introduced important changes in the theatre, such as helping to
dismantle the star system and improving the status of the playwright
by assuring him a fair share of the profits. However, aside from *London Assurance* which was recently and happily revived on Broad-
way, only his Irish plays, *The Colleen Bawn* (1860), *Arrah-na-Pogue*

(1864) and *The Shaughraun* (1874) continue to be performed today. Ireland had produced other and better playwrights before Boucicault, namely Farquhar, Congreve, Goldsmith and Sheridan, but they wrote mainly for the English theatre, and their comedy of manners was hardly appropriate to the Irish experience in the nineteenth century.

As a consummate showman, Boucicault caught and held the popular eye, drawing unprecedented numbers to his Irish plays. Most of the ingredients that he used were standard elements of nineteenth century melodrama, but according to such discriminating critics as Bernard Shaw and Henry James, when Boucicault himself appeared in the title role, he brought a kind of magic into the theatre. Henry James spoke of his writing and stagecraft as "hard cleverness, polished and flexible with use," while his acting was "very like genius."[6] His blend of farce and melodrama, his use of historic material and of the song and dance routines of the music hall, his identification with the man at the bottom of the social heap became basic ingredients in Sean O'Casey's plays, and they survive in the work of Samuel Beckett, Brendan Behan and such new and promising playwrights as Ron Henderson, author of *Says I, Says He*.

Boucicault's rogue is an amiable entertainer, full of passionate blarney for pretty women, fond of whiskey and a good joke. Like Rory O'More, he is a *comedtherin schamer*, and a witty and persuasive talker. His "Irishness," still associated with ignorance and the ubiquitous pig, was obviously intended to amuse the audience. In this respect, and in his fundamental decency and optimism, Boucicault's rogue is related to Handy Andy. He has little of the toughness or the pagan, anarchic spirit of Phelim O'Toole and Billy Dawson.

Each of Boucicault's rogues is linked to an aristocratic figure, usually an Irish rebel chief, for whom he risks his life. Their relationship suggests the traditional one of jester and king, but the Irish rogue is far more deferential than the medieval jester and his descendants, like Moliere's Scapin, who bully and exploit their employers and delight in exposing their weakness and folly. The rebel chiefs are actually Victorians in disguise, while the "rogue" is articulate, good natured, fun loving, an irrepressible *élan vital*. This pattern is most evident in *The Shaughraun*[7] where Robert Ffolliott, echoing Wordsworth, refers to Conn as his "loving play fellow" and his "wild companion." It is striking how persistently the myth makers relegate the English peasant to solid virtue and his Irish counterpart to merry irresponsibility.

While no one of Boucicault's comic heroes is a thorough rogue, Myles-na-Coppaleen in *The Colleen Bawn,* which appeared in 1860 in New York, comes closest. He is a poacher, an ex-convict, a maker of bootleg whiskey. He is sly and nimble as a fox, capable of listening at key holes and windows and of carrying forward his own particular schemes with considerable success. He is unencumbered by the usual obligations, living from day to day in congenial and irreverent idleness. His first entrance on stage, singing, with a keg of whiskey on his shoulder, demonstrates the kind of broad humor which is characteristic of Boucicault:

> *Corrigan.* What's that on your shoulder?
> *Myles.* What's that to you?
> *Corrigan.* I am a magistrate, and can oblige you to answer.
> *Myles.* Well! It's a boulster belongin' to my mother's feather bed.
> *Corrigan.* Stuff'd with whiskey!
> *Myles.* Bedad! How would I know what it's stuff'd wid? I'm not an upholsterer.
> *Corrigan.* Come, Myles, I'm not so bad a fellow as ye may think.
> *Myles.* To think of that now!
> *Corrigan.* I am not the mane creature you imagine!
> *Myles.* Ain't ye now, sir? You keep up appearances mighty well, indeed.
> (1.2.)

Like Rory O'More, Myles is fond of playing on words and is equally artful at dodging the main issue. He picks up on terms used by the magistrate, twisting their meaning or offering a completely preposterous answer (the "boulster" to his "mother's feather bed"). The trick achieved partly by feigned ignorance or simplicity is to throw his questioner off the scent and then double back and trap him in a snap of wit: "I am not the mane creature you imagine!"/"Ain't ye now, sir? You keep up appearances mighty well, indeed."

Myles is romanticized by the fact that he has broken with society, giving up a thriving business as a horse dealer (hence the name, Myles of the Horses)[8] because of his hopeless love for Eily O'Connor, the Colleen Bawn. He is opposed dramatically by Hardress Cregan, a gentleman and a scoundrel, who wins the Colleen Bawn, but does not acknowledge her as his wife because he is ashamed of her peasant ways.

Eily isn't much of a character. I suppose her innocent girlish charm had some appeal to Victorian audiences, but she is self-effacing and self-sacrificing to the point of nausea. Excessively apologetic about her origins, she accepts all the criticisms her husband has to offer on points of grammar. After a time one begins to look forward to the drowning scene with some hope of its success.

Boucicault borrowed his plot from *The Collegians* (1829) by Gerald Griffin, who in turn had based his novel on an actual case of a young peasant woman who was seduced and then murdered by a man of affluence and position. In the real tale, lurid accounts of which may still be read on the walls of pubs in Kerry where the crime took place, the guilty man and his accomplice were both executed; in Boucicault's version the gentleman repents and is reunited with his long suffering colleen.

That reunion is arranged by Myles, who has rescued Eily from various crises, including an attempt on her life. He hands her back to Hardress Cregan with a sly reservation: "When ye cease to love her may dyin' become ye, and when ye do die, lave yer money to the poor, your widdy to me, and we'll both forgive ye." There is little doubt that Eily has chosen the lesser man and that Myles is the true hero of the play. For all his devotion, however, he remains the most independent of the rogues, without a wife or property, or allegiance to any cause.

The marriage between peasant and aristocrat, which is confirmed at the conclusion of the play, is a highly romantic confection in view of the social history of the times. The feudal world represented by Eily and Hardress crumbled during the great famine. While the independent farmer eventually took the place of the peasant, the "Big House" deteriorated more slowly but quite as irrevocably throughout the nineteenth century.

Many of the landlords ruined themselves through extravagance; others were ruined by taxes or by their efforts to help their tenants during the famine. Their property was taken over by local entrepreneurs, represented in Boucicault's plays as Malvolio types, who eventually come to a bad end. Boucicault was probably influenced by Shakespeare's comedies in other aspects as well. He divides his world into similar polarities: the aristocrat who is treated seriously and the peasant, who is invariably comic. In contrast to *As You Like It* or *A Midsummer Night's Dream*, there is little possibility of any fruitful merging of these oppositions. The social gap is much too large. There are, however, two interesting exceptions to the generally wooden representatives of the upper class. They have the energy and spontaneity, if not the limitations, of Boucicault's peasants. Anne Chute is a witty foil to Eily O'Connor, and The O'Grady is a forceful and exuberant character in *Arrah-na-Pogue*. One of Boucicault's most popular creations, O'Grady evidently made a strong impression on Sean O'Casey, who echoes his sentiments in *Juno and the Paycock*: "If there be one thing that misleads a man more than another thing, it is having a firm conviction about anything."

Boucicault was clearly attempting to repeat his success with Myles, as the comic heroes of *Arrah-na-Pogue* and *The Shaughraun* are basically variations on this original character. One interesting difference, which also sets them apart from Rory O'More, is that they are much more obviously clowns. They aim to please, and at the slightest provocation break into a song or a jig. Many of their songs, like "Cruiskeen Lawn," "Brian O'Linn," "The Wearing of the Green," and "The Pretty Girl Milking Her Cow," are based on traditional Irish airs. This practice of interweaving music and dance into the action of the play was adopted by Sean O'Casey and Brendan Behan, who even rouses a corpse to sing in the finale of *The Hostage*.

Conn "the Shaughraun", or "Wanderer", is the true *bodagh*, that is, a comical vagabond, who keeps up a steady barrage of songs and tricks to amuse and confound. Like Myles, Conn has spent time in jail, but his experience does not in the least deter him from further breaches in the shaky structure of the law. He rescues or "poaches" the Fenian, Robert Ffolliott, at least twice in the course of the play and is extremely adroit in eluding all forms of authority. Of all the rogues he is most addicted to knockabout comedy, which proves useful in dodging the police as well as his "ould mother"; Conn turns the poor old woman topsy turvy, exposing her foolishness along with many another's. At the height of his antics, he presides at his own wake, slyly emptying the whiskey jug while the keen is raised over the "corpse." The scene is sheer burlesque as Boucicault reflects little of the macabre found in folk tales and ballads. With an unerring instinct, he catered to the taste of the middle class. The humor of the peasant or the Dublin tenement dweller was darker, more ferocious, much more vital.

Like Phelim O'Toole, Conn has an eye for pretty women, and one of them, Moya, is determined to have him for a husband despite his mother's warning. Her response suggests their basic affinity:

> *Mrs. O'Kelly.* Conn niver did an honest day's work in his life — but dhrinkin', an' fishin', an' shootin', and sportin', and love-makin'.
>
> *Moya.* Sure, that's how the quality pass their lives. (1.3.)

The appeal of such rascals was undoubtedly related to the very serious business of social and economic survival. At the beginning of the nineteenth century early marriage had led to an unprecedented growth in the population from approximately 6.8 million in 1821 to eight million in 1841, the majority of whom lived in poverty, subsisting mainly on the potato. When blight destroyed the potato crop in the late 1840's, a million perished from famine and disease. Those who survived were determined not to make the mistakes that led to disaster for a previous generation. Early marriage was discouraged and economic considerations tended to take precedence over romance. Many young women were forced to accept elderly husbands who could provide them with sustenance, a situation which is the tragic basis of Synge's *Shadow in the Glen.* The appeal of the rogue was the appeal of the forbidden, the daring and romantic choice.

All of Boucicault's rogues are wonderful talkers, whether it be in teasing women or easing themselves out of a difficult situation. Even Shaun, the more predictable hero of *Arrah-na-Pogue* (Arrah of the Kiss)[9] is full of passionate words for the women he loves:

> *Shaun.* Wid the love in my heart that makes every minit a fortune, sure rest is only a waste of time, and to shut my eyes on the sight of your face before me is sinful exthravagance, my darlin'. (1.1.)

There was undoubtedly some identification between Boucicault, an unconventional and articulate man who in his sixties took a third wife half his age, and his roguish heroes who are irresistible to women. The sheer exuberance of Shaun's language is similar to that of Synge's vagabonds, only Shaun is more erotic, a rare quality in fiction and drama of this period. In this play, which appeared in Dublin in 1864, there is a particularly good trial scene, which, as David Krause has noted, so impressed Bernard Shaw that he borrowed it for *The Devil's Disciple*. In the course of this scene Shaun confuses the legal proceedings, creating an uproar in the court, which is trying to convict him of armed robbery. The comedy depends on Shaun's real and pretended ignorance as well as on his ability to create a thicket of language which those conducting the trial (none too bright themselves) can scarcely penetrate:

> *Major.* Now, prisoner, are you guilty or not guilty?
> *Shaun.* Sure, Major, I thought that was what we'd all come here to find out. (2.5.)

In the nineteenth century the "brogue" was associated with ignorance and poverty, and the typical stage Irishman only confirmed that opinion. In Boucicault's plays, however, it became something of an asset, partly no doubt because Boucicault himself played the rogue in what Shaw described as fine "sloothering" tones. The brogue was still considered comical — because of his accent it was assumed that Boucicault could never play tragic roles — but it was becoming the mark of the skillful and persuasive talker, the man whose good humor takes the sting out of his victory in any verbal dueling match. In America H.L. Mencken attributed the new influx of "Irishisms" to the enormous popularity of Irish plays, particularly those of Boucicault. He concluded that such plays encouraged the absorption of Irish pronunciation as well as elements of syntax and grammar into the American language.[10]

Boucicault does manage to work in a few "bulls" from the stage Irish tradition:

> *Regan.* Not a human crature could rache that barrin' he was a saygull" (*Arrah* 3.11.)

And there is still a certain amount of joking about the peasant's failure to grasp English:

> *Claire.* Did they bring him home insensible?
> *Mrs. Kelly.* No, Miss — they brought him home on a shutter . . .
> (*Shaughraun* 3.1)

But this kind of humor has taken a more interesting direction. Unlike most people testing out a foreign language, the Irishman did not feel limited to a basic vocabulary but helped himself to a generous assortment of syllables for their sheer sensory pleasure. William Carleton is the most skillful of Irish writers in exploiting the comic possibilities in this tendency; it is an essential ingredient in the work of Boucicault, Synge and O'Casey as well.

In Boucicault's plays the values attached to standard English and to Irish English are curiously reversed. The speech of the peasants is not only comical, but witty and imaginative, while that of the upper classes — with the exception of Anne Chute and The O'Grady, who might have stepped out of Restoration Comedy — is devoid of resonance or feeling. Most of it is so bad that it reads like camp: "Do you know the place where these ruffians resort?" This is not living speech, but the contrivance of a stage Englishman, who is as bad as Sean O'Casey's wooden representatives of the middle class. It is very likely that no conscious judgment was involved, that Boucicault simply failed to create plausible upper class characters (though he succeeded in *London Assurance*); the consequences nonetheless modified public attitudes toward the Irish countryman.

In fashioning his Irish plays, Boucicault made more explicit use of historic than of legendary material, though there are curious juxtapositions of the two traditions. Finn MacCool appears in *Arrah-na-Pogue*, for example, as Beamish MacCoul, an aristocrat with a price on his head. In the opening scene he is a witty Robin Hood figure who unfortunately lapses into a conventional posture once the action is under way. Both *Arrah-na-Pogue* and *The Shaughraun* take place in 1798, the year of the ill fated rising commemorated by Yeats in *Cathleen ni Houlihan* and Tom Flanagan in *The Year of the French*. As a result of his role in that short-lived effort to wrest control from the English, MacCoul is declared an outlaw, and like the earlier *rapparees*, becomes a highwayman in order to recover some of the money from his estates. Boucicault complicates the plot by yet another episode from Irish history. In 1803 Robert Emmet was involved in a brief military skirmish in the streets of Dublin. Although he might have escaped, he returned to see his sweetheart, Sarah Curran, was captured and subjected to a brutal public execution. Emmet has been memorialized by writers from Tom Moore to James Joyce, who lingers with grisly humor on the implements of execution in the Cyclops chapter in *Ulysses*. In Boucicault's play the renegade hero also returns to see his sweetheart, placing his life in jeopardy. But, unlike the "bould Robert," he repents of his revolutionary activities and receives a full pardon from Dublin Castle.

There is no mention of revolution in *The Colleen Bawn*, but the ghost of Robert Emmet reappears embodied in the Fenian hero, Robert Ffolliott in *The Shaughraun*. Ffolliott, a most unlikely Fenian, surrenders rather than allow a priest to lie in order to conceal his whereabouts. Like MacCoul, he adheres to a gentleman's code of honor and is finally pardoned at the critical moment and reunited with his sweetheart. There is no hint in this play of the bloody fracas in Manchester in 1867 which led to the execution of three ordinary men, the so-called Manchester martyrs, or to the explosion in Clerkenwell prison that killed twenty people and leveled a row of tenement houses — both desperate efforts to free Fenian prisoners.

Irish attitudes toward the law permeate Boucicault's plays and provide the melodramatic feats of the major characters with some authentic scaffolding. Popular resistance to authority is real enough as is the response to hunted men. And although Boucicault romanticizes his revolutionaries and makes his outlaw heroes comical — they have much in common with Finn the trickster — he occasionally reveals the grimmer side of popular sentiment. In *The Shaughraun*, for example, the informer, Harvey Duff, commits suicide to escape being torn to pieces by an angry mob.[11]

Boucicault's use of historic material contributed to the popularity of his plays not only in Ireland but in England and America, where there was a growing interest in Irish affairs. Since its initial production *The Colleen Bawn* has been staged more than three thousand times, has been translated into French, and has been made the basis of an opera, *The Lily of Killarney*. *Arrah-na-Pogue* was given a command performance at Dublin Castle and was admired by Queen Victoria. The only serious policital objection to any of Boucicault's work came in response to a song in *The Shaughraun*, "The Wearin' of the Green," which was prohibited in Great Britain because of the tragedy at Clerkenwell prison.

Boucicault's plays undoubtedly had a mollifying effect on public opinion regarding the "wild Irish." Besides their value as entertainers, his comic heroes have virtues which Victoria would have approved of. They are all figures of exceptional courage and daring, all too willing to sacrifice themselves for the women they love or the chief to whom they owe their allegiance. Although they may stretch the truth, they are basically honest with firm loyalties and a core of moral conviction. Unlike the legendary rogue, they are chaste as well as chivalrous and either marry the girl of their choice or save her life. They may be admonished for laziness or drinking or poaching, but these are minor failings after all. Despite their status as outlaws, there is nothing threatening or brutal about these rogues; indeed they are a curiously humble lot, apologetic for their ignorance and respectful toward the upper classes. At one point Arrah admonishes Shaun, in reference to one of the gentry, "to do as you are bid." There is no anger in any of them and no sense of irony. Instead, Boucicault's comic heroes express an optimism, which completely ignores the bitter conditions of postfamine Ireland.[12]

Ned Lebow has discussed how the poverty of the Irish was largely attributed to their reputed indolence, while the British poor were considered victims of impersonal economic forces beyond their control. Despite the wretched conditions under which the Irish lived, particularly in the early nineteenth century, they were considered to be generally happy with their lot; therefore the argument was advanced: why should any effort be made to alter their lives?[13] Boucicault's gentle rogues confirmed the stereotype of the happy, child-like indolent Celt, which has currency even today.

It is very much to the point that for all their heroism, unlike Rory O'More, they are not regarded as men, but as "boys." It is the same phenomenon experienced by American Negroes and dramatized by Richard Wright in *Black Boy* (which in other repects is very different in content). In the work of Boucicault and Wright neither Irish peasant nor Negro is fully emancipated. The Irishman may defy the law and live merrily on the fringes of the community, but he is scarcely a threat to the status quo and hardly fit for Home Rule. No wonder he was popular with audiences weary of agitation and alarmed by the Fenian "menace." They responded to these figures as they had responded to Lady Morgan's Wild Irish Girl and Thomas Crofton Croker's leprechauns, all of them innocent and amusing diversions.

The fact remains that these plays of Boucicault were also popular with Irish audiences and they are still performed today. That tireless playgoer, Joseph Holloway, tells us the people who flocked to the Queens Theatre, the traditional house of Irish drama, were so familiar with Boucicault's work that they could supply the appropriate line if an actor missed his cue. He speaks of an 1897 revival of *The Colleen Bawn* as a "magnet," which was as

> potent as ever on this occasion and drew a thoroughly good-humored, closely-packed, big-hat-and-feathered, mostly country audience within the walls of the theatre . . . The audience enjoyed it as thoroughly as if they had never witnessed it before, although I am sure most of them almost knew it by heart, so frequently have they revelled in its many excellencies.[14]

Speculation of this sort is always open to question, but it seems likely that the Irish had begun to enjoy the notion of themselves as roguish charmers. Moreover, Boucicault's romantic drama allowed them to forget the more brutal facts of peasant life while appealing to their sentimental patriotism. He did nothing to question or criticize their traditional values and their sentimental attachment to the old Catholic Gaelic world.

In Boucicault's plays the bulwark of authority is the parish priest. He is an unassailable father figure, the *senex*, whom the comic hero does not dare to overturn. Conn or Myles may tease the priest or slip a little whiskey into his "tay," but they acknowledge his superiority, and in any conflict the priest invariably prevails. At the conclusion of *The Shaughraun*, Father Dolan actually takes Conn by the ear and returns him to his mother, thus sealing his fate as a perennial adolescent.

Within the limits of romantic comedy, Boucicault again strikes a note of realism. By the nineteenth century the ordinary peasant was so completely stripped of his rights under the old system of land tenure that he had lost all personal sense of autonomy. Authority was vested in the Church or in the school master or in any representative of the Big House. The more adventurous or the more desperate emigrated. Many who remained tended to accept the traditional wisdom that because they were ignorant and poor, they were inferior.

Although Boucicault was not interested in any serious analysis of Irish history, he was never simply a showman; his melodramatic schemes are always shaped by a real political consciousness. Public approval meant financial success — and his gross receipts were enormous — but it also meant public sympathy for the Irish people, public support for new laws governing health, old age pensions and ownership of the land. John Synge, the first major playwright to emerge during the Revival, ignored political questions entirely and produced riots in Dublin and in the United States. By that time the age of compromise had passed and the stage was being set for an authentic revolution.

4. The Comic Hero

I N *A Portrait of the Artist as a Young Man* the development of
Stephen Dedalus as artist-priest is directly related to his
growing command of language. This theme, among the most
significant in modern Irish literature, emerges from the resistance of
the Gael to an alien language and mode of thought. That resistance
is evident in Stephen Dedalus, set apart despite his education from
the culture of Shakespeare and Ben Jonson because he was born in
Dublin:

> How different are the words *home, Christ, ale, master,* on his lips
> and on mine! I cannot speak or write these words without unrest
> of spirit. His language, so familiar and so foreign, will always be
> for me an acquired speech. I have not made or accepted its
> words. My voice holds them at bay. My soul frets in the shadow of his
> language.[1]

William Carleton (1794–1869) was probably the first Irish
writer to establish a link between the development of the hero and
an increasing skill with language. His response is less complex and
less ironic than that of Joyce, but his sense of a divided heritage gave
him also a sensitivity toward language, a way of distancing himself
from the dialect which he developed as a literary medium.

A peasant's son, who spoke Irish as well as English and Latin,
Carleton was born, the youngest of fourteen children in Clogher, a
small parish in County Tyrone, Ulster. Carleton, too, considered the
priesthood as a vocation and picked up what education he could
from itinerant school masters. There were no Jesuits available and
certainly little in the way of formal schooling. As a result or possibly
from inclination, much of his youthful energy took a different direc-

tion: "I attended every wake, dance, fair, and merrymaking in the neighborhood, and became so celebrated for dancing, hornpipes, jigs and reels, that I was soon without a rival in the parish."[2] The wonderfully comic "Denis O'Shaughnessy Going to Maynooth" is based on Carleton's memories of himself as a "local phenomenon." Like Joyce he changed his mind about the priesthood, and instead of settling into the uneventful life of a small farmer, young Carleton set out for Dublin with a copy of *Gil Blas* in his pocket, determined to make a name for himself.

He gradually discovered that there was a market for the kind of story he knew best. And so he began to write for various Dublin journals, drawing on his memories of Clogher and the old tales he had heard from his father, a born story teller with an inexhaustible fund of "charms, old ranns, or poems, old prophecies, religious superstitions, tales of pilgrims, miracles, and pilgrimages, anecdotes of blessed priests and friars, revelations from ghosts and fairies. . . ."[3]

William Carleton recorded a particular page of Irish history with passion and vividness, but his writing — and certainly his novels — is very uneven. *The Black Prophet* (1847) and *The Emigrants of Ahadarra* (1848) contain elemental scenes of great power, similar to those of Thomas Hardy in *Tess of the D'Urbervilles* or *The Return of the Native*. Other novels, such as the sentimental romance *Jane Sinclair* (1841), are scarcely palatable to a modern audience. His best work is undoubtedly *Traits and Stories of the Irish Peasantry* (1830; second series, 1833), which won him an international reputation during his life time. These stories vary a great deal in tone and subject matter. In "Wildgoose Lodge" he probably produced the most horrifying tale to come out of nineteenth century Ireland. It is based on an actual event, the murder of an entire family, bludgeoned and burned to death by a gang of Ribbonmen.[4] Reprisal was equally brutal. Carleton, himself, had seen the bodies of those executed, bound in tar sacks and gibbeted as a public warning. No modern writer equaled Carleton's ability to convey the cruel realities of Irish life until Yeats sat down to write his denunciation of war in "Nineteen Hundred and Nineteen." Few of Carleton's stories, however, are unrelieved by comedy. His own theory was that no one ever possessed a "higher order of humor whose temperament was not naturally melancholy." In Carleton's prose, melancholy and mirth "frequently flash together"[5] in the manner of gallows humor.

Like many of his contemporaries, Carleton became embroiled

in controversy; much of his fiction was written with a particular issue in mind. He contributed to Caesar Otway's *Christian Examiner*, notorious for anti-Catholic propaganda, and to politically conservative journals such as the *Dublin University Magazine*. Later in his career when he began to associate with Thomas Davis and the staff of the revolutionary journal, *The Nation*, he publicly apologized for anything he had written earlier which might have offended the Irish people. With Davis's encouragement, he wrote *Valentine M'Clutchy* (1847), an attack on landlords and the system of rackrenting. In *The Black Prophet*, dedicated to the British prime minister, he describes the terrible effects of famine in rural Ireland. Through this fascinating, frequently lurid, but intensely compelling book, he both attacks the grain profiteer and apologizes for the violence of the poor. He could be a harsh and sometimes questionable judge of his own people, inclined to sermonize, as in "Parra Sastha" and "Larry McFarland's Wake," on the virtues of industry and good hygiene.

Carleton has a tendency to pause in midnarrative to argue about a political or social issue, a tendency which not only undermines the structure of his fiction but contributes to a lack of coherence in tone or point of view. Some of his characters, as in "Shane Fadh's Wedding" and "Ned McKeown," are crude and downright offensive stereotypes.[6] Despite these and other failings, he wrote two or three of the best modern Irish stories, and his work is an enormously rich source of information on folk customs and beliefs.

Carleton was particularly sensitive to the issue of language, vehemently objecting to the notion that the speech of the ordinary Irishman was nothing but "an absurd congeries of brogue and blunder."[7] More than any of his contemporaries, he helped to dispel that notion. His narratives contain many Gaelic phrases, explained and translated, to demonstrate the quality of native speech. His dialogue, at its best, metaphorical, rich, peppery, and highly inflected, expresses the energy and wit of the Irish country people. Carleton explained that his method of writing Irish English was to "transfer the genius, the idiomatic peculiarity and conversational spirit of the one language into the other, precisely as the people themselves do."[8] "Denis O'Shaughnessy Going to Maynooth," like "Phelim O'Toole's Courtship," is marred by narrative and structural defects, but these are far outweighed by the pleasure afforded through the wonderfully comic language.

As a young man destined for the seminary at Maynooth, Denis is the focal point of family and community. He expresses the dearest wish of the Irish peasant: to have a son chosen for the priesthood. By virtue of his intelligence and piety, Denis is early regarded as a paragon, and much of the humor in the story revolves around his intellectual pretensions, which are furiously encouraged by family and friends. There is, of course, a sizable gap between claim and reality. A man in his position is expected to discourse on all subjects, and Denis, depending on the gullibility of his listeners is never at a loss for words; indeed his rhetoric grows more extravagant in proportion to his lack of information: "I vow to Demosthenes, if you provoke me I'll unsluice the flood-gates of my classicality, an' bear you off like a sthraw on the surface of my larned indignation."[9] Speaking of that period in his own life upon which he based the character of Denis, Carleton observed that he had affected "a lofty dignity which would have thrown a penetrating man of common sense into convulsions of laughter. My style was as fine a specimen of the preposterous and pendantic as ever was spoken."[10]

In this story much of the humor is in the talk; one is struck again and again by the Irish love of rhetoric and argument, even for rules of grammar and for obscure forms of knowledge. This was natural in an oral culture where the story teller was an important source of information and entertainment, and the ordinary means of education were unavailable to the mass of people. In Ireland this aptitude for language was further cultivated by the bardic schools with their elaborate rituals of instruction and the courts of poetry which kept the Gaelic traditions alive through the eighteenth century.[11]

Carleton anticipates not only Joyce, but Synge and Shaw in conceiving of language as a dynamic process reflecting growth and change within an individual character. As Christy Mahon's development into an authentic hero is expressed primarily through his mastery of language, so Denis's development is reflected in three fairly distinct levels of expression.

As a "young priest" Denis speaks Latin and English with a strong trace of the brogue, which tends to undercut his most solemn pronouncements. He misuses words and delivers wildly erroneous statements in a highly formal syntax and utterly pompous tone. The very extravagance of his language as well as his claims are comical indeed. We are told that "when a lad is designed for the priesthood, he is, as if by a species of intuition, supposed to know more or less of everything. . . ." He is egged on by his father, "ould Denis," who engages him in verbal combat to show him off to the neighbors. He is determined that Denis will "tread in his own footsteps," having observed that his son possesses "as bright a talent for the dark and mysterious" as he does himself:

> Why, you don't know at all what I could do by larnin'. It would be no trouble to me to divide myself into two halves, an' argue the one agin the other.
> You would, in troth, Dinny. . . .
> Or read the Greek Tistament wid my right eye, an' translate it at the same time wid my left, according to the Greek an' English sides of my face, wid my tongue constrein' into Irish, unknownst to both o' them.
> Why Denis, he must have a head like a bell to be able to get into things.
> Throth an' he has that an' 'ill make a noise in conthroversy yet, if he lives
> (978).

This passage is a good example of the kind of verbal energy that distinguishes the story. The language is highly metaphoric and witty with that flair for the fantastical which Vivian Mercier believes inherent in the Irish comic tradition.[12] There are no boundaries to Denis's imagination nor to his self-importance, which is slyly pricked by his audience. Irish humor frequently takes pleasure in such distortion of bodily features, which goes far beyond ordinary caricature, suggesting a link with the ancient practice of satire, often a form of intense ridicule aimed at specific parts of the body. Irish humor — and this is particularly true of Carleton — also makes use of extended figures of speech (or one figure capped by another) that are ironic or ambivalent in meaning. Thus the clause, "He must have a head like a bell," ostensibly suggests clarity, but there is a secondary implication of emptiness and noise, which is picked up (capped) in the last line and joined with a typical macabre joke: He'll "make a noise in conthroversy . . . if he lives." Irish fondness for a good story is frequently expressed in a willingness to elaborate on the bare bones of the truth — or to dispense with it altogether. Carleton, himself, observed that what the Irish lack in material prosperity they compensate for by richness of imagination. In his own fiction this sometimes takes the disconcerting form of narratives within narratives. One such "divarshin" within this story presents Martin Luther as an Irishman inventing Protestanism with the help of the devil. The tale begins with Luther seated at his desk with an ample supply of wine and whiskey punch when in walks the devil, "a grave-looking man, in the garbage of a monk," and they begin to discuss the plight of the poor clericals who "can't afford to be licentious for want o' money." "Thrue; an' I would wish to see it made chape," says the other," if it was only to vex the wealthy." The tale, generally characterized by dreadful puns and the playful rearrangement of history, is probably drawn from folklore.[13] The comedy here, and throughout "Denis O'Shaughnessy Going to Maynooth," also depends to some extent on the ignorance and superstitiousness of the country people.

In his autobiography as well as in his fiction, Carleton wrote about the extremely poor condition of education in Ireland (a national system was not introduced until the 1830's) despite the reverence of the people for learning of all kinds. As a young man eager for classical training, Carleton was forced to make do with meager and frequently interrupted instruction under various masters who usually met their pupils in barns or in roadside shelters, the so-called hedge schools. In two stories, "The Poor Scholar" and "The Hedge School," he gives us an account of the style of education available in those days when the position of master was determined publicly through a battle of wits.

The skills of such men must have varied enormously, but many were trained in rhetoric and argument, were excellent mathematicians and very often acquainted with Latin and Greek as well as much knowledge that was highly esoteric. The world for them was a literary battlefield. They were forced to be on the defensive, for their scholarly reputations were open to challenge, and they could be ousted at any time by a more skillful debator. To protect themselves, they resorted to rather remarkable advertisements of their achievements as may be observed from the following excerpt:

Spelling, Reading, Writing, and Arithmetic, upon altogether new principles, hitherto undiscovered by any excepting himself, and for

which he expects a Patent from Trinity College, Dublin; or, at
any rate, from Squire Johnston, Esq., who paternizes many of the
pupils; Book-keeping, by single and double entry — Geometry,
Trigonometry, Stereometry, Mensuration, Navigation, Guaging,
Surveying, Dialing, Astronomy, Astrology, Austerity, Fluxions,
Geography ancient and modern — Maps . . . Natural and Moral
Philosophy, Pneumatics, Optics, Dioptics, Catroptics, Hydraulics . . .
Physic, by theory only, Metaphysics practically . . .[14]

Many of these itinerant schoolmasters were "spoiled" priests or
wandering poets like Owen MacCarthy in *The Year of the French*.
They had a reputation for radical politics, seducing women, and,
naturally, a gargantuan thirst. Their highly eccentric manner and
their fondness for hyperbole undoubtedly contributed to the portrait of young Denis.

As his story progresses Denis, extremely conscious of social position, begins to adopt "a gloomy formality," which is intended to
conceal his real feelings. We are told that "his nose was set upon his
face in a kind of firm defiance against infidels, heretics, and excommunicated persons." His pompousness becomes even more
outrageous once he has acquired a horse and a good suit of clothes.
He begins to refer to himself as "Dionysus," a name which, he
believes, carries more dignity than the common "Denis." His choice,
is, of course, ironic in view of his status as a "young Priest." But
"Dionysus" has been quick to observe that piety has material as well
as spiritual rewards. At home he insists on meat instead of the
customary meal of potatoes, and the neighbors are amused to note
that his learning "blazed with a peculiar lustre whenever he felt
himself out at elbows." This point brings us to the satirical core of
the story, which is an attack on the worldliness of certain priests.
With considerable relish, Carleton describes their fondness for food
and drink and merrymaking. His satiric thrust is sharpest in describing the maneuvers by which Denis is finally selected as a candidate
for the seminary at Maynooth. His family must first bribe the local
priest and then the bishop, himself, before Denis is accepted.
Despite the humorous dialogue, there is no doubt of the seriousness
of Carleton's criticism. Had Denis been a poor boy, he would have
been rejected.

Many critics, notably Benedict Kiely in *Poor Scholar*, have ob-
jected to Carleton's treatment of the clergy. And "Denis

O'Shaughnessy" has been singled out because it first appeared in Caesar Otway's *Christian Examiner* (1831) and contained more anti-Catholic sentiment than appeared in later editions of the story.[15] There is undoubtedly ground for objection, but in the more complete version which appeared in *Traits and Stories* (1833) the satire is well honed and skillfully aimed and, if anything, strengthens the artistic merit of the piece. Furthermore, the evidence suggests that Carleton lost sight of his Protestant readership as he became absorbed in his characters, creating the elder O'Shaughnessys in the pattern of his own parents. The story, for all its satirical qualities, turns out to be a celebration of Irish life.

As Denis prospers, his language becomes more consciously rhetorical and Latinate, more heavily studded with literary and theological allusions. There is less evidence of the brogue and fewer blunders in usage, and his flights of fancy are usually reserved for family and friends. This, for example, is a passage in which Denis warms to the prospective pleasures of his life as a priest:

> Thus we go on absolving in great style, till it is time for the
> matutinal meal — vulgarly called breakfast; when the whiskey,
> eggs, toast, and tea as strong as Hercules, with ham, fowl,
> beef-steaks, or mutton-chops, all pour in upon us in the full tide of
> hospitality. Helter-skelter, cut and thrust, right and left, we work
> away, till the appetite reposes itself upon the cushion of repletion;
> and off we go once more, full and warm to the delicate
> employment of adjudicating upon sin and transgression, until
> dinner comes.
> (1002).

In the presence of more educated people, he tends to be modest, though tenacious and shrewd in argument. His sheer delight in language is still very much apparent as is his wish to impress. After he has offered the bishop his "most supercilious thanks," the latter advises him to "use plain words;" that advice is not heeded until Denis is finally converted into an ordinary citizen. His conversion, like Christy Mahon's, is effected through the medium of a pretty woman but, while the playboy is freed, Denis is bound fast.

Although he initially tries to discourage her, Denis eventually realizes that he loves Susan Connor, whom he has long enjoyed impressing with his eloquence. In an elaborate conversation which becomes increasingly preposterous the more he is drawn to Susan, he admits his ambition to distinguish himself through the Church. In keeping with the solemn and pietistic role he has chosen, he does not admit to any personal loss but sympathizes with Susan, who is forced to retire in the face of such arguments as:

> The Irish hierarchy is plased to look on me as a luminary of almost superhuman brilliancy and coruscation: my talents she pronounces to be of the first magnitude, my eloquence classical and over-whelming, and my learning adorned by that poor insignificant attribute denominated by philosophers unfathomability!
> (995).

Having bargained his way into the seminary at Maynooth, and having observed the life style of the clergy on an intimate basis, Denis realizes he has made a serious mistake. As he becomes trapped in his own posturing, the story becomes more serious and less interesting. Denis, the imposter, is a wonderfully comic figure, but once he begins to regret his ambitions, his desire to soar over the heads of the neighbors, to achieve the lofty eminence of a bishop, his language loses some of its imaginative force. Denis finally emerges a wiser human being with some experience of the world and some self-knowledge:

> I have mingled with those on whom . . . I looked with awe, as on men who held vested in themselves some mysterious and spiritual power. I have mingled with them, Susan, and I find them neither better nor worse than those who still look upon them as I once did.
> (1024).

His (relatively) plain English, spoken without a trace of the brogue, suggests a more sober and realistic nature.

Having accepted the role of the hero, Denis must go through with the necessary denouement. He is caught and caught fast in the net which a more wary Stephen Dedalus will take care to avoid. He has accepted the values thrust on him by his father, enjoyed his sense of superiority, even received the tribute of the people in the form of some fairly astonishing gifts on the eve of his departure for Maynooth. Along with such items as an oak sapling for clinching arguments "wid a visitation upon the kidney," he acquires an assortment of old books including "Irish Rogues and Rapparees" and "Garden of Love."

Thomas Flanagan has suggested that the story should have ended with Denis's triumphant return home with the bishop's endorsement of his candidacy for Maynooth.[16] Instead, Carleton provides us with a florid romantic scene and then compresses the events of two years into three pages in which Denis leaves Maynooth after his father's death and marries Susan. It seems to me, however, that Carleton's instinct was basically sound. His story does require a comic resolution: the imposter, like Moliere's Tartuffe, must be unmasked. His mistake was to sentimentalize, to treat his mock hero seriously and then to push the concluding scene off stage in a kind of epilogue.

Perhaps the problem lay even deeper, in the conservatism of Irish culture. In traditional comedy the hero overcomes the *senex* figure, the father or his surrogate, and thus the dynamic renewal of the community is assured. In Carleton's comedy there is no fundamental conflict between *senex* and hero; the son accepts the values of the father. And in choosing marriage instead of the priesthood, Denis also confirms the tradition into which he was born. He develops sufficient insight to recognize his own foolishness, but there is neither rogue nor rebel in young Denis; he depends on the ties that bind him to the community. It was not until years had elapsed and much of the vitality had been sapped from the Irish rural community that Synge's playboy was able to break those ties and accept the challenge of the open road.

Like the legendary rogues, Synge's hero is an "outsider," a "man on the run," but his character and growing mastery of language also link him to the boastful, egocentric Denis O'Shaughnessy.[17]

Synge's decision to make Christy an "outsider" was directly influenced by the homeless men he met in his own solitary wanderings. In "The Vagrants of Wicklow" he admires the unusual vitality of these people as well as their distinctive temperament: "In all the circumstances of the tramp life there is a peculiar value for those who look at life in Ireland with an eye that is aware of the arts also."[18]

The tramp has an interesting history in Ireland, where society was highly mobile prior to the seventeenth century. Poets, brehons (judges or law givers), priests and kerns, all traveled the roads. The people were accustomed to following their grazing herds over vast

areas which were held in common; in the summer they lived in
booleys, temporary camps which, according to the English, often
sheltered the outlaw or the thief. The Elizabethans were so ap-
prehensive about Irish rovers, they executed many of them and ex-
erted considerable effort to make the Irishman into a farmer, rooted
in one spot, highly visible and subject to English law. In the nineteenth century the roads were again swarming. Many had been
driven from their homes during famine periods and, according to
writers as disparate as William Carleton and Maria Edgeworth, they
were treated sympathetically. Religion reinforced the native inclination to be hospitable. Itinerant workers were also a common sight
tramping the roads in search of seasonal employment. As farms
were consolidated at the close of the century, however, and the
landless man was forced to emigrate, the tramp was a more unusual
phenomenon, and one to be suspicious of. Associated with the
tinkers, who were regarded as promiscuous thieves, they had
become outsiders, threatening to the small farmers and the slowly
emerging middle class. So the tramp becomes an appropriate symbol for Synge and Beckett, artists who set themselves in opposition to
conventional society.

At his initial appearance Christy Mahon is a slight figure, dirty
and exhausted, wanting only to sit by the fire and gnaw a turnip in
peace. At this point he bears little resemblance to Denis
O'Shaughnessy. Shy and awkward and none too bright, Christy is "a
middling scholar only." Before he struck the famous blow with the
loy, he was clearly a scapegoat figure, despised by his father and
isolated from the community at large because he failed to measure
up to their standards of manliness. Christy supposedly lacked
courage, was a clumsy worker, and, worst of all, had no stomach for
alcohol. Much is made of his sexual arrestment and his timidity
toward women, whom the father tells us made sport of him as the
"looney of Mahon's."

To be sure the father is a questionable witness, given his bouts
with drink and insanity, as well as his fury toward his son. But Christy's own account of his past life, as well as his obvious terror of his
father when the latter catches up with him, suggests the basic truth
of this characterization.

That The Playboy is a comic version of the oedipal theme has
long been recognized.[19] If he is ever to become a man, Christy must
rebel against his father, must slay him symbolically and ritualistical-

ly. The critical moment comes when the father, in a reversal of the classical oedipal situation, tries to force Christy into marriage with the woman who nursed him as a child. Christy strikes his blow to escape the implication of incest with this "walking terror," weighing over two hundred pounds, and thus starts on the difficult journey that will lead him to autonomy.

Mayo, like much of Ireland at the turn of the century, is a world in the grip of the fathers. Michael James for all his drinking and carousing is conventional enough in his demands; his daughter Pegeen has little choice but to manage his business in a thrifty and tough-minded fashion. Her proposed marriage to Shawn Keogh is the only escape route she has managed to secure, and that marriage with its promise of heifers offers to be more beneficial to Michael James than to his very angry daughter. Mayo is dreary and monotonous, but beyond its immediate boundaries the outer world appears threatening. No one offers to go to the aid of the stranger, who turns out to be Christy, apparently dying in the ditch outside the shebeen.

Religion and the family, the institutions that shored up the foundations of Carleton's world, have become sterile and constricting, and the sense of community has deteriorated. One is more conscious of the characters as individuals because of their personal isolation and animosity toward one another. They are manipulative and competitive, qualities encouraged by the money economy that was slowly becoming established and which Synge believed was corrupting the simple life of the people which, despite its difficulties, was in many ways beautiful. In *The Shadow of the Glen* he sets up a similar dichotomy: Dan Burke and Michael Dara are primarily interested in money, while the tramp offers Nora Burke the possibility of returning to a simpler, freer life, though it poses many hardships.

In *The Playboy* spiritual authority is represented by Father Reilly, whose presence is constantly being evoked by the pious Shawn Keogh. The priest is merely censorious, a very different figure from the hearty and compassionate men who appear in the work of Lover, Boucicault and even Carleton. His energies seem to be entirely focused on preventing any premarital sex among his parishioners. Keogh is terrified at the thought of being alone with Pegeen and is ridiculed for his timidity. By completely giving up his authority to the priest, he becomes another kind of fool. When Father Reilly learns that Christy has appeared on the scene, he is quick to send in the Widow Quin to "protect" Pegeen. When that doesn't work, he cuts through the red tape, delaying her marriage, "dreading that young gaffer" who, unlike Keogh, is sexually potent. It is interesting that the priest never actually appears on the stage; his physical presence is unnecessary as his spiritual authority over Keogh is absolute.

Given the dreary lives of the people of Mayo, bound fast by poverty, custom and religion, it is little wonder that they are attracted by a man who has committed a violent and revolutionary act. The fantastical and the unexpected has occurred, and Christy is hailed as a heroic and, above all, a manly figure. As an outlaw he enjoys celebrity as well as protection from the police. He represents freedom and energy; he is a man who might well revitalize a community in which chastity is the highest virtue and the wake a central ritual.

The conflicting images of death and resurrection which dominate *The Playboy* do in fact recall the traditional observances of the Irish wake. Death for the devout Christian is never a matter entirely for grief; in Ireland even the poorest families provide food, drink, and tobacco, and memories of more ancient and pagan customs still linger. Until well into the nineteenth century funeral games, including kissing and mock marriages, evidently originating in obscure rites of fertility, were as essential a feature as the keen or ritual crying of the mourners.[20] In *The Playboy*, therefore, it is not surprising that activity shifts back and forth between the courting of Pegeen and Kate Cassidy's wake. Unlike the traditional rites, here there is plenty of drinking but little celebration: "When we sunk her bones at noonday in her narrow grave, there were five men, aye, and six men, stretched out retching speechless on the holy stones." Death rather than life dominates the people of Mayo. Their talk, often fantastical, is strongly tinged with the macabre:

> . . . when I was a young lad there was a graveyard beyond the
> house with the remnants of a man who had thighs as long as your
> arm. He was a horrid man, I'm telling you, and there was many a fine
> Sunday I'd put him together for fun, and he with shiny bones,
> you wouldn't meet the like of these days in the cities of the
> world.
> (Act 3)

They are delighted in details of the supposed murder which encourages comparison with such grotesque incidents as: "a party was kicked in the head by a red mare, and he went killing horses a great while, till he eat the insides of a clock and died after." Such ferocity and savage humor seem to distinguish the best Irish comic writing. These qualities are deeply embedded in the folklore and are reflected in the work of Carleton, Joyce, O'Casey, Beckett, and Flann O'Brien.

Regeneration for the people of Mayo must come from outside, possibly through Christy Mahon, whose association with the image of the rotting corpse is paradoxical. "Christy" suggests "Christ," the mystery of the dying and reviving god, that ancient symbol of eternal return. Christy is, in a certain sense, the resurrected spirit of his father — a fierce and potent man. He is first introduced as "a queer fellow above going mad or getting his death maybe." His revival is linked to images of murder and decay which emerge even in the love scene introduced by Pegeen, who has an affinity for the morbid or grotesque: "You're right daring to go ask me that, when all knows you'll be starting to some girl in your own townland, when your father's rotten in four months or five." Her first suitor, Sean Keogh, is linked with the "west room," the room traditionally reserved for parents who have given up their authority in the household, anticipating old age and death. Only a man as joyous as Christy could win her over to the side of life.

David Krause has made the interesting observation that Christy Mahon is similar in spirit to Oisin, who represents the ancient vitality and lustiness of pagan Ireland. In the "Dialogue Between Oisin and Patrick," a long poem of over a hundred ballad stanzas probably written in the sixteenth century, Oisin emerges as an

> eloquent champion of pagan freedom. . . . The satiric portrait
> of St. Patrick and the clergy, while it may be unhistorical, reflects
> the emergence of a spirit of anti-clericalism and irreverence in
> the common people and the folk bards of medieval Ireland. And
> apparently this spirit, symbolically projected by Oisin, developed
> into a cumulative literary tradition which, though a minority voice
> in the country, has remained alive in modern Ireland. . . .[21]

Krause takes issue with Daniel Corkery's complaint about the pagan, "un-Irish" quality of Synge's writing, arguing that it is this very pagan and erotic quality that links Synge to the bardic tradition.

Christy is also related to the poet-fool who appears in the twelfth century *Aislinge Meic Conglinne* (*The Vision of Mac Conglinne*) and to the "playboys" who are remembered in Irish folklore from the eighteenth century. Because these figures are quite calculating in their assumption of a comic mask, however, they will be discussed in the chapter on Tarry Flynn, who shares this quality.

As Christy begins to understand his new position, he is gradually transformed: the country fool emerges as an authentic hero. Responding to the demand of the Mayo people, he is increasingly given to great leaps of imagination and daring. The "middling scholar," who doesn't understand the names of certain crimes, becomes as eloquent as the fabled rogue. The bare story of his one single blow: "I just riz the loy and let fall the edge of it on the ridge of his skull," increases in drama and savage detail: "He gave a drive with the scythe, and I gave a lep to the east. Then I turned around with my back to the north, and I hit a blow on the ridge of his skull, laid him stretched out, and he split to the knob of his gullet." With a little more encouragement, he achieves mythic proportions as "a gallant orphan cleft his father with one blow to the breeches belt."

The dialect that made Andy Rooney the butt of the upper classes becomes here the potent instrument of the hero. Christy Mahon is a peasant and a comic figure, but a hero nonetheless by virtue of his willingness to challenge all comers and to defend his new concept of himself. One begins by laughing at him, as one laughs at the earlier clowns, but is eventually won over to his point of view. Christy's gift for language, which always tends to be comical in its extravagance, recalls that other prodigious talker, Denis O'Shaughnessy. Each is able to impose his own particular vision of himself upon the people around him. Synge, who revised *The Playboy* at least ten times, was a far more careful writer than Carleton, and so there is a closer and more dramatic correlation between Christy's development as poet-hero and his growing mastery of language. The verbal genius of both Denis and Christy lift them above the ranks of ordinary men, but Denis in a way characteristic of the Irish comic character uses language to dazzle and evade, to create a mask which conceals his true nature. Christy is the exception, the man who finally becomes the antithetical self,[22] the hero he is reputed to be.

Synge learned a good deal about the use of Irish English from Douglas Hyde and Lady Gregory who took more care to render it accurately than most of the writers who preceded them. Moreover, earlier writers, even William Carleton, chose standard English for prose narrative. Irish English was reserved for dialogue, particularly for its comic effects. In *The Love Songs of Connacht* Douglas Hyde provided a translation that captured the spirit of the Gaelic original by stretching the possibilities of the dialect as a literary medium. In Lady Gregory's *Cuchulain of Muirthemne* the heroes of the ancient sagas speak in the language of the Galway peasants with which she had been familiar since childhood. Synge was to adopt the same technique in *Deirdre of the Sorrows* in which both Conchubor and his attendant speak in dialect.

Synge had studied Irish as a student at Trinity College, but at Yeats's suggestion went to the Aran Islands and there improved his understanding of the language. This experience — as is well known — was the turning point in his career, for it provided him with material out of which he fashioned the plays that made him the foremost dramatist of the Abbey Theatre. His journals of travels throughout Ireland and, particularly, his account of the Aran Islanders, who lived under conditions of awesome simplicity, contain dialogue, stories, and descriptive details which appear again, sometimes with little alteration, in his plays. Synge tells us that his inspiration for *The Playboy of the Western World* came from the story of a man who had actually killed his own father and was protected by the islanders until he could escape to America. "Such a man, they say, will be quiet all the rest of his life, and if you suggest that punishment is needed as an example, they ask, 'Would any one kill his father if he was able to help it?' "[23]

Faced with mounting controversy about his use of the idiom, Synge claimed that he never used a phrase he had not heard among the country people and that "the wildest sayings and ideas in this play are tame indeed, compared with the fancies one may hear in any little hillside cabin in Geesala, or Carraroe, or Dingle Bay."[24] Critics have pointed out minor errors in Synge's syntax and vocabulary, but these simply attest to the difficulty of mastering a dialect which was still being developed as a literary medium.

In *The Playboy* Synge uses a heightened, poetic concentration of "those elements which distinguish Anglo-Irish from standard English, and which render it more flexible, more expressive, and more potent in its rhythm."[25] It is language remarkable for its flights of extravagant fancy, its metaphor and its economic phrasing, its use of images which are strange to the modern sensibility because they reflect the remote, primitive life of the people of Connemara. The language reflects Irish influence to a far greater degree than that of Samuel Lover or Dion Boucicault. Thus, for example, there is a much higher incidence of rhetorical questions and of emphatic constructions: "It's that you'd say surely." The English perfect tense is discarded in favor of such forms as: "And you walking the world telling out your story to young girls or old" and "I'm after going down and reading the fearful crimes of Ireland." Many phrases are literal translations of the Irish. For example, in the statement, "I stood a while outside wondering would I have a right to pass on or to walk in and see you," the phrase "have a right" is used to mean "should". The word is a translation of the Irish *coir* and is used in the sense of the proper or permissible thing to do.[26] The rich texture of Synge's idiom also derives from the fact that it contains many Latinate constructions as well as a residue of English as it was spoken by seventeenth century Cromwellian settlers. Critics have also pointed out the fact that Synge, who wrote poetry, particularly toward the end of his life, cast many lines in blank verse.

Referring to the special quality of Synge's work, William Butler Yeats said that until he read Synge he had believed that the dialect was capable only of "obvious roystering humor and this error fixed on my imagination by so many novelists and rhymers made me listen badly." However Synge found the dialect so rich, he began translating into it fragments of the great literature of the world. "It gave him imaginative richness and yet left to him the sting and tang of reality."

In *The Playboy* much of the "sting and tang of reality" is provided by women, who are far more outspoken and aggressive than the local men. Their behavior recalls Synge's own experience with the "wild and capricious" young women of Aran, who delighted in teasing him. Very soon Christy has both the Widow Quin and Pegeen Mike battling for his affections.

The Widow Quin is a potent figure, who represents qualities which are normally opposed to one another. She is both outsider and mother figure. Choosing her would mean regression, abandoning the role of the hero, because Christy would be easily dominated by her. The widow stresses the important affinities between them. She has literally — though, we assume, unintentionally — killed her husband and is consequently feared by the community. Her fate foreshadows his. She is a passionate, unconventional, but lonely woman, who unabashedly admits her longing for the "gallant hairy fellows" abroad on the sea. Next to Christy, she is the most imaginative figure in the play, quite able to transform her "little houseen" into a likely habitation for a young poet:

> I've nice jobs you could be doing, gathering shells to make a
> whitewash for our hut within, building up a little goose-house,
> or stretching a new skin on an old curragh I have, and if my
> hut is far from all sides, it's there you'll meet the wisest old men, I
> tell you, at the corner of my wheel, and it's there yourself and
> me will have great times whispering and hugging.
> (Act 2)

Unlike Christy, the Widow is also a realist, and once she sees that he is determined to woo Pegeen, she makes a good bargain with him, agreeing to help in exchange for certain favors.

As clever as the Widow Quinn may be, she is no match for the fierce malice of Pegeen: "Doesn't the world know you reared a black ram at your own breast, so that the Lord Bishop of Connaught felt the elements of a Christian, and he eating it after in a kidney stew?" She cruelly taunts Shawn Keogh once she has rejected him, and his warning to Christy has merit: "She wouldn't suit you, and she with the divil's own temper the way you'd be strangling one another in a score of days." Pegeen is drawn to Christy as a man of spirit, worthy of a woman as passionate as herself.

As the play develops, not only is Christy more and more able to act a vital and decisive part, he is able to hold out to Pegeen, a girl, after all, with the stink of poteen about her, the possibility of a comparable transformation. She will become worthy of the hero, beautiful and mild mannered, no longer "the fright of seven town lands for her biting tongue." In creating Pegeen, Synge drew upon a fundamental Irish archetype. She has little in common with those sweet faced colleens served up by Dion Boucicault and other nineteenth century writers of fiction and drama. In early Irish society, women enjoyed considerable authority; some had real political power as well as several husbands. While the great epic wars of Greece and Ireland were both initiated because of a woman, Maeve, unlike Helen of Troy, drew up the battle plans.

When Christy is first employed by the Flahertys, he is pleased

by the prospect of relative ease and prosperity, but as he expands into his new role, he is less interested in such realities. He has no
material possessions to offer Pegeen. And it is a measure of the
change worked in her that she agrees to marry him for his courage
and imagination. For the short time of their courtship, she is able to
turn her back on a world that has restricted and infuriated her.

While Christy gradually emerges as the hero of the play, there
is one element in his character which is fairly constant. From the
beginning he is an outsider and a lonely man. ". . . I was lonesome
all times, and born lonesome, I'm thinking, as the moon of dawn."
This note permeates Synge's work, expressing both the writer's personal mood and the peculiar quality of the Irish countryside even today. The landscape, particularly in Connemara or in the hills of
Kerry, is both beautiful and desolate. Traveling through those misty
hills, with here and there a scattering of ragged sheep or a small cottage, often abandoned and falling into ruin, one's usual associations
drop away and one has the sense of moving backward in time.
Synge's journals reveal that he sought out remote areas like the
Great Blaskets, the outlying, western tip of Europe, to enjoy a splendid isolation overlooking the "wild islands and the sea . . . alive with
the singularly severe glory that is in the character of this place."[27]

Even when he was back in the vicinity of Dublin, Synge's life
was one of relative isolation. His immediate family never approved
of his work in the theatre; none of them ever attended a performance of his plays during his lifetime. He had some few loyal men
friends, notably Yeats, but his associations with women were
troubled. An early love affair ended, ostensibly, because the young
woman, Cherry Matheson, could not accept Synge's unorthodox
views on religion. While he was writing *The Playboy* he was much
tormented by his relationship with the actress Molly Allgood whom
he wished to marry. His letters to her, signed "Your Old Tramp,"
are full of jealousy, desperation, and feelings of rejection — very different emotions from those expressed publicly or to his male acquaintances. His journals as well as other letters express a forceful
and witty intelligence as well as a keen pleasure in living, elements of
his personality which enter into *The Playboy* as much as his sense of
personal alienation.

In *The Playboy*, up until the critical second blow against the
father, there is a very good likelihood that Christy will wed Pegeen
Mike. But in terms of the basic mythic structure of the play, Christy

must overcome his da in order to establish his prerogatives as a man. His task is complicated by the vitality of Old Mahon, who keeps springing to life again, and who has made his own version of the assault quite profitable, retelling his tale to all who will listen for the price of a few drinks or a night's lodging. Their mutual ability to produce a "gallous story" emphasizes the similarity between father and son, both rogues, both imaginative and resilient comic figures.

In making the second assault against his father, Christy not only establishes the validity of his heroic posture, but expresses the will of the authority ridden community. However, by acting publicly, he exposes both the repressed hatred of the people of Mayo and their fear of retribution. So they turn on him violently to punish him and, of course, themselves. The hero becomes the scapegoat-pariah, who takes upon himself the burden of communal guilt.

Pegeen realizes that her loss of Christy will be irreparable, but she is unable to bear the humility of public exposure. At the critical moment she brands Christy with the burning turf, symbolically attempting to castrate him, to render him powerless in the hands of the mob. Furiously rejecting her, Christy frees himself from the tyranny of the community.

Until the conclusion the play tends to follow the pattern of ancient Greek folk drama which involved the death or sacrifice of a hero-god (the old year), the rebirth of a hero-god (the new year), and a purging of evil by driving out a scapegoat. During these rites the strength and fertility of the young hero were tested; he underwent a form of "questioning" after which he achieved "recognition" — *anagnorisis* or new knowledge. In *The Playboy*, as we have observed, Christy is both scapegoat and hero, while old Mahon plays the dual role of the old king and the *alazon* or intruder, who is finally confounded in the "struggle." The Greek drama, which was in fact a fertility ceremony, ended with a triumphal procession or *komos*, with songs of joy. From this ceremony is derived the traditional conclusion of comedy, the union of hero and heroine, which assures the continuing vitality of the community.[28]

This is rarely the case in Irish comedy after Carleton and Boucicault. There appears to be a fatal conservatism in the community and a fatal disjunction between the sexes. Leopold Bloom, surviving a long and troubled journey, returns home to rest, not in the bosom of Molly-Penelope, but next to her feet. Separated from Pegeen, Christy will never father a generation of "little gallant swearers." Creativity for the solitary man can be experienced, as it was for Synge, himself, only in terms of the imagination.

Once Christy has discarded the role of fool or omadhawn, and begun to act like a hero, he is increasingly threatened with madness. His father, also a great talker and a wild and solitary man, has at times completely lost his senses and been institutionalized. This fate, like that of Patch Darcy in *The Shadow in the Glen*, is what haunts the man of imagination and the man who chooses the solitary life. Of course, in the view of Michael James, Christy is already mad, and we've been told that maniacs, like any threat to the community, must be expelled. So the life Christy chooses is a dangerous one, but safety in terms of the play means stagnation and the death of the imagination. In the final scene Christy is denounced as a liar and an attempt is made to force him back into the earlier role of "idiot" and "fool." But strong in the discovery of his own powers, he can subdue his father and leave the community behind, denouncing them in turn as "the fools" of Mayo.

In many primitive cultures the madman has been regarded as a visionary. In the Dionysian revels, throwing off all customary restraints and yielding oneself to the orgiastic rites was to obtain access to the god, to be imbued with divine madness, creativity, poetry, the authentic self. Irish legend preserves the account of Suibhine (Sweeny) doomed to torment and madness but gifted with the power of prophecy and poetry. In terms of this play, however, the threat of madness in its extreme form is the threat of self-destruction. While Christy is indeed "mad", that is, estranged from the point of view of Michael James, he has still the power to revitalize the people of Mayo and does for a time impose his vision of reality upon all of them, including Michael James. Old Mahon, on the other hand, in his drunken revels is isolated, enfeebled, terrified by the hallucinations he experiences.

In the earlier works we have examined, the virtue of self-sacrifice was admired. Even after Denis O'Shaughnessy realizes he has no religious vocation, he allows family obligations to propel him toward Maynooth. By Synge's day the peasant was being replaced by the enterprising small farmer, and the more independent young people were leaving the farm altogether. This shift in values is expressed in *The Playboy*, which is truly modern because of its emphasis on personal freedom and choice. Those who remain behind in the community of "fools" are trapped in a narrowing circle of existence. There is no possibility of prosperity or change while the people are dominated by custom and religion that have grown sour and lifeless, and drunkenness is the main source of relief.

No discussion of Synge's play is complete without a comment on the riots which broke out during the original production in Dublin and afterwards in America. However, as so much has already been said, I shall be brief. First of all the famous allusion to the word "shift," which triggered the violence, has always seemed to me an excuse for rather than the real cause of the rioting. The Irish were hardly pleased by images of themselves as ignorant, backward, weak-spirited fools. They had suffered long and bitterly from derogatory images both at home and abroad, and it should be noted that the emphasis in the early productions was on *realism*; emphasis on the comic and the fantastic came at a later date. Maurice Bourgeois observed in 1913 that the Irish people as they are portrayed in *The Playboy* "are anything but fit for self-government. Synge's comedy when viewed in this light, certainly constitutes the most tragic exposure of his fellow-countrymen's besottedness."[29] Quite understandably, the strongest reaction to Synge's play came from nationalists like Arthur Griffith, who were carefully developing the image of the heroic and high minded patriot.

While Dubliners were deeply offended by *The Playboy*, they continued to enjoy the antics of country clowns related to that original archetype, Handy Andy. They were a regular feature of music hall entertainment in Dublin and London where Irishmen themselves laughed at clowns with a thick brogue and a shillelegh, who for all their misadventures, invariably landed on their feet. Their laughter probably expressed ambivalence toward that old Gaelic world; affection mingled with contempt for what seemed outmoded, clumsy, primitive.

Whether creatures of farce, like the inhabitants of Lady Gregory's little village of Cloon or the more clever and engaging heroes of William Carleton, Boucicault, or Synge, the Irish comic character usually reveals a gift for language. The countryman may blunder or misinterpret events, but he usually exhibits a boldness in invention and a narrative flair. As the countryman developed fluency in English, however, he was more often represented on stage, in fiction, and in popular stereotype as a wit or witty rogue. By the latter part of the nineteenth century the brogue came to be regarded as something of an asset, associated with "blarney" rather than "blundering" and with the ability to perform and to improvise. If anything, according to such disparate observers as Matthew Arnold and William Carleton, the Irishman's fault lay in an excess of imagination, a tendency to prefer sound over sense, to resist the "despotism of fact."

The importance of speaking well was rooted in an oral tradition in which poet and storyteller played central roles, stimulating the minds of the people despite the severe hardships they endured. As Lady Gregory pointed out, in the isolated rural communities where there was little commerce and few books, good conversation was highly prized. It was a world whose tightly drawn physical boundaries were everywhere transcended by a belief in the supernatural. Irish fancy transformed animals and birds into restless and sometimes malignant spirits. Ghosts traveled the dark winding roads at night. The stone rings and forts of prehistoric Ireland were the dwelling place of fairies. The humblest task as well as the central passages of marriage, birth and death were steeped in ritual originating in the distant past.

Although Gaelic had been largely displaced by English by the close of the nineteenth century, the native pleasure in speech, which had been nurtured by the cadences and the rhetorical subtleties of both poet and storyteller, remained. Of the characters we have discussed, Denis O'Shaughnessy best embodies the values attached to the competing language systems. He displays that sense of power in the spoken word and the passion for rhetoric and arcane knowledge associated with the bardic schools. However his growing influence and maturity as well as practical success are linked to a mastery of English. Carleton was suspicious of Irish glibness and love of fantasy, and so his hero is treated satirically and must suffer a penalty for his excess.

The modern comic writer has inherited this dual sense of cultural identity. He tends to be both suspicious of his rhetorical heritage and at the same time thoroughly capable of exploiting it. The character he creates tends to resist the physical limits of the world in which he finds himself by taking refuge in fantasy and disdaining practical success. Like the rogue, he prefers to remain outside the mainstream, on the periphery of the community. He is critical, self-conscious, evasive, often ill at ease with the opposite sex. His sense of humor cuts two ways; it has none of the genteel forbearance and sentimentality of Boucicault or what passed as

"Irish humor" in the nineteenth century. It is savage, satiric, sometimes self-lacerating. It has the darkness and vitality of the folk.

II

The Masque
of Satire

Introduction

SATIRE in Ireland is of ancient and uncertain origin, but evidence suggests that it developed out of a belief in magic and incantation. In "Satirists and Enchanters in Early Irish Literature" Fred Norris Robinson tells us that the poets "who freely mingled natural and supernatural processes" are not clearly separable from the druids in the old Irish period (600-900): "Destructive spells and poems of slander or abuse were all thought of together as the work, and it sometimes seems almost the chief work, of the tribal man of letters."[1] He was typically employed to satirize the enemies of a patron-king, and if he was not sufficiently compensated for his labors, he might well satirize his patron, raising boils on his neck or demeaning him forever with an invidious nickname or verse:

> O Flannáin, you slow mare, you one-legged goose;
> You crooked bolt in face of the war-cry of the foreigners.
>
> O Dallan, you undistinguished, unlucky man;
> You twisted, withered-handed, shaggy-dog-haired crooked one
> You hungry, thirsty, troublesome one;
> You odious, comic carrier of a little bag with cold hands![2]

Some of the more drastic examples of the power of the satirist have to do with the legendary figure of Aithirne, who demanded and received the single eye of the king of Connacht. Aithirne then journeyed to Leinster where he demanded to sleep with the queen. In this curious tale the king's honor as well as his life can be preserved only through the prostitution of his wife. The king's response is recorded: "Thou shalt have the woman for my honour's sake.

Nevertheless there is not in Ulster a man who could take her unless I gave her to thee for my honour's sake."[3] There is no record of the queen's response.

So strong was the belief in the power of satire to cause injury and even death that attempts were made to banish the poets from Ireland and specific admonitions against the misuse of their powers were codified in brehon law. Seven kinds of satire are listed for which an "honor-price" is appropriate: "a nickname which clings; recitation of a satire of insults in his absence; to satirize the face; to laugh on all sides; to sneer at his form; to magnify a blemish; satire which is written by a bard who is far away, and which is recited." Here there is no clear distinction made between magical incantation and mockery or invective; in the Irish language the same words (commonly *aer* and its derivatives) are employed.[4]

Satirists were numbered among the divisions of the army which one Gaelic king might send to destroy another. In *The Táin* they make several appearances prophesizing defeat for Maeve and attempting to subdue Cúchulainn:

> "Give me your javelin," the satirist said.
> "I'll give you any gift but that," Cúchulainn said.
> "Other gifts I don't want," the satirist said.
> Cúchulainn struck him, for refusing what he chose to offer.
> Then Redg said he would take away Cúchulainn's good name unless he got the javelin. So Cúchulainn flung the javelin at him and it shot through his head.
> "Now that is a stunning gift!" the satirist cried.
> So Ath Tolam Sét got its name — the Ford of the Overwhelming Gift. . . .[5]

In the middle ages satire took on a sophisticated literary form, which employed a sustained narrative and an elaborate system of parody. It reveals a delight in mockery and wit and an emphasis on "word play" rather than "word magic." Two of the best examples attest to the early rivalry betwen poet and priest. In *Tromdámh Guaire* (*The Burdensome Bardic Company*) the poets are mocked for their impossible demands upon a king of whom it is said that one arm had grown longer than the other from being extended in hospitality. Among their many strange and unpredictable desires are: "a bowl of the ale of sweet milk, with the marrow of the anklebone of a wild hog; a pet cuckoo on an ivy tree . . . a girdle of yellow lard of an exceeding white boar . . . a garment of the spider's web . . ." At one point their leader, Senchán, is carried off by a giant cat, whom he has satirized as a "hanging down cowtail." Rescued by a holy man, he is not only ungrateful but furious because, had he been slain, Guaire the king would have been justly satirized for a failure of hospitality. Finally, Marvan, the saintly brother of Guaire, invites the bardic company to a test of skill in which Senchán is forced to chant until one eye pops out onto his cheekbone. Peace is then restored — along with Senchán's eye — through the power of St. Marvan.[6] In *Aislinge Meic Conglinne (The Vision of MacConglinne)*, which I will discuss in more detail in the chapter on *Tarry Flynn*, the situation is exactly reversed: the clergy retreat before the inspired cunning of the poet. Despite the mockery on both sides, it should be noted that many priests were themselves poets, and there was often close collaboration between the two orders, both, for example, being present at a marriage or at the investiture of a king.[7]

Cormac's Glossary, which dates from the ninth or tenth century proposes that the term *fili*, or poet, derives "from poison (*fi*) in satire and splendour (*li*) in praise."[8] While the etymology is fanciful, this dual function did in fact ensure the prestige of Irish poets who established themselves as a wealthy, hereditary class. From prehistoric times they apparently gathered together in schools headed by an *ollamh* or principal man of letters, like the worthy Senchán, who had himself gone through years of arduous training to achieve mastery of his craft. Although our discussion has thus far emphasized his vindictive qualities, the poet played an indispensable role in recording the history and praising the deeds of the Gaelic aristocrat. In *The Hidden Ireland* Daniel Corkery observes that the great bulk of verse from the middle ages is panegyric: "each great house had its *dunaire*, or collection of poems, written in its honour." Until the seventeenth century, prose was not even considered an art form.[9] Fearing that poetry inflamed the military ardor of the Gael, Sir Henry Sidney, father of the poet Philip Sidney and Lord Deputy of Ireland, issued a proclamation in 1566 stating that anyone could take a "rhymer" and "spoil" him.[10] The real downfall of the bardic institution came, however, with the defeat of the Tyrone rebellion in 1603 and the subsequent diaspora of the leaders who had been the patrons of Gaelic music, poetry and learning.

According to Daniel Corkery, poets continued to gather together in "courts of poetry" throughout the eighteenth century and thus kept alive some of the old learning and the elaborate prosody of their forebears. Many took to the road earning their living as day laborers, often depending on the hospitality of ordinary people, who offered them food and lodging in return for poems and stories. In this way, as well as through the circulation of Gaelic manuscripts, the art of poetry and its ancient association with magic were preserved in the oral tradition. It was believed that the poet had a unique nature, that his gift was from God and was usually expressed in a spontaneous flow of language. This idea is demonstrated in the following account of Diarmaid na Bolgaí Ó Sé of Kerry:

> "Are you a poet?" said the priest?
> "I am a really good poet," said Diarmaid.
> "Would you compose a song for me?" said the priest.
> "I will if you like!"
> "Have it ready for me in a week," said the priest. Diarmaid stuck his staff into the ground immediately, letting the priest know that he did not want even that respite, and he produced a song of twenty-seven stanzas in one single stream.[11]

In *Poets and Dreamers* Lady Gregory offers an account of one of the last of the wandering bards, Raftery (1784–1835), whose tribute to Mary Hynes is remembered by Yeats in "The Tower." The tales which Lady Gregory gathered in the west of Ireland reflect both affection for the man, who was blind, and respect for his powers. The fact that the beautiful Mary Hynes had an unhappy life and died young is, oddly enough, associated by the country people with Raftery's love poem: "No one that has a song made about them will ever live long." A more characteristic tale describes the misfortunes of those who had informed against a man subsequently hanged in Galway. Raftery was present at the execution and composed a poem praising the victim but pronouncing a curse upon his enemies, who thereafter lost their land and whose children died. His powers, like those of the *fili* who could, apparently, blight the land and cause rivers to overflow their banks, were said to extend to nature as well. A widely circulated story has to do with a bush under which Raftery sought shelter. He "praised it first; and then when it let the rain down, he dispraised it, and it withered up, and never put out leaf or branch after." Lady Gregory had seen the actual curse in an Irish manuscript ("I pronounce ugliness upon you. That bloom or leaf may never grow on you.") preserved in a stone cutter's cottage.[12]

In *The Irish Comic Tradition* Vivian Mercier presents a much more comprehensive study of the development of satire. This brief introduction in primarily intended to illustrate the role of the Gaelic poet or man of letters as well as the conservatism of the culture which retained a lingering belief in "word magic" into the twentieth century. Modern Irish writers have expressed their consciousness of standing at the edge of a great divide, hearing nothing but silence from the nineteenth century, when Gaelic literature is finally stilled.[13] There is no question, however, that their sense of the power of language has been shaped by a culture in which it has been immensely valued. Their alienation takes on a special significance in view of the close tie between poet and people and the respect and generous hospitality the former received in Gaelic Ireland.

In place of a coherent literary heritage modern writers have had thrust upon them a series of myths about the Irish people. The very genius of the language itself has been falsified, turned into "glibness" or "wit" or "blarney." And popular audiences have come to expect this. Joyce speaks directly to the problem in rejecting the role of "court jester" to the English. The writers to be discussed in Part II are those, like Joyce, who respond to the popular image of the comic Irishman or the performing Irishman. While some exploit his legendary charm, most use satire as a means of exploding what they perceive as a debasing myth. Their work draws upon Gaelic literature and the oral tradition, and it shares certain features of the early satire.

Vivian Mercier discusses the fact that Gaelic satire "contains a great abundance of lampoons framed as alliterative epithets aimed at an individual rather than at folly or vice in general." It is distinguished by word play: "the quantity of synonyms and nonce-words which it employs makes it the despair of editors and translators." He goes on to illustrate the Gaelic delight in the absurdity of a tale and the Gaelic inclination toward the fantastic and the macabre, qualities which are very much in evidence in the literature discussed in Part II. He believes that much of the finest Anglo-Irish literature is comic because it has absorbed the archaic outlook — "the play-spirit" — of the older culture.[14] The modern satirist also enjoys skewering a literary rival by mimicking and mocking not only his art but his physical appearance; his delight in pure destruction often seems the equal of his literary forebear's. Thus "James Joyce is never more Irish than when he violates the bounds of good sense, good taste and even sanity for the sake of a jest."[15]

Unlike early satire, however, modern literature is full of self-mockery and distrust; it is also extremely derisive of social and political process. One result of the endless myth making to which the Irish have been subjected is an acute concern for what is valuable and worth retaining in Irish life. Satire is used to achieve perspective against contemporary pressure to romanticize and sentimentalize history and tradition.

In Synge's *Playboy of the Western World* criticism is balanced against a joy that springs from the sheer exuberance of creation, embodied in the emerging hero. In Flann O'Brien's *At Swim-Two-Birds* there is no hero, only a kind of underground man fleeing a society which is provincial, censorious, narrowly pietistic, hostile toward the arts. This brilliant, caustic satire is the work of a man familiar with the older literature and thus all the more conscious of his humiliating position. Until the sixties the best modern European and American literature was banned in Ireland, and every native writer of talent sooner or later found himself censored. After the overthrow of an English government which had systematically destroyed much of the Gaelic culture, the effort of Irish statesmen to institutionalize Victorian standards was painfully ironic. It should be noted, however, that writers also complained about the lack of a sophisticated reading public and felt compelled to seek publication in London as a mark of literary distinction.

Discussing his own penchant for satire, Patrick Kavanagh relates it to that "furious enthusiastic hatred which is a form of love."[16] After centuries of oppression and war of the most devastating kind, the long awaited free nation turned out to be an impoverished, backward looking, embittered land, but a land nonetheless cherished to which the artist felt himself bound even in exile.

The tendency of Irish publishers to reflect Victorian standards was one reason for the life long exile of James Joyce. The original manuscript of *The Dubliners* was pronounced unsuitable when it was submitted for publication and was subsequently destroyed by the printer in 1912. Thereafter the work of Ireland's most famous writer was published abroad. The treatment Joyce received inspired him to lampoon his publisher in an angry but witty broadside, "Gas from a Burner," which he had printed at his own expense. In Part II, I will discuss Joyce's use of satire because that aspect of his work has received relatively little attention from critics and because the focus of this study is the comic or performing Irishman, who in *Ulysses* is best represented by Buck Mulligan. For Joyce satire is merely one facet in the larger comedy; the writers who came after him, or were younger contemporaries, were less optimistic.

Samuel Beckett's Murphy, who is to some extent a parody of Stephen Dedalus, flees to London, hoping to eradicate his past history. He is a threadbare philosopher, torn between his desire for a pretty prostitute with bourgeois inclinations and a need for absolute freedom. Through his jaundiced eye, Irish political and cultural institutions become a crazy patchwork of reflex activity, pernicious in influence, obstinate in tracking down the expatriate. He is gradually ensnared by a group of demented Irish, including a poet modeled after Austin Clarke, who mastered the craft of the Gaelic poets and employed their techniques in writing English. Murphy escapes them only when he absent-mindedly propels himself into oblivion, leaving his ashes to be flushed down the w.c. at the Abbey Theatre — preferably during a performance.

Flann O'Brien's *At Swim-Two-Birds* is an assault on the Joycean novel and the Joycean concept of art. (He used to complain that Joyce had reduced the world of letters to "a chronic state of exegesis.") The narrator, who also resembles Stephen Dedalus, is a student who escapes the stultifying climate of modern Dublin, not by going into exile but by retreating into a world of fantasy peopled by an assortment of figures from legend, myth, romance, and popular fiction. At the center of this increasingly bizarre, but brilliantly and mordantly comic tale, is the isolated artist maddened by his efforts to make poetry out of modern Ireland.

Writers coming of age after the Revival found they had to contend with yet another version of the comic Irishman. While the peasant had been ridiculed for his brogue, his modern counterpart was encouraged to produce one as part of "the witty Celtic act." He was expected to be morose, impulsive, fiery, loquacious, literary, and, of course, thirsty. Flann O'Brien observed that Irish writers, "fascinated by the snake-like eye of London publishers, have developed exhibitionism to the sphere of acrobatics." He attributed much of the blame for the new myth of Irishness, "doing the erratic

but lovable playboy," to John Synge: "This trouble probably began
with Lever and Lover. But I always think that in Synge we have the
virus isolated and recognisable . . . I have personally met in the
streets of Ireland persons who are clearly out of Synge's plays. They
talk and dress like that, and damn the drink they'll swally but the
mug of porter in the long nights after Samhain."[17]

In a similar vein Patrick Kavanagh used the term "buck lep" to
characterize the act of a man "eager to display his merit and exuberance as a true Gael." The "buck lep" appears to be a modern
equivalent of the "salmon leap" favored by Cúchulainn; it is allegedly performed by leaping into the air with a shout, causing the heels
to strike hard against the buttocks.

> The bucklep or the bucklepper may be found in many areas
> of Irish life but is especially notable in literature and may
> take many forms: a gratuitous reference to Cúchulain,
> an affected quaintness of phrasing, a pious nod toward
> 1916 and all that stage-Irish characterization, the cliché
> mixture of melancholy and sentimentality, false bravado such
> as showy contempt for the Church, or the reverse, false piety.[18]

He asserted that "Irishness" was a "form of anti-art, a way of posing
as a poet without actually being one; this became the theme of a
mocking, parodic poem, "The Paddiad," which consigns his contemporaries to the devil of mediocrity.

When Patrick Kavanagh first came to Dublin in 1939, he
observed that the peasant had acquired a mystique — partly
because of the emphasis on peasant plays at the Abbey. He was
himself hailed as a "peasant poet," a title he found offensive and
restrictive; he believed that the Irish poet was being encouraged to
play the role of a public clown. Like Flann O'Brien, he complained
that the Irish government was spending large sums of money on such
enterprises as the preservation of Gaelic, while serious modern
writers received no support whatsoever.

Seeking an explanation for the new stage Irishman, Kavanagh
also attacked the work of Synge in language as heated as anything
heard during the riots of 1907. But as Brendan Kennelly has pointed
out: "A poet's critical judgments are always, at bottom, necessary
justifications of his own most dearly held aesthetic."[19] In *Tarry
Flynn* Kavanagh offers his personal critique of the poet: Tarry is a

visionary, passive, detached, a wise fool in contrast to the ebullient playboy.

The novel is wonderfully humorous in its earthy dialogue and its account of another young man struggling for independence. A more serious element, understated in *The Playboy*, but explored very honestly here, is the emotional and sexual frustration endured by great numbers of men and women because of the religious, social, and economic pressures peculiar to rural Ireland. In this novel the atypical comic pattern still holds true. The real focus of interest is the conflict between generations. In modern Irish literature, lovers tend to be secondary figures (reflecting the social pattern) as young men and women try to come to terms with the older, disparaged culture. There are many fine portraits of women, but they are often practical, realistic people and thus threatening to the male dreamers around them.

While the writers discussed so far have reacted against the stereotype of the comic Irishman, both Sean O'Casey and Brendan Behan exploited that stereotype as many Irish playwrights like Ron Henderson continue to do. O'Casey's characters are entertaining precisely because of the colorful rhetoric, their outrageous postures, and the song and dance routines from the music hall, but they are the maimed survivors of economic and social breakdown, retreating behind a verbal screen and refusing to come to terms with the demands of the world around them.

O'Casey is a satirist who uses colorful Dublin slang to puncture the romantic concept of Ireland with its mystique of war. He shows us the teeming, disease ridden tenements of Dublin, where more than two-hundred citizens died in the crossfire of the Easter Rebellion in 1916 and where neighbors murdered one another in the Civil War of 1922-23. O'Casey's proleteriat are a people cut off from their Gaelic and agrarian roots, and their emotional impoverishment is as real as the physical hardship they endure. The women by and large survive because of perseverance and courage, but the men tend to be ineffectual and evasive dreamers. O'Casey exposes the "gay, improvident Celt" as a twentieth century anachronism.

Brendan Behan, whose plays derive from Sean O'Casey's, was himself imprisoned for many years for IRA activities. He hits hard at Irish nationalism in *The Hostage*, presenting the latter day IRA as a motley group of the sexually and socially maladjusted. In the free wheeling atmosphere of a Dublin brothel, he creates innumerable

opportunities for satirizing aspects of Irish life: the language movement, the temperance movement, religion, the upper classes, James
Joyce, the Gaelic tradition and Eamon de Valera. His wit is more
genial than Sean O'Casey's, more dependent on the irreverent one
liner:

> Pat. . . . your real trouble when you go to prison as a patriot, do
> you know what it will be?
> Officer. The loss of liberty.
> Pat. No, the other Irish patriots, in along with you . . .
> — (The Hostage, 1)

Like O'Casey, his sympathies are in favor of the working class
English as well as Irish who turn out to be pawns in an international
struggle that has become wholly impersonal and wholly destructive.

In The Borstal Boy Behan provides us with a rather different
perspective about the consequences of being born into an Irish family with strong republican sympathies as well as artistic talent.
Behan was early applauded as a bright and entertaining youngster,
and the same qualities assured his popularity inside the British
borstal to which he was confined after he was discovered carrying
explosives into London at the age of sixteen. He relates how he
quickly adopted the role of the congenial and amusing "Paddy," accepted by British and Irish alike. The facts of Behan's later life suggest that, unlike Kavanagh, he enjoyed public popularity, welcomed
it, and was gradually consumed by it. He became the proverbial
comic Irishman, boisterous, hard drinking, witty, a public performer, lionized in the pubs, and conspicuously avoided by the
"respectable" Irish at home and in America. His career points to the
tragic dimension, the consciousness of death concealed by the comic
mask, which will be more fully explored in Part II.

5. James Joyce and Buck Mulligan

A S A YOUNG MAN James Joyce took a skeptical view of Ireland's preoccupation with the past, with her ancient literature and her chronicle of ancient wrongs. He was impatient with nationalists who affected contempt for the whole of Anglo-Saxon civilization and sought to revive the spirit of the Gaels by isolating themselves from contemporary influence. Joyce heaped scorn upon the efforts of W. B. Yeats, Augusta Gregory and John Synge to achieve a true Anglo-Irish synthesis by creating a literature in English which drew its inspiration from the Gaelic world. He was rather premature in judging that world as dead as that of ancient Egypt, as having expired with the poet James Clarence Mangan (1803–1849).

Joyce's remarks on Mangan, generally thought of as a forerunner of the Revival because of his translations and his adaptation of Gaelic modes of composition, reveal a good deal about how he regarded his own position as a writer. He speaks of Mangan as an isolated figure who "sums up in himself the soul of a country and an era" as "one of those strange abnormal spirits who believe that their artistic life should be nothing more than a true and continual revelation of this spiritual life, who believe that their inner life is so valuable that they have no need of popular support. . . ."

Joyce maintains that Mangan was obsessed by a broken and divided tradition and that even in his most passionate moments the history of his country enclosed him so narrowly that he could "barely reduce its walls to ruins."[1] This vehement image has as its referrent a passage from Mangan's translation of "O'Hussey's Ode to The Maguire" which describes the revenge of an Irish chieftain who was despoiled, driven from his own land and declared an outlaw:

Hugh marched forth to the fight — I grieved to see him so depart;
And lo to-night he wanders frozen, rain drenched, sad, betrayed —
But the memory of the lime-white mansions his right hand had laid
In ashes warms the hero's heart.

I suspect the fiery inspiration of The Maguire in Joyce's resolution to attack those who threatened his own autonomy. Instead of a torch, however, he turned to a more Irish mode of destruction.

While he was still a student at University College, Dublin, in 1901, Joyce publicly condemned the Irish Literary Theatre for what he perceived as provincialism, accusing Yeats of surrendering to the rabble because of his "treacherous instinct of adaptability," his "floating will."[2] As he matured as a writer, he acquired a taste for satire, which he used with increasing skill against the objects of his indignation: the writers who formed a circle of influence in Dublin, who were to establish the Abbey Theatre and provide a new direction in literature. They must have been fairly astonished at the caricatures etched by Joyce in his Swiftian lampoon, "The Holy Office." Assuming the role of Katharsis-Purgative, he wittily and arrogantly mocks the key figures of the Revival as overly romantic, effusive, out of touch with the human condition:

That they may dream their dreamy dreams
I carry off their filthy streams

Reducing his fellow Dubliners to a motley crew of eccentrics, he pictures Yeats as appeasing

His giddy dames' frivolities
While they console him when he whinges
With gold-embroidered Celtic fringes —

His stance is reminiscent of the contentious spirit of the Gaelic bards or the hedge school masters, who engaged in elaborate battles of wit and erudition to show off their skills and to lay claim to a disputed position. In the spirit of such controversy, Joyce pictures himself as a heroic, defiant, isolated figure, "steeled" in the school of Aquinas and Aristotle, and then discharges an extraordinary fusilage, accusing his rivals of cowardice, jealousy, deception, and philistinism:

Where they have crouched and crawled and prayed
I stand the self-doomed, unafraid

The quarrel comes to a fine boil in *Ulysses* where Joyce uses the most extreme forms of ridicule to discredit political as well as literary forms of Irish nationalism. Before concentrating on Buck Mulligan, who is the subject of this chapter, I would like to consider the Cyclops scene briefly in order to illustrate more fully Joyce's tactics as a satirist.

In this scene, which takes place in a pub, Joyce links the Irish capacity for heroic gesture with the Irish capacity for porter. Here, Homer's bloodthirsty and none too intelligent giant, Polyphemus, and Finn MacCool, the Irish epic hero, are ironically associated with the central figure of the citizen. Giantism is the structural principle of the chapter, but that it is a spurious giantism is evident in the character of the citizen, who is petty, malicious, ignorant, "all wind and piss like a tanyard cat." The citizen is a jaundiced portrait of Michael Cusack, founder of the Gaelic Athletic Association, which was a primary means of organizing nationalist sentiment at the turn of the century. Rejecting "foreign sports," Cusack encouraged the young men of Ireland to take up hurling and Gaelic football; the Association from its inception had strong ties with the Fenian movement.

Loud in complaint, the citizen boozily commemorates the patriotic dead, becoming more and more furious with Leopold Bloom's efforts at reason and moderation. His posture is so offensive that he would be an intolerable character if he were not rendered comic through the perspective of the narrator as well as the flow of ironic and parodic associations accompanying the dialogue in Barney Kiernan's pub. In the rapidly shifting context even the citizen's considerable power of invective ("those tonguetied sons of bastards ghosts") has a comic effect as does his contempt for "the brutal Sassenachs and their patois." His blind unreasoning fury leads us to conclude that Sein Fein is a form of madness and the citizen a victim of Irish "syphilisation."

In this chapter Joyce treats the Revival as one more comic manifestation of Irish nationalism. The legendary Finn appears as an overblown leprechaun, swollen to monstrous proportions, ostensibly through the misguided efforts of translators like Augusta Gregory. Joyce's description is very much in keeping with the oral tradition which had a tendency to debunk such heroes. Superimposed upon the citizen, who identifies himself with militant Fenianism, Finn appears as a "broadshouldered deepchested stronglimbed frankeyed redhaired freely freckled shaggybearded widemouthed largenosed longheaded deepvoiced barekneed brawnyhanded hairylegged ruddyfaced sinewyarmed hero."

Joyce plays humorously upon the incongruities and sheerly fanciful quality of the early sagas:

> Lovely maidens sit in close proximity to the roots of the lovely trees singing the most lovely songs while they play with all kinds of lovely objects as for example golden ingots, silvery fishes, crans of herrings, drafts of eels, codlings, creels of fingerlings, purple seagems and playful insects.[3]

He parodies the epic fondness for hyperbole, for "word cataracts," long strings of descriptive phrases or fanciful catalogues of food, possessions or the attributes of heroes. Such catalogues probably served to display the virtuosity of the poets, giving pleasure in the prospect of sheer abundance and in the intricately woven patterns of assonance and alliteration. At the extreme verge of this shaft of ridicule aimed at Douglas Hyde, founder of the Gaelic League, is the dog Garryowen reciting Irish verse which "recalls the intricate alliterations and isosyllabic rules of the Welch englyn." (That "verse" turns out to be a curse upon Barney Kiernan for not providing him with drink.)

The citizen's reference to the heroic dead and his tendency to speak in hackneyed patriotic formulas become in turn the basis of a memorable passage of macabre humor. Its subject is Robert Emmet, one of the more romantic figures in the panoply of Irish saints and martyrs.

In Joyce's parody of the execution, a vast and sentimental multitude assemble, among them an assortment of foreign delegates, one of whom is assisted to his seat with the aid of a steam crane. Rapid excursion trains are provided for the thousands eagerly swarming in from the country. Even the children at the Foundling Hospital are invited to "the day's entertainment," "a bit of real Irish fun without vulgarity." Prior to the execution, an "animated altercation" over the correct birth date of St. Patrick, involving cannonballs, scimitars, umbrellas, stinkpots and the like is happily resolved in favor of the 17th of March.

When the "headsman" appears in "faultless morning dress," he is greeted with enthusiastic applause, cheers from foreign delegates, and a flurry of waving handkerchiefs. The executioner, his face concealed in a ten-gallon pot, tests the knife for the disemboweling by decapitating "in rapid succession a flock of sheep." Also standing by, waiting to carry off the blood of the "martyr" as well as his internal organs, is the steward of the "amalgamated cats' and dogs' home."

A romantic tableau is provided when the "blushing bride elect" flings herself upon the bosom of the hero, kissing various suitable areas of his person. Even the police are reduced to tears. In real life Robert Emmet's beloved Sara Curran, the subject of a plaintive ballad by Tom Moore, eventually married an Englishman; in Joyce's version a handsome Oxonian steps forward, presenting his bankbook and genealogical tree to claim the hand of the lady.

Thus Joyce debunks a popular idol, whose eloquence and courage have been held up as a model to generations of Irishmen, many of whom learned as children the famous speech from the dock. By presenting the death of Emmet as a theatrical event arousing the mob to a pitch of sadistic and erotic frenzy, Joyce implies that Irish nationalists betray their heroes by exploiting them to create a mystique of death.

The absurd strain of humor in the execution scene, with its blend of merriment and savagery, is akin to that of the Dublin street singers who amused audiences with "The Night Before Larry Was Stretched," "Johnny I Hardly Knew Ye," and "The Kilmainham Minuet," ballads about hanging and mutilation.

The macabre, little in evidence in nineteenth century fiction and drama which was attuned to the middle class, emerges with a vengeance in the twentieth century. Often joined to satire, which is fiercely critical because of a fierce disappointment with the quality of modern life, it provides a cutting edge against despair and a defense against the maudlin or the sentimental. Among those who wield the "cold steel pen," notably Samuel Beckett, Flann O'Brien, Sean O'Casey, Brendan Behan, Edna O'Brien and M. J. Molloy, none is so devastingly accurate in pricking national self-esteem as James Joyce.

While Joyce delighted in ridiculing those who were creating new Irish myths, his most brilliant satire was directed at a more intimate foe in the character of Buck Mulligan.

The name of Malachi (Buck) Mulligan is rich in associations, many of them ironic, which particularly fit him for the role of *Schlagfertig* or striking wit.[4] First of all, as is well known, the character is modeled after Oliver St. John Gogarty, at one time a friend of Joyce and a celebrated Dublin wit, a surgeon and a man of letters. Mulligan is associated with St. John Chrysostomos, "the golden mouthed," a brilliant speaker. (So is Mulligan, but the gold is to be found mainly in his teeth.) The name Malachi is linked primarily with the last prophet in the Old Testament who denounced corrupt priests and with St. Malachy, a twelfth century Irish prelate reputed to have the gift of prophecy. It is also the name of two Irish kings who played key roles in the defeat of the Vikings. The first Malachi, according to legend, destroyed his enemies by trickery, drowning their leader after his daughter, accompanied by fifteen Irish warriors disguised as women, had arranged a tryst with the Vikings. Malachi II, or Malachi Mór, was a heroic figure and a bitter rival of Brian Boru, whom he succeeded as Ard-Ri or High King after the battle of Clontarf in 1014.

The surname Mulligan is also of distinguished origin. The chiefs of the sept of Ó Maolagóin were the lords of Tír MacCarthain in County Donegal until they were dispossessed in the Ulster plantation in the seventeenth century. In Joyce's time, however, the name had acquired a humorous connotation because of Jimmy O'Dea, the Irish comedian who entertained Dublin audiences with sketches of "Mrs. Mulligan, the Pride of Coombe."[5]

The most interesting and probably the most significant historic association is with the Anglo-Irish rakes or "bucks," who were notorious in the eighteenth century because of their riotous behavior. The bucks were spoilers, members of a ruling class which inflicted injury and insult on the ordinary citizen and which was rarely prosecuted. A great many stories about Buck Whaley, Buck Jones and Buck English, most of them quite fanciful, still circulated in Dublin in the early twentieth century. There are newspaper accounts in the Dublin National Library and the Royal Irish Academy dating from 1907 and 1908. Joyce may have received copies of these or of *Buck Whaley's Memoirs*, which were published in 1906. In any event he would have heard of the exploits of Burnchapel Whaley, whom he mentions in *A Portrait*, at University College, Dublin, whose main building was at one time Whaley's residence.

The Dublin bucks formed various clubs, among them the so-called pinkindindies who wore their swords with the tips exposed and amused themselves by "pinking" or slashing the unlucky passer-by who got in their way. Others took the names of Indian tribes, like the Iroquois, who were known for their cruelty. The most notorious was the Hellfire Club founded in 1735 by Richard Parsons, the first Earl of Rosse, and James Worsdale, the painter. Its object, according to the newspaper accounts, was "drinking, debauchery and sacrilegious mockery of religion." Evicted for setting fire to the Eagle Tavern on Cork Hill, where they usually met, the members established themselves in a house owned by Parsons on the top of Montpelier near Rathfarnham, which is southwest of Dublin. Legends about the orgies of the Hellfire Club multiplied over the years, particularly after the house was destroyed by fire. They may have furnished Joyce with some material for the Circe chapter in *Ulysses*.

The rites of the Hellfire Club centered around devil worship and the celebration of the Black Mass. The president, dubbed "King of Hell," was garbed like Satan and enthroned in the drawing room of the Montpelier house, which was ornamented by horns, hooves, human skulls, and the like. Several deaths were attributed to the Club, but most of the victims apparently died of their enthusiasm for *scaltheen*, a potent brew concocted out of whiskey and butter to test the caliber of the membership. The club was supposedly abandoned after a fiery encounter with a local priest who had been tried by a jury of thirteen members and sentenced to death. Granted time to pray, the resourceful clergyman exorcised their black cat. According to one account, "as the Priest finished speaking a great crash was heard overhead, the room became red and the lamps fell down and set fire to the table."[6]

Whether this has anything to do with Stephen Dedalus's apocalyptic thrust at the chandelier or Mulligan's role in the Black Mass, I have no way of proving; however, the term *buck* was certainly intended to evoke memories of these riotous adventurers of an earlier age. As Anglo-Irishmen, the bucks were "usurpers," members of the ruling class which had impoverished and degraded the native Irish. Like Mulligan, who brings in Haines, thereby hastening Stephen's departure, they collaborated with the English to deprive the native Irish of their rights.

The term *buck* has yet another connotation, that of the dandy or fop, linking Mulligan with his primrose waistcoat to Oscar Wilde and the aesthetes of the 1890's, the yellow decade. Mulligan's narcissism and concern with dress, his witty, epigramatic style, the hint of homosexuality ("manner of Oxenford"), all suggest the decadent mode of the fin de siècle, which Stephen must reject if he is to become an artist of the first rank. The most characteristic trait linking Mulligan to Wilde is, however, a propensity for clowning, the need to perform, to wear a mask.[7] Early in his career Wilde deliberately attracted the attention of the public through his eccentric manner and dress, the famous knee breeches, the velvet coat, the sunflower boutonniere. He sought out the rich and the famous to exploit them, if only for their publicity value. His open disdain for the bourgeoisie set him apart as an isolated and notorious figure long before the unfortunate scandal of the Wilde-Queensberry trial. He was pleased to find himself caricatured in *Punch* and in Gilbert and Sullivan's *Patience*, which brought him an offer to tour America. "Asked in effect to sell his notoriety, his aesthetic clothes and mannerisms, his resemblance to a comic character in a light opera and his appeal to public curiosity of the lowest sort, Wilde replied by cable, 'yes, if offer good.' "[8]

In his essay on Oscar Wilde, Joyce observed that it is in the tradition of Irish writers of comedy from Sheridan and Goldsmith to Bernard Shaw to play court jester to the English.[9] It was a role that he emphatically refused to play though he was well equipped to do so. Not only was he a brilliant wit, but as both *Ulysses* and *Finnegans Wake* demonstrate, Joyce was thoroughly familiar with the stage Irish tradition; he knew the songs, the jokes, the pantomimes, and had a talent for mimicry and burlesque. By all accounts he also had a fine tenor voice and seriously considered a musical career. It is very much to the point that Stephen — as Mulligan reminds us — is the "loveliest mummer of them all."[10] I suspect that Joyce defended himself against the pull of the stage Irish tradition, against an instinctive pleasure in "mere performance," by projecting some of its worst aspects onto Mulligan.

Mulligan demonstrates his talent as a performer in the opening chapter of *Ulysses* where he plays the role of mock priest, celebrating Mass with a bowl of shaving cream, a mirror and a razor. Mulligan's gaiety and his pleasure in the physical world counterbalance Stephen's tragic, introspective mood. He is used as a foil to reveal certain limitations in Stephen's character, his obsession with death, his fears, inflexibility, and pride.[11] In the course of the day he adopts various postures, plays many roles, appearing, for example, first to side with Stephen and then with Haines. He rarely lets slip the actor's mask, so there is little indication of what, if anything, he believes in. His mockery continually stirs Stephen's self-doubt. James H. Maddox believes that the mercurial Mulligan is a particularly threatening figure to Stephen because "he calls into question the very concept of a self . . . thus establishing a theme central to both Stephen and Bloom: the question of the continuity of the self in time."[12] Stephen's enormous labors to free himself from the mesh of religious and cultural values which are smothering him appear meaningless to Mulligan. Most particularly his agonizing guilt over the death of his mother is made to seem a monumental egotism: "I see them pop off every day in the Mater and Richmond and cut up into tripes in the dissecting room. It's a beastly thing and nothing else. It simply doesn't matter . . . Humour her till it's over."

Mulligan's emotional detachment, his resistance to personal introspection, to philosophy and religion, is probably meant to reflect a scientific mentality, though he shows little evidence of scientific training or of the larger issues behind scientific research. Immersed in the external and measurable world, the catalogue of the senses, Mulligan views the most profound of human experiences as ephemera, devoid of lasting significance. He thus represents a powerful attraction for Stephen, struggling to erect a new system of values on the ruins of his faith. To one formed by the rituals of Catholicism and nurtured on the subtleties of scholastic philosophy, all other forms of religion, as Stephen observes in *A Portrait*, seem poor substitutes. It is very tempting to plunge instead into complete cynicism and conceal one's despair by mocking all forms of belief.

As the *Schlagfertig*, Mulligan not only penetrates Stephen's defenses, he strikes at values central to Irish culture. His assault is invariably comic, but the hostility beneath the jester's mask is never quite concealed. Mulligan's parody of the Mass is an excellent device for ridiculing Stephen's moral seriousness, but it also allows Mulligan to dominate, to force Stephen into the role of acolyte, who must carry first the shaving bowl and then the food which is offered around in a kind of communion feast. In ridiculing Catholicism Mulligan is typically blasphemous or obscene, as in the "Ballad of Joking Jesus":

I'm the queerest young fellow that ever you heard
My mother's a jew, my father's a bird. . . .

That note of anti-Semitism will be heard frequently in the course of the day, but none will sound it more persistently than Mulligan.

Another favorite target is the sexual taboo. In a society which is remarkably discreet in avoiding references to sexual matters, Mulligan draws attention with his ribaldry. He appears insatiably curious about the erotic preferences of other people and is quick to make damaging insinuations ("Is she up the pole?"). Sex, like death, has supposedly little mystery for Buck Mulligan, who insists that it is comic in the Bergsonian sense of something mechanical encrusted upon the living.[13] His jests are intended to shock the Victorian Irish merely by exposing the bare facts of anatomy.

Joyce repeatedly links the derisive wit of Mulligan to that of Swift, another "mocker" and "a hater of his kind." In "The Oxen of the Sun," Mulligan presents an "immodest proposal" for setting up a national fertilizing farm where he will offer "his dutiful yeoman services for the fecundation of any female of what grade of life soever. . . ." Underneath his clever parody of Swift, in which he reduces women to cattle who need "servicing," there is an evident misogyny. Within the context of the chapter, his speech is a crime against motherhood, that most cherished of Irish institutions. The fact is that Mulligan treats women everywhere with contempt as objects to be exploited sexually and financially. His posturing as the quintessential Irish bull is very likely an elaborate screen; Mulligan's obsessive mockery of sex, and particularly sexual perversion, suggests maladjustment rather than an easy intimacy with women. One never actually sees him in their company, and for all his boasting about virility, he does not accompany Dedalus and Lynch to Bella Cohen's brothel.

Mulligan's satiric assault on the Irish Revival provides further clues to his character. In the opening chapter he mocks the new art as pretentious, hence "snot green." In the library he is more openly contemptuous, providing a counterpoint to Stephen's theory about the emotional life of Shakespeare by jesting about the homosexuality of Irish writers.

At his entrance he is greeted with smiling acknowledgment by all except Stephen; he is expected to provide a comic interlude: "Shakespeare? he said. I seem to know the name. . . . To be sure, he said, remembering brightly. The chap that writes like Synge." In his parody of Synge, Mulligan uses the brogue for comic effect, playing on the old stereotype of the Irish drunk:

It's what I'm telling you, mister honey, it's queer and sick we were, Haines and myself, the time himself brought it in. 'Twas murmur we did for a gallus potion would rouse a friar, I'm thinking, and he limp with leching. (198–199)

The point here is that art which focuses on the Gaelic world is necessarily pretentious, limited in meaning, hardly to be taken seriously. Since the peasant represented to Joyce a culturally impoverished but oddly self-satisfied condition of life, he was critical of those who made the Irish countryman and his language the focus of their work. Thus it is not surprising that Synge's use of the dialect as an exclusive medium for dramatic expression is singled out for ridicule.

While Synge is ridiculed for his interest in folk dialect and customs, W. B. Yeats, John Eglinton, George Moore and George Russell (A.E.) come in for their share of the assault.[14] Mulligan's performance here has a compulsive quality about it. By disparaging Stephen's audience and asserting his own authority, he betrays an anxiety to confirm the personal bond which is beginning to dissolve. One reason for its dissolution is that Mulligan comes to represent the homosexual world to the still immature Stephen Dedalus, whose adventures with Fresh Nelly and Rosalie, the Coalquay whore, are far from satisfying. Wilde's "love that dare not speak its name" is a persistent minor theme in the chapter, raised initially by Stephen's response to the librarians and then taken up and elaborated upon by his rival. The marked affinity between the two young men, always evident in their exchange of wit, suggests that Joyce uses Mulligan to explore ideas or obsessions which Stephen will eventually discard. Mulligan typically acts as a "comic chorus,"[15] offering mocking or subversive variations on Stephen's expression of personal, religious, philosophical or artistic commitment or belief.

Mulligan first raises the subject of pederasty in relation to Bloom who, he warns, is "Greeker than the Greeks." He passes quickly from a similar jest about Shakespeare to a prolonged and increasingly distasteful attack on the new Irish writers as, for example, in the parody of Yeats's "Baile and Aillinn":

And that filibustering filibeg
That never dared to slake his drouth
Magee that had the chinless mouth.

Being afraid to marry on earth
They masturbated for all they were worth.
(216)

He refers to the Mechanics Hall, which after renovation became the
Abbey Theatre, as the "plumbers' hall," punning about perform-
ances there as the "pubic sweat of monks." Homosexuality is used in
an offensive, stereotypical manner as an emblem of weakness: thus
the Revival is dismissed as effete, decadent, amateurish, an echo of
the fin de siècle in England.

The bad odor generated by Mulligan's wit recalls Swift's "Letter of Advice to a Young Poet": "When Writers of all sizes, like
Freeman of the City, are at liberty to throw out their *Filth* and *Ex-
crementious Productions* in every Street as they please, what can the
Consequence be, but that the Town must be *Poyson'd* and become
such an other *Jakes*, as by report of great Travellers, EDINBO-
ROUGH is at Night. . . ."[16] It is possible that Joyce is interested here
in the function of satire as a "less obvious form of dirt."[17] For
Mulligan's wit is neither liberating nor life affirming as is the great
tradition of comedy to which Joyce — for all his use of satire —
finally belongs. Although he is often comic, Mulligan's purpose is to
negate or destroy, and he seems less and less entertaining as the day
wears on.[18] In this scene he "soils" the character of the men whose
invitation he has just accepted. And it is very much to the point that
he continues to associate with them. Despite his role as provocateur,
he is basically a conventional man, well aware — and this may be
one reason for his anger — that he is not the *Uebermensch*. Unlike
Stephen, he is incapable of creating or discovering an alternative to
the social and cultural milieu he so insistently derides.

As they leave the library together, Stephen perceives the basic
impotence in Mulligan, recognizing also that his hostile jests are a
projection of his own fear of sexual inversion: "Jest on. Know
thyself." Observing Bloom, Mulligan erupts with new virulence: "O,
Kinch, thou art in peril. Get thee a breechpad." By linking Stephen
to Ophelia, suggesting to him a feminine as well as a passive role,
Mulligan attempts to implicate his rival in his own probably unconscious homosexual feelings. It is not until the Circe chapter that
Stephen finally exorcises Mulligan, parrying that striking wit with
his own buoyant and ironic humor.

In the library scene, however, Stephen's separation from Mulligan is not yet complete. He is still being exploited, having finally agreed to buy that "gallus potion" that Mulligan has been waiting for. More significant, his own derisive attitude toward Eglinton, Best, and Russell still links him to the "brood of mockers" from whom no worthwhile concept of art or philosophy of life may be expected. Stephen's earlier pronouncement about Irish art as "the cracked looking glass of a servant" makes it clear that he shares Mulligan's skepticism about the efforts of new writers to draw upon Gaelic sources rather than the traditional English ones. In the library he reduces A.E., a complex and energetic man who gave practical advice to Irish farmers and was one of the few intellectuals to champion the workers in the transport strike of 1913, to a fuzzy minded ineffectual dreamer: "Through spaces smaller than red globules of man's blood they creepy-crawl after Blake's buttocks into eternity of which this vegetable world is but a shadow." Thus while it is clear that Mulligan's performance is intended to seem offensive, the culminating effect of the combined mockery of the two young men is to dismiss the work of the Revival as effete and pretentious. No effort is made to distinguish such elements as the hard clarity of newly translated Irish lyrics or George Moore's realistic fiction from the romantic effusions of the Celtic Twilight.

In "Nighttown" Mulligan appears as a mocking spectre, who is finally exorcised when Stephen turns Mulligan's own weapons against him. He turns up first as the "sex specialist," who pronounces Bloom "bisexually abnormal" and proceeds to deliver a grotesque indictment which combines his own neurotic tendencies with those of Bloom: "There are marked symptoms of chronic exhibitionism. . . . He is prematurely bald from self abuse, perversely idealistic in consequence, a reformed rake, and has metal teeth." In the company of other medical students, as one of the goosestepping "beatitudes," Mulligan represents the bluntly physical: "beer, beef . . . buggerum" as opposed to intellectual or spiritual values. He appears again in the costume of a jester weeping tears of molten butter before the putrefying corpse of Stephen's mother.

Edmund Epstein has pointed out that "brightness" is paradoxically associated with Stephen's enemies. Mulligan, "tripping and sunny like the buck himself," Haines with his pale eyes, John Eglinton with his "rufous" hair, Richard Best's brightness and lightness — all are regarded with antagonism. Stephen himself feels an affinity for the darkness, associated with the Jews and the Moors (Averroes and Moses Maimonides) and that "obscure soul of the world, a darkness shining in brightness which brightness could not comprehend." It is in the darkness that the soul is nourished, only the darkness that is fruitful. The prophetic moment of illumination is given to those who are not externally illuminated, that is, prosperous or acclaimed in the eyes of the world. Thus it follows that, while Mulligan is dressed in white and gold and primrose, Stephen and Bloom are in black.[19]

In the final apocalyptic vision of "Nighttown" in which Dublin gives up its dead, Mulligan appears in the guise of Fr. Malachi O'Flynn, celebrant of the Black Mass. "Dressed in a long petticoat and reversed chausable, his two left feet back to front," Fr. Malachi reflects not only the inversion of the Black Mass but the contradictory nature of mercurial Mulligan, the effete concealed behind the exhibition of virility, the seriousness of the mock priest. The Black Mass is the celebration of God as Dog, the exaltation of matter over spirit, the offering of the damned. Malachi O'Flynn is assisted by the Rev. C. Haines Love, who holds over the celebrant's head the umbrella-prophylactic for which there is little need. At the moment of consecration: "This is my body," the bare buttocks of Malachi are revealed, a carrot protruding, in mockery of "the love that dare not speak its name."

Robert Adams tells us that this may be taken as a parody of the climactic scene in *The Lake* by George Moore in which the hero, Fr. Oliver Gogarty, having decided to leave the priesthood, strips off his garments. Adams concludes by judging the larger parody of the Mass as "odious,"[20] but surely that is to entirely ignore the ironic spirit in which it is conceived and the fundamentally comic exposure of Mulligan. It is here that his "striking wit" is most brilliantly parried.

Joyce's quarrel with Oliver St. John Gogarty and the rest of the Dublin literary circle has been amply described by Richard Ellmann.[21] The only point I wish to emphasize is that Joyce's use of ferocious mockery directed against specific individuals is very much in keeping with the spirit of Irish satire. He carries his jest to ludicrous extremes, making little attempt in the case of the Gaelic enthusiasts to respond to the complexity of his subject. He diminishes the Dublin literati by ridiculing not only their intellectual and artistic capability but their physical traits and most particularly their virility. Joyce's strategy with Buck Mulligan is more complicated because of his affinity with Gogarty. In this case satire is used both to discredit an intellectual and artistic rival and as a defense against the lure of "mere performance." The mercurial Malachi is consigned to the circle of dilettantes who gather at the home of George Moore. In casting off Mulligan, Joyce probably achieved some kind of psychic balance just as Leon Edel assures us Tolstoy did in pushing Anna Karenina under a railroad train. It may simply have been the equanimity and perspective that come with distance and time. But Joyce certainly felt more free to draw upon Irish myth and folklore and to fully exploit the stage Irish tradition in fashioning the great comic epic of *Finnegans Wake*.[22] Shem the Penman and Shaun the Post finally turn out to be facets of the same personality.

There is a curious epilogue to the tale of Buck Mulligan and Oliver St. John Gogarty. In *Surpassing Wit* James Carens proposes that critics have all along tended to confuse Gogarty and Mulligan. Gogarty became trapped by the assumption that his talents were primarily those of a ribald, a mocker and a clown, and as a result he has not received adequate recognition for his accomplishments as a poet and a man of letters. The purpose of this new book is to reevaluate the work of Gogarty, to free him in turn from the spell of that archdruid, James Joyce.

6. Samuel Beckett's Murphy

I N ESTABLISHING the Abbey Theatre, W.B. Yeats set out to prove that Ireland was not "the home of buffoonery and of easy sentiment."[1] Neither he nor James Joyce fully displaced the stage Irish tradition, but along with other writers of the twentieth century, they succeeded in generating a much more potent mythology by recasting the ancient tales in modern form and transforming the real landscape of modern Ireland into something more rare and beautiful. That grey Anglo-Norman tower in Gort is filled with echoes of Red Hanrahan. And it is no longer possible to visit the Isle of Howth without imagining the head of the sleeping giant Finnegan or Molly Bloom among the rhododendrons. In "The Geography of Irish Fiction" John W. Foster speaks of Connemara and the Aran Islands as "places of solitude and retreat (flight and succour), of passion and timelessness" which exist in a "permanent recess of the Irish psyche." He proposes that the writer's preoccupation with place is a preoccupation with the past without which Irish selfhood is apparently inconceivable.[2]

Samuel Beckett is the one major writer of fiction who moves in a widening trajectory away from the mythical landscape of Ireland, shedding language, history, custom, the all too resonant particularities of time and place. The journey begins with *Murphy*.

In this ironic and playful novel, Murphy is presented as irrational man, drifting through a Newtonian world of mechanical lust and mechanical action. The modern day cities of London and Dublin function like Newton's clockwork universe wound up by a divine flick of the wrist and condemned to perpetual motion. They are cities inhabited by grotesques, both English and Irish, totally absorbed in activity that has little if any meaning: a crowd disperses, "the better to gather elsewhere."

The seventeenth century, like our own time, was a period of intellectual and religious crises as traditional beliefs collapsed under the impact of men like Copernicus and Newton. It was increasingly difficult to accept either the authority of the Church or the evidence of the senses that led one to assume that the sun revolved around the earth. The seventeenth century thinker had therefore to become a skeptic, questioning all forms of authority and all knowledge that depended on the elaborate theorizing of the scholastics. Reason, however, led Newton to conclude that the universe could be explained through mechanics; even man was to be regarded as a machine, highly sophisticated, but a machine nonetheless. Descartes, attempting to preserve the concept of a soul free from the mechanical laws of the universe, postulated a dichotomy of mind and body.

As we look at the Newtonian and Cartesian models, which appear absurd from the perspective of modern physics and psychology, we are brought face to face with our own limitations in the person of Murphy. Beckett's novel, like *Gulliver's Travels*, is in the tradition of the Menippean satire which deals less with people than with intellectual attitudes. Murphy, who is something of a self-parody, is a variant of the *philosophus gloriosus*, a highly stylized character committed to a rigid, though anything but rigorous, system of ideas. He is pointedly referred to as a "surd," that discovery of modern mathematics which provides a convenient though irrational means of positing space-time relationships and consequently a four-dimensional universe to replace the Newtonian model. Beckett implies that our contemporary obsession with the irrational simply replaces an earlier obsession with the rational, which replaced a still earlier obsession with faith.

The most eccentric of our Irish comic figures, Murphy views physical reality with contempt, preferring the higher pleasures of the mind conceived more or less after the Cartesian model as quite separate from the body. Unfortunately, his "body" is attracted to one Celia Kelly, a pretty Irish prostitute who tries to rehabilitate Murphy and provide him with a proper social identity. The question of identity, a major preoccupation of the Irish for centuries, is treated as an irrelevance by Beckett except when it can be used as the target of a joke. Thus Murphy's name, in slang, "a potato" and his association with Murphy's Law: if anything can go wrong it will. Murphy sheds his past as easily as he sheds his clothes, disgarding the whole burden of Irish history, the heavy freight of bitterness, tragedy, old hatreds, and class systems. We know that he was born in Dublin and that he was a dubious sort of theology student, but when we first encounter him idling about in London, he has left Dublin for good.

Murphy is, in fact, a kind of anti-Irishman, who speaks only when absolutely necessary in a fairly formal, often pedantic style. His suit has a green shimmer, but it is the aeruginous green that comes from long wear. He is resolutely unromantic and unsentimental in his relationship with the prostitute Celia. He is solitary rather than gregarious, stingy with money and never drinks. If he is idle and rebellious against the "despotism of fact," it is purely by calculation. If he has the old Irish yearning for freedom, it is of the most absolute, purely philosophical kind.

Murphy is indifferent to people, ambition, surroundings in general. Though, like Yeats and his followers, he resists the establishment that demands "quid pro quo," his rebellion is modeled on the Dantesque figure of Belacqua, who was content to languish on the steps of Purgatory rather than begin the journey toward salvation. In place of the romantic ideal of Ireland, Murphy's aim is "the accidentless One-and-Only called Nothing," achieved by strapping himself naked in a rocking chair and rocking away until he is oblivious to all sensation. Rejecting Irish puritanism, Murphy believes that physical craving must be appeased, never repressed, if the mind is to be free. In this novel, unlike the work that follows, the problem is treated ironically and humorously.

With Murphy's mind, imagined as a "large hollow sphere, hermetically closed to the universe without," three modes of pleasure are possible. Within the first, elements of physical experience could be arranged. Here, for example, his landlady can be sexually assaulted by a drunken Irish bard. The second phase consists of the pleasures of phantasy and contemplation, the bliss of Belacqua. The third phase is the most desirable; here is absolute formlessness, where Murphy becomes a "mote in the dark of absolute freedom." Samuel Mintz explains how the ideological basis for Murphy's belief in a mind-body dichotomy is to be found, not in the work of Descartes, but in that of one of his followers, Arnold Geulinex, who believed that the mind was wholly ineffectual outside its own sphere, but within that sphere the individual was wholly free.[3] This helps to explain both Murphy's quest for happiness and his rather feeble grip on reality. Geulinex explained mind-body coordination as a miracle of divine intervention. A man no more given to mental than to physical exertion, Murphy ignores the problem that bedeviled Berkeley, the "idealist tar," by assuming some kind of congruence between mind and body. He vaguely believes in "supernatural determinism," but the problem is "of little interest." We are told that as he grows older, he is more and more convinced that his mind is a closed system, "self-sufficient and impermeable to the vicissitudes of the body." On this delusion much of the exceedingly macabre humor of the book rests.

The philosophical determinism underlying the structure of the novel as well as the implacable rhythms of the prose style provide an ironic counterpoint to Murphy's longing for absolute freedom. Murphy is the most evasive and desultory of comic characters. A kind of mock saint, he regards freedom not as the right to choose, but as the absence of all desire. While the other characters in the novel move with brisk purpose toward specific ends, Murphy drifts, procrastinates, allows himself to be propelled by accident. He is forced to admit to certain weaknesses — for food as well as for Celia. In one scene he calculates that if he could overcome his craving for ginger biscuits, his lunch (consisting of five biscuits), would be edible in 120 ways. While he struggles with a temptation worthy of St. Anthony, his lunch is swallowed by a dachshund (who regurgitates the ginger biscuit).

It is likely that Murphy's efforts to become a "mote in the dark of absolute freedom" is also intended as a parody of Stephen Dedalus's struggle toward intellectual and artistic stasis.[4] Stephen seeks the freedom to create, to give to experience a shaping form; Murphy seeks formlessness. His dualism may be regarded as a comic extension of Stephen's spiritual alienation. The latter constructs a theory of art on the scaffolding erected by Aquinas and Aristotle, while Murphy, a former theology student who reads Latin, depends on astrological charts to guide his sublunary motions.[5] Both men are impoverished, solitary figures living in exile and both are determined to eschew action or aggression. The correspondences between them are typically farcical, however. Stephen is haunted by images of a dog-panther-fox; Murphy is victimized by the dachshund who swallows his lunch.

While all of the figures in Part I were engaged in some kind of struggle with authority, Murphy wants only to retreat quietly back into the womb or as near a state of unthinking bliss as he can achieve. Birth is viewed as the supreme calamity; Murphy never wears a hat because it reminds him poignantly of the caul. His desire to return to the womb or what it represents — a subconscious wish for death — is treated comically. One of the funniest scenes in the book occurs when Murphy literally goes off his rocker and lands on his head, bare backside up, totally unable to extricate himself from his bonds. There he remains, muttering to himself, until Celia rescues him.

An exceedingly pretty young woman, Celia would prefer to stay with Murphy because she loves him and because she finds prostitution a bore. Associated ironically with both Jonson and Swift, Celia is viewed by Murphy as a deterrent to the long slide down to the tomb. She is described solely in terms of her physical attributes as nothing else about her concerns Murphy, who bewails the fact that the part of him he hates loves Celia.

The initial phase of their relationship is fairly harmonious. Murphy proposes marriage; Celia accepts, but unfortunately his little scheme of petty fraud, which enables him to live very modestly without working, will not support another person. Hence the tragic ultimatum: Murphy must go to work, expose himself in the local "slave markets" if he expects the "music" with Celia to continue.

Reluctantly, Murphy agrees to work, but only when the stars decree that the moment is propitious; for the only system outside of himself in which Murphy professes to have any faith is astrology, a peculiar aberration in a man aspiring to absolute freedom. Murphy has his chart cast by a mysterious swami and sallies forth, "keeping a wary eye out for publishers, quadrupeds and tropical swamps, as these may terminate unprofitably for the Native."

Murphy seeking employment again demonstrates an inimitable style. Dressed in a suit that is green with age and sporting a lemon bow tie, he is "content to expose himself vaguely on the fringes of the better-attended slave market." Murphy, like Mulligan and Stephen Dedalus, is associated with the fin de siècle, but in a highly ironic way. In this scene he appears as a caricature of the dandy, having attended meticulously to the details of his dress — such as they are. However, his weary disdain and self-preoccupation have no basis in an aesthetic ideal. Despite his look of posturing, the attitude with which he faces the world is real. Murphy is in genuine revolt against what Oscar Wilde termed "the sordid perils of actual existence."

Despite his evasive tactics he is offered a job in a mental hospital by a very desperate Irish bard. This job not only allows him to elude Celia, but provides him with a glimpse of what he assumes to be the perfect existence, that of the schizoids, aloof in their padded cells. The patients become a "sign post" for him; he decides that "nothing less than a slap-up psychosis could consummate his life's strike."

Murphy is quite happy tending his patients despite the physical labor involved. During his working hours he is a great success with the patients, proving to Murphy his compatibility with them. The best part of his day hinges on a game of chess with Endon, one of the "schizoids." The two players avoid facing each other directly; communication is effected through a long, unaggressive series of moves in which hours pass without either player losing a piece or even checking the other. An ideal relationship.

Depression overcomes Murphy only when he leaves the hospital at the end of his work shift. Although totally alone now, he is unable to find peace in the accustomed manner. The outer world is cloudy and exhausted; he is visibly breaking down, responding to the tug of insanity. Having finally surrendered to Endon with much difficulty in the symbolic game of chess, Murphy retreats at the critical moment, consistent in his inconsistency. Staring into the utterly opaque eyes of Mr. Endon, he sees himself reduced to a speck in the unseen. Realizing that his own mental powers are deserting him and that he does not, after all, wish to be irretrievably sucked into the void, he bolts from the hospital, shedding his clothes along with his responsibilities. He makes his way back to his garret and rocking chair, vaguely thinking of returning to Celia.

The dilemma is resolved by his timely death. In one sense, all the gas generated by a flatulent existence finally explodes, taking Murphy along with it. In this rather crucial instance, Murphy is again strapped in his rocking chair, seeking to become a "mote in the dark of absolute freedom," and he quite literally succeeds — propelled by the physical reality he has tried to ignore. Gas seeps into his make-shift radiator (turned on by accident in the bathroom below), and is ignited by a candle. The scene ends on an exceedingly macabre note:

> The rock got faster and faster, shorter and shorter, the gleam was gone, the grin was gone, the starlessness was gone. . . . Soon his

body would be quiet soon he would be free. The gas went on in the w.c., excellent gas, superfine chaos. Soon his body was quiet.[6]

All the characters who pursued Murphy, thinking only he could satisfy their needs, now content themselves with one another. There are various and peculiar couplings, notably that of the Irish bard and the head male nurse of the Magdalen Mental Mercyseat, and immediate physical relief for Cooper who can now take off his hat and sit down. Like Hairy in *More Pricks than Kicks*, who similarly benefits from the death of Belacqua, Cooper has absorbed some of Murphy's qualities. In a Newtonian world, motion is never lost.

At the coroner's inquest, Murphy's acquaintances gather together to view the charred remains of our poor hero, who can be identified only by a large birthmark on his buttocks. Murphy's corpse becomes a rather ludicrous object under the gaze of the "17 eyes" (Cooper has only one). The occasion is marked by curiosity, self-satisfaction, and the amorous declaration of Ticklepenny and the male nurse. An Irish wake originally included phallic ceremonies; here of course they are somewhat inverted.

At the finish Murphy is cremated, and his ashes are scattered over a barroom floor by the drunken, improvident Cooper:

> By the closing time the body, mind and soul of Murphy were
> freely distributed over the floor of the saloon; and before another
> dayspring greyened the earth had been swept away with the sand,
> the beer, the butts, the glass, the matches, the spits, the vomit. (275)

So Beckett treats with wry contempt Murphy's efforts to withdraw from the "colossal fiasco," to escape ordinary human experience. In his best work *Waiting for Godot* and *Molloy*, Beckett's characters achieve a Sisyphian nobility by their willingness to confront an existence which is lonely, agonizing, and apparently bereft of meaning.

Despite his foolishness, Murphy has been somewhat better off than the characters who move perpetually toward some desired end. In this Newtonian world he is a tangent touching the circle of their affairs. The others go blithely on, engaged in a series of motions and countermotions, which cancel one another out with the nicety of a mathematical equation. Motions and events are interchangeable; if one partner is unavailable, another will do. Desire, according to

Beckett, is fairly mechanical in its circuit of effects: "The old endless chain of love, tolerance, indifference, aversion and disgust." Ms. Counihan professes to love Murphy, but accepts the amorous advances first of Needle Wylie then of Neary, who no sooner finds a woman than he loses interest in her.

The one character who seems to have a fairly serene if moribund existence is Celia's grandfather, Willoughby Kelly; seamed and withered and bed ridden, he "doesn't look a day over 90." Kelly has much in common with Murphy, being antisocial and unconventional and having spent his life in "dingy, stingy repose." Though he believes himself fond of Celia, he scarcely opens his eyes to look at her and is certainly indifferent to the fact that she is a prostitute, even congratulating her on her skill at attracting customers.

Kelly's one obsession is kite flying, and the kite is to Kelly what the soul is to Murphy. It is his link to the infinite, his principal pleasure in life. Once the kite is lost in the final chapter, and Kelly is completely earthbound, he is a doomed man. The tension between dream and reality, mind and body has been destroyed. Ludicrous though he is, Kelly has maintained the crucial balance that Murphy would not concede possible.

One reason may be that physical decrepitude that links him to Moran, Malone and the Unnamable. Kelly can maintain his equilibrium precisely because his physical needs are so few. Inured to physical decay, he can transcend it. In the same way a better Moran begins to emerge with the onset of age and death. Murphy's dilemma is that of a young man trying to appease the body, which continually craves Celia, ginger, and so on.

With *Murphy*, Beckett emerged as a master of comic style, particularly adept at providing the unexpected in terms of language, character and situation. In *More Pricks than Kicks*, Beckett's first important work of fiction, the language tends to be abstract and abstruse. The sentences strain toward effect, and there is little that is remarkable about the imagery aside from the central reference to Dante's indolent friend Belacqua, who becomes the prototype of Murphy and, as A. J. Leventhal has observed,[7] that of all Beckett's major characters.

With *Murphy*, published four years later in 1938, the style has become witty and precise. A major source of comedy is the disparity between Beckett's irrational and fairly grotesque characters and their formal, balanced, Latinate speaking style.[8] Even the landlady,

Miss Carridge, speaks like an academic. Beckett plays on the disparity, not only between character and speaking voice, but between his own carefully controlled narrative style and a plot that is patently absurd.

The lethargic, almost catatonic meanderings of Murphy are described with brisk energy. Take, for example, his meeting with Celia which, like most events in his life, is sheerest accident. However, the tone and the rhetoric with its echoes of Swift's *Modest Proposal* suggest necessity or the direct intervention of fate. Details of their surroundings are woven ironically into a framework for the occasion. The prose is highly formal, even didactic, a steady progression of two-part descriptive phrases pronouncing the inevitable coupling of Murphy and Celia: ". . . sculptors and statuaries, critics and reviewers, major and minor, drunk and sober, laughing and crying, in schools and singly, passed up and down." (14)

Minor characters are revealed in terms of their obsessions — typically sex and alcohol. The comedy frequently fits Henri Bergson's definition: "the effect of the mechanical encrusted upon the living." This is a description of Neary in love:

> There he sat all day, moving slowly from one stool to another until he had completed the circuit of the counters, when he would start all over again in the reverse direction. He did not speak to the curates, he did not drink the endless half-pints of porter that he had to buy, he did nothing but move slowly round the ring of counters, first in one direction, then in the other, thinking of Miss Counihan (56).

Beckett is also fond of the pun: "Why did the barmaid champagne? Because the stout porter bitter." Another comic effect is produced through the inverted cliché: "Murphy, unable to believe his ears, opened his eyes," or "he now told her all about them (his heart attacks), keeping back nothing that might alarm her." Beckett's characters, like those in Edward Albee's *American Dream*, make no effort to conceal their selfishness or avarice or their lewd designs on one another. One laughs at the exposure of feelings, which the more sophisticated among us have learned to suppress or conceal: "Miss Counihan pressed her bosom with vague relish against the lesser of two evils."

In the final chapters the comic tone of the novel[9] takes on an incresingly macabre quality. The characters are afflicted with various indignities, among which death is merely a bad joke. While Murphy expires in flames, his upstairs neighbor slashes his throat with a razor, and the disposal of his body is presented as a triumph of economy and bureaucratic efficiency. His landlady, Miss Carridge, stages an attack of hysteria, attracting the police and thus avoiding a doctor's fee. They in turn deposit the "old boy" in an ambulance, proving he still lived,

> for it is a misdemeanour to put a corpse, no matter how fresh , into
> an ambulance. But to take one out contravenes no law, by-law,
> section or sub-section, and it was perfectly in order for the old boy to
> consummate, as he did, his felony on the way to the hospital. (136)

The "dianoetic laugh" echoes in Synge and Joyce but is most clearly sounded in the work of Samuel Beckett. Joyce, and even Synge, reflects an optimism that chooses eros over death, while Beckett, like Swift, is scatological, emphasizing the progressive deterioration of the body and the sexually grotesque. In *Murphy* the human body is generally presented as deformed, malodorous, or simply irritating. Sexual desire, even for the delightful and excep-tional Celia, is viewed as comical necessity. Men and women eye one another as quarry, and emotional feelings are seldom reciprocated. From the oyster kisses of Needle Wylie and Miss Counihan "inclin-ing her bust no more than was necessary to preserve her from falling down backwards," we are not far removed from the grotesque coupling of Moll and MacMann.

Beckett employs that ancient mode of comedy: laughter at the physically abnormal. Murphy, who has the attitude of one "frozen in the middle of a hornpipe" is derided for his ungainly physical ap-pearance, which causes people to accost him and small boys to im-itate him. Although he is pursued by women, it is his "surgicial quality" they admire, masochists, every one. Aside from the beautiful Celia, the characters in the novel are all physically deformed in some way. The romantic Neary is covered with sores, literally as well as figuratively. Cooper, Neary's dipsomaniac ser-vant, has one eye and can neither remove his hat or sit down. Even the animals are abnormal. Such a procession of the diseased and the deformed reflects a profound distaste for the physical world which is set apart from and opposed to the inner world of the self. Action is regarded as "a dreary ooze of being," hopeless, futile, without consequence. Beckett's attitude, although expressed in an ironic and self-mocking tone, is very like that of Roquentin in *Nausea* shrinking from the image of the chestnut tree.

In *The Irish Comic Tradition* Vivian Mercier talks about the life-hating aspects of the Irish grotesque and suggests that the Sheela-na-gig, a primitive Irish figure of a very ugly woman with enlarged genitalia and shrunken breasts, reflects a fear of sexuality that has been preserved into modern times.[10] It is certainly true that Beckett emphasizes the grotesque aspects of sexuality by linking it with age, impotence and deformity. But aside from Swift, I can think of no other major Irish writer with similar inclinations. In the work of Joyce the relation between men and women is often comic, but it is also the profound source of all creative life. Poetry in Irish, as well as the sagas, suggests that the Gaels were a lusty people, and the folk tales still being collected in the Gaeltacht have an undeniably earthy strain. Irish puritanism is a relatively recent development, which may be linked both to the influence of the Victorian middle class and to the hegemony of Maynooth.

While Irish writers in exile tend to recall their native land with some degree of passion, Beckett's response is a mocking detachment edged with contempt. For Beckett, an Anglo-Irishman who witnessed the ravages of the civil war, the Free State was never part of the civilized world. So it is not surprising to find in *Murphy* certain features of Irish life exaggerated and otherwise exposed to ridicule. Cathleen ni Houlihan, the traditional figure of Ireland, for example, becomes Cathleen na Hennessey, a bar maid. The Cork philosopher Neary has learned to stop his heart in situations beyond endurance as "when he wanted a drink and could not get one, or fell among Gaels and could not escape. . . ." While Murphy himself is a teetotellar (another means of stripping away that Irish identity), most of the lesser characters are exceedingly fond of their pint of plain. Beckett even resurrects the nineteenth century stereotype of the Irish brute in the person of Miss Counihan of the "low breasts and high buttocks," who is "exceedingly anthropoid even for Cork." With true Dublin prejudice, Cork is identified with the worst aspects of provincial life ("I say you know what women are . . . or has your entire life been spent in Cork?")

Like Joyce, Beckett takes special aim at the Revival. Murphy's last wish is that his ashes be flushed down the w.c. during a performance of the Abbey Theatre. Neary, reaching the limits of Cork endurance, attempts suicide in the G.P.O. by dashing his head against the bronze backside of Cúchulainn (erected there in memory of the 1916 uprising). Miss Carridge, a most practical and most malodorous landlady, secretly reads A.E.'s *Candle of Vision*. Beckett's sharpest satire is directed against Austin Clarke, who at the time *Murphy* was written was writing poetry using Gaelic models. He appears in the novel as Austin Ticklepenny, an "Olympian sot," who has brought himself to the verge of mental breakdown by composing pentameters in the Irish mode, "as free as a canary in the fifth foot." He is seeking a cure by working for the Magdelen Mental Mercyseat, "emptying the slops of the better-class mentally deranged." In terms of the novel he is an amusing eccentric, though helpless and hopeless, quite driven to despair out of a mistaken notion of his duty to old Eire. Like Murphy, whom he draws in this wake, he finds refuge among the insane.

After *Murphy* the comedy of Beckett becomes increasingly bleak, the true *humour noir*. There are fewer references to things Irish as he pares his subject down to its essentials, stripping away the traditional structures of time, place and individual history. Perhaps the most interesting residue is to be found in the relationship between Molloy and Moran, which reflects among other things, the conflict inherent in the dual heritage of the Anglo-Irish. Molloy, who lives in Bally and talks obsessively is evidently intended as Irish — Hugh Kenner refers to him as the "wilder, Irish" personality; whereas the rigid, authoritarian Moran lives in an English world, appropriately labeled "Turdy."[11]

Molloy, along with the other major work, notably *Waiting for Godot*, was written in French after World War II and then translated into English. It has been suggested that Beckett turned to French to express the darker, negative strain in his personality. Thus even while he was writing *Murphy* in English, which despite its grotesqueries is a very funny book, Beckett was composing bitter and violent poems in French like "La Mouche."[12] Beckett has explained to Lawrence Harvey that by writing in French he was able to rid himself of the nuances of the Anglo-Irish idiom and the consequent "temptation to rhetoric and virtuosity." In comparison to the richness of his native tongue, the "asceticism of French semed more appropriate to the expression of being, undeveloped, unsupported somewhere in the depths of the microcosm."[13]

Beckett's early work, and this is certainly evident in *Murphy*, is full of verbal wit and playfulness. His growing conviction of the inadequacy of language sets him apart from other writers: "If you really get down to the disaster, the slightest eloquence becomes unbearable. Whatever is said is so far from experience."[14] Beckett was the first major Irish writer to respond to the inferno of World War II. Joyce, living in exile in Trieste and Paris, took no part in the war and turned back to the Ireland of his youth for inspiration. Beckett in Paris joined the underground along with Alfred Peron, a close friend who was eventually caught and executed by the Nazis. His later work reflects the agony of the cataclysm; all the certainties, the very structure of language itself has broken down.

7. Flann O'Brien and Mad Sweeny

I N RECENT YEARS with new editions of *At Swim-Two-Birds,*
The Third Policeman, The Dalkey Archive and *An Béal*
Bocht available, Flann O'Brien has begun to receive the
recognition he deserves as one of the finest modern satirists. His
comic masterpiece *At Swim-Two-Birds* was originally published in
1939,[1] a bleak period in world history and a time of disillusionment
in a partitioned Ireland, where the promise of cultural and political
revolution seemed to have failed completely. Old political feuds still
smoldered, and there were occasional, violent reprisals which encouraged the reactionary tendencies of the new government.
Because of the stultifying effects of censorship, it was a difficult time
for writers.

Fluent in Irish, with a first-hand knowledge of the old
literature, O'Brien explored the relation between past and present,
between mythic Gael and the cautious citizen of Dublin. Like Joyce
he was passionately concerned with the imaginative life of the artist
in a culture divided against itself. And while Joyce satirized the
leaders of the Revival in order to define his own position, O'Brien
satirized Joyce for much the same reason.[2] His fiction is filled with
mocking echoes of the great artificer. With an uncanny ear for
dialogue and for the nuances of both poetry and prose, O'Brien was
as skillful at parody as Joyce had been before him.

O'Brien's concern with the nature of language took many
forms. As a purist, he issued a catechism of clichés to rebuke the
man in the street. He also opposed government efforts to revive Irish
as an impractical scheme, which worked against the best interests of
Irish speakers by isolating them from the modern world. He did not
argue against the ability of the language to absorb modern or scien-

tific concepts; in fact he demonstrated its ingenuity and flexibility in *The Irish Times*, but he was skeptical of the way the language was being tied to an archaic and impoverished life style. This became the subject of *An Béal Bocht*, translated by Patrick Powers in 1973 as *The Poor Mouth*. As a master of "smooth learned Gaelic," O'Brien made fun of contemporary autobiographical accounts of life in the Gaeltacht, those remote regions of the west which preserve what remains of the native culture. Because of its parodic nature and the fact that some of the humor depends entirely on linguistic puns and allusions — as Mr. Powers, himself, conceded — no translation can be wholly satisfactory. However, the central theme, which is relevant to this study, is certainly clear enough in the English version, which is the basis of my commentary.

The main character is Bonaparte O'Coonassa, an *omadhawn* if ever there was one, who spends his days in idleness among a lively collection of pigs in the "backside of the house." His ignorance is as extreme as his poverty and his pessimism as pervasive as the sullen downpour and the unending dreariness of life in Corkadora. His understanding of the world comes to him in the form of folklore and gossip and the musings of the "old grey fellow" who augments their diet of potatoes by "hunting," that is, thieving from the neighbors.

The Gaels in *The Poor Mouth* seldom venture into "foreign parts" and have little understanding of the modern world. Their attitude is very like that of Joyce's countryman in *A Portrait* smoking philosophically on his pipe and muttering that "there be queer creatures indeed at the latter end of the world." They are, however, sly at manipulating the occasional government official and the scholars, who descend in droves bringing "happiness and money and high revelry." An ironic equation is drawn between purity of language and a lack of worldly goods. The Corkadorans have the "choicest poverty and calamity," and hence the finest Gaelic, but their "Gaelicism" eventually proves too much even for the scholars, who abandon them for milder climates.

O'Brien's characters seem to take a perverse pleasure in the extreme misery of their lives. Everything is done very slowly with reflection according to what has been written down in the "guid books." Their activities have little to do with reality; a major point of the satire is that Irish peasants have been so much the subject of myth that their actual history has been obscured. O'Brien observes rather acidly that the people themselves have begun to emulate literary patterns, to act according to prescriptions set down by anthropologists, historians, folklorists, writers of fiction and poetry. Thus they are resigned to "truly Gaelic famine" and "truly Gaelic hardship" of every kind. Bonaparte marries (despite considerable confusion about the facts of life) and is eventually bereft of wife and child; to seal his misfortune, he is wrongly accused of crime and sentenced to twenty-nine years of imprisonment in a court where only English is spoken and where consequently the proceedings are entirely incomprehensible to him. On his way to jail he meets a feeble old pauper, who turns out to be his father, returning home after serving a similar sentence under similar circumstances.

One might say that with *An Béal Bocht* the comic treatment of the Gaels has come full circle. In O'Brien's story most of the elements associated with the nineteenth century figure of Paddy reappear with a vengeance. There is the squalor and idleness, the pigs nestled in with the family, the incessant talk, the primitive customs, the innocence in worldly matters. But the people of Corkadora are grim and melancholy; in their weakened condition, dancing or whiskey, though rarely forthcoming, is often fatal. The sun never shines on their remote country, and there is so much rain that fishermen make their way through the fields netting an occasional pig. O'Brien isolates and exaggerates features of Irish life, particularly as they have been presented in folklore and literature. An integral part of the tradition, after all, is the complaint about the hard life, and here it is crystalized at its most terrible and — through modern eyes — most ludicrous.

The writers who created the comic Irishman of the nineteenth century evoked laughs from a distance by emphasizing the poverty of the Gael and his failure to meet English or Anglo-Irish standards. They had little understanding of Gaelic culture itself and so exploited what they saw as its "quaintness" for the sake of entertainment. O'Brien proposes that the modern Gaelophile has achieved a comparable falseness by idealizing the "pure Gael,"[3] making a virtue out of poverty and ignorance and collecting reels of utter nonsense under the label of folklore.

His quarrel was with those who sentimentalized the life of the Gaeltacht and whose efforts to create a new literature in Gaelic he found insufferably dull. While O'Brien did not believe that there was any real prospect of a broadscale revival of Irish, in a letter to Sean O'Casey he agreed that it was "essential" for a writer: "it supplies that unknown quantity in us that enables us to transform the English language and this seems to hold of people who know little or no Irish, like Joyce."[4]

During his lifetime Flann O'Brien, whose actual name was Brian O'Nolan, achieved considerable recognition in yet another guise — that of Myles Na gCopaleen, a sardonic recreation of the popular hero of *The Colleen Bawn*. For nearly twenty-five years he wrote as many as six columns a week for *The Irish Times* under the heading "Cruiskeen Lawn" (literally "the little full jug"), which is the name of a folk song favored by Boucicault's hero. He ranged widely in subject matter, even altering the persona of Myles, whose death and resurrection were duly reported, to allow himself as wide a scope as possible. He was enormously inventive and entertaining, fond of the most unlikely jokes and puns — the worst having to do with the adventures of Keats and Chapman, who has a pigeon named Homer. He was provocative and with time increasingly critical of social, cultural, and political affairs. It was said that he finally began to see himself as a latter day Swift with "a mission of chastising the folly and hypocrisy of contemporary Ireland."[5]

As a student at University College, Dublin, O'Brien was typed as a "funny man," and his more serious nature and abilities were often overlooked. This pattern continued in his professional life, which was marked by increasing frustration and division. He was a full-time employee in the Department of Local Government from 1935–1953, a period in which he turned out a prodigious amount of fiction and journalism, reflecting still further division. From the time of his undergraduate days at UCD, he wrote under many different guises, but the two most significant are those of Myles Na gCopaleen and Flann O'Brien. As the former he achieved immense popularity; as the latter he was relatively unknown.

Skeptical about the qualities that ensure success, Myles had a number of caustic things to say about the exhibitionism of Irish writers. He was scornful of the "bought-and-paid-for" Paddys on the B.B.C. who, he believed, were exploiting the myth that because they were Irish they were automatically "gifted" or "poetic." He complained about the egotism of writers, and the enormous waste of ink, urging that poetry in particular be banned since it had the unfortunate effect of stimulating still more poetry — most of it bad.[6] He had little patience for humbug or self-flattering pretensions to eloquence or talent of any sort; however, his words suggest a degree of self-mockery. The increasingly barbed tone of his column undoubtedly had complex roots, but it was also a way of distancing himself from the stereotype of the comic Irishman and Boucicault's Myles-na-Coppaleen.

In *At Swim-Two-Birds* Flann O'Brien considers the dilemma of a serious writer in a culture where language making has become an obsessive performance, a disease of the imagination. He proposes that an Irishman can no longer keep still when there is an opportunity for "melodious discourse," and the Revival only made matters worse. Reading *At Swim-Two-Birds*, one is alternately buffeted and exhilarated by cataracts of words issuing in a wildly incongruous medley of voices. The tone shifts rapidly from ordinary conversation to fantasy, poetry, folk tale, and western yarn, mimicking and mocking the conventions of speech and literature and none more effectively than the Irish epic tale.

The legendary hero Finn MacCool appears in O'Brien's work as a sleepy giant, who torments the Plain People of Ireland with interminable tales of the heroic past. While the People affect a cultivated regard for literature, they secretly prefer the limericks of Jem Casey, who eulogizes a "pint of plain" as the only friend of the working man. Derided as a crotchety and implacable old bore, Finn is nonetheless a compelling figure. The bardic tradition — and here O'Brien reveals his ambiguity — is still a marvel of the imagination. The strangeness and richness of the language is a delight to the ear weary of contemporary clichés.

Much of the impetus of O'Brien's satire comes out of a lifelong quarrel with James Joyce.[7] In contrast to the artist-priest transmuting ordinary experience into the "radiant body of everlasting life," O'Brien posits a writer who is in full flight from ordinary experience. And little wonder. Modern Dublin is a dreary, provincial city of perpetual rainfall, where religion is no longer a powerful or even an oppressive force, merely an inexhaustible source of moral and social platitudes.

O'Brien's Dubliners also belong to the lower middle class, but they are suffering from a far more advanced case of paralysis. Their range of experience is extremely limited, their views puritanical, self-righteous, wholly unimaginative. There are no echoes of recent history, nothing of the socio-political consciousness of the thirties. The talk is amiable, conciliatory and incessant; no breach of decorum, no dissenting opinion is tolerated. This is hardly a realistic portrait of Dublin, as Ann Clissman maintains,[8] but a satire of its worst tendencies, considerably enlivened by the author's zany and malicious humor.

Like Murphy, O'Brien's nameless narrator is in many respects a parody of Stephen Dedalus. He is an outsider, uninterested in competition, material progress, the usual middle-class virtues. He is shabby, indigent, long suffering and so indifferent to personal hygiene that he smells. Obstensibly a student at University College, Dublin, he rarely attends classes, preferring to remain in bed when he is not visiting the local pubs. By resisting social and academic pressure, he is free to develop his own fairly remarkable imaginative life. In the monkish retreat of his bedroom, he is engaged in "sparetime literary activities," that is, the anti-novel whose conclusion more or less coincides with the inexplicable completion of his degree.

O'Brien's hero is continually at odds with his uncle, a caricature of the petite bourgeois, narrow minded, dogmatic, obtrusive, a "holder of a Guinness clerkship, the third class." He talks incessantly, and there is no subject that he does not fail to trivialize, to reduce to simplistic and intolerable formulas. He is an immediate spur to the fantastic imagination of his nephew. In a scene that is wittily reminiscent of *Ulysses*, his singing to the tinny accompaniment of a gramaphone provokes his nephew first to seek out the comfort of Byrne's pub and then to execute a series of prose passages that culminate in the description of an extraordinary chorus ranging from Cuban love songs to the liturgical music of Bach, Mozart, and Handel.

O'Brien's proposal that Irish art is an elaborate ruse to escape the boredom of Irish life becomes irresistible in terms of his own fiction. The perpetual drizzle exactly reflects a psychological climate which undermines sanity. To maintain his precarious balance, the narrator in *At Swim-Two-Birds* becomes a master at passive resistance, at avoidance and manipulation; thus Joyce's dictum "silence, exile and cunning," takes on new implications. This latter day artist is firmly bound to the motherland; there is not the slightest echo of a cosmopolitan world beyond the Irish sea. His own alternative is to escape into a world of fantasy, which is richly comic and which possesses the energy and variousness which Dublin itself so audibly lacks.

Like *Finnegans Wake*, which echoes through the O'Brien canon, *At Swim-Two-Birds* is intensely concerned with the process of its own creation. In an early chapter the narrator presents his manifesto: "a satisfactory novel should be a self-evident sham . . . The modern novel should be largely a work of reference . . . thereby excluding persons of inferior education from an understanding of contemporary literature." Continuing his assault on the Joycean establishment, the narrator offers three beginnings to the novel within the novel he, himself, is writing. Once underway the story is frequently and arbitrarily broken up by extrapolations from various prose works, by Middle Irish poetry, by commentaries on the fiction-in-progress, by plot summaries and by rhetorical and structural analyses. The artifice of fiction is continually stressed while the various personae of the writer are exposed to a lacerating satire, which betrays a terrible sense of futility at the root of O'Brien's art.[9]

The principal character created by the student narrator is Demot Trellis, himself a writer, pimpled and corpulent, who spends most of his time in bed. The experience of Trellis, like that of Sweeny, whom we shall come to shortly, parallels that of the narrator in certain key respects, and each new projection of the writer is more ludicrous and more eloquent under stress. While Trellis is writing a book "on sin and the wages attaching thereto," he compels his characters to live with him at the Red Swan Hotel so that "he can keep an eye on them and see that there is no boozing." His control relaxes only when he is asleep, a fact which is soon taken advantage of by his characters, who not only drug him in order to lead independent lives but plot to destroy him in collusion with his son (the curious offspring of an assault by Trellis on an attractive female character). That son, Orlick, has an inherited talent for writing, and so the torment of Trellis will be yet another layer of fiction embedded in the original structure. Orlick provides "a nice simple story with plenty of the razor," which is revised over and over until the pain is sufficiently horrible. In a literal application of the ancient technique of Irish satire, in which words alone are used to inflict harm, Trellis is torn to pieces. Every bone in his body is broken again and again, and the torture continues all the while he is being interrogated by a panel of fictional characters, most of them his own. He is compelled, not only to accept his sufferings without protest, but to respond eloquently to his judges. The emphasis in this exceedingly sadistic scene is on the macabre. The catalogue of Dermot's agonies, which are clearly beyond the range of endurance, proceeds in mock heroic style:

> The man in the bed was beleaguered with the sharpness of razors as to nipples, knee-rear and belly-roll. Leaden-hard forked arteries ran speedily about his scalp, his eye-beads bled and the corrugations of boils and piteous tumuli which appeared upon the large of his back gave it the appearance of a valuable studded shield. . . .[10]

His tormentor is the Pooka MacPhellimey, "a courtly member of the devil class," also given to eloquent discourse:

> . . . To inquire as to the gravity of your sore fall, would that be inopportune?
> You black bastard, said Trellis.
> The character of your colloquy is not harmonious, rejoined the Pooka, and makes for barriers between the classes. Honey-words in torment, a growing urbanity against the sad extremities of human woe, that is the further injunction I place upon your head. . . . (255)

Through such mockery, O'Brien contends that the artist is mutilated by the act of creation; he becomes the victim of an "inverted sow neurosis wherein that the farrow eat their dam." O'Brien parodies Joyce, but the comedy grows more and more corrosive as it turns inward, revealing the self-doubting anguish which is its driving force. In place of the artist-priest, he focuses on a much older concept, that of the poet as inspired clown or lunatic. Who else but a madman could hope to transcend the human condition or fashion out of it something permanent or original or beautiful? O'Brien's artist is ridiculed as compulsive, infantile and ego-centric. His passivity is merely a mask for the extreme violence of emotions, which finding no normal outlet become inevitably self-destructive.

While O'Brien quarrels primarily with Joyce, he also aims a glancing blow at Keats (a favorite target of Myles Na gCopaleen). In one scene the narrator is indulging in "a drop of the hard stuff," evidently still a redeeming feature of Irish life and a staple of Irish jokes. He observes that "the mind may be impaired by alcohol . . . but withal it may be pleasantly impaired" and wonders what "mad pursuit," what "wild ecstasy" will follow. He thereupon plunges into a round of blind vomiting drunkenness followed by three days of writing and recuperation in bed. The art that emerges is fragmentary, iconoclastic, grotesquely comic; the very antithesis of Keats's vision of eternal beauty in "Ode to a Nightingale."

I mentioned earlier the immense power of the Gaelic poets, a hereditary and wealthy professional class, who were feared and respected for their satire and "word magic." That world provides an ironic yardstick against which to measure the role of their modern counterparts. In an early scene in *At Swim-Two-Birds* Finn appears in the midst of his tribe reciting tales which magnify his own reputation (he refuses to recite anything else). He is preposterously self-indulgent, vain, boastful and longwinded, all of which is encouraged by a circle of admirers.

In the student's imagination that irrepressible Finn becomes "old Storybook," dispossessed of his power, his wealth, his followers, and — worst of all — his audience. He is one of several figures who express O'Brien's sense of internal exile, the artist dispossessed in the midst of his own people.

While O'Brien's wrath at his own predicament is evident in the savagery of his wit, his response is often broadly comic or farcical. His own brilliant verbal resources are a source of much pleasure, which mitigates the harsher elements in his satire. At one point, for example, Finn complains about his treatment in *Ulysses*: "Who but a book-poet would dishonour the God-big Finn for the sake of a gap-worded story?" Who indeed? O'Brien extends Joyce's parody in "The Cyclops," also imitating and exaggerating the more ornate features of Middle Irish poetry and prose. Throughout this work he displays a love of rhetoric and every kind of linguistic embellishment. The play of language, intended as mockery, becomes an end in itself:

> With that he rose to a full tree-high standing, the sable cat-guts which held his bog-cloth drawers to the hems of his jacket of pleated fustian clanging together in melodious discourse. Too great was he for standing. The neck to him was as the bole of a great oak, knotted and seized together with muscle-humps and carbuncles of tangled sinew, the better for good feasting and contending with the bards. (16–17)

In order to weave his own "book-web," O'Brien places in the mouth of Finn the most peculiar tale in the book: that of the legen-

dary Sweeny, who best expresses his concept of the artist as absurd
mad man. Along with all of Finn's stories, it is subject to comic in-
terpolations by the Plain People of Ireland.

According to the legend at the battle of Magh Rath in 637, the
hot tempered Sweeny, King of Dal Araidhe so injured Ronan, a
clergyman, that he cursed Sweeny. Whereupon Sweeny assumed a
bird-like form and took to wandering over the hills of Ireland, lodging only in trees, bereft of any companionship or comfort. In his
madness and torment he recited a remarkable series of lyric poems,
one of the most beautiful (it is not included in the novel) was
associated with the church as Snamh-da-en or Swim-two-Birds by
the Shannon River.

The tale of Sweeny, the *Buile Suibne*, was translated in 1910 by
J.G. O'Keeffe for the Irish Texts Society. O'Keeffe worked primarily
with a manuscript written by Daniel O'Duigenan between 1671 and
1674 and estimates that the original version in Middle Irish was written between 1200 and 1500. In his introduction he observes that the
account of Sweeny's madness "bears some resemblance to the widely
dispersed story of the Wild Man of the Woods of which the Merlin
legend is perhaps the most conspicious offshoot."[11]

As a master's candidate at University College, Dublin,
Flann O'Brien also translated the *Buile Suibne*, and the lyrics which
he includes in his book are for the most part actual translations;
there are minor variations for the sake of developing theme and
tone.

The comedy associated with Sweeny is of a decidedly macabre
nature and develops largely out of the context. The mad poet
lacerated by thorns and wracked by cold and rain composes
quatrain after elegant quatrain in praise of nature, and the more he
suffers, the more eloquently he sings. In selecting detail, however,
O'Brien tends to emphasize the ludicrous rather than the poignant
features of the legend. At one point, for example, Sweeny is pursued
and captured by a kinsman, Linchehaun, who restores him to sanity. Unfortunately, it turns out that Sweeny is as vain as he is quick-
tempered; he engages in a leaping contest with a hag, traveling
great distances and reaching new heights of lyricism "with the hag at
her hag's leaps behind him." There is no respite until in desperation
Sweeny leaps from the summit of Dun Sobhairce in Ulster, and the
hag, attempting to follow him, is dashed into "small bits" and "fine
pulp" on the rocks below.

The "steely Latin line" and the pure lyric note of the original are certainly evident, but they seem crazily incongruous in the context of Sweeny's sufferings; indeed so intense is his suffering and so strange his predicament that his story even at its most literal always verges on the fantastically comic. O'Brien's translation concentrates on the grotesque aspects of the Sweeny legend as does his emphasis on the interminable recitation of poetry indulged in, not only by Sweeny, but by every character, madman or clergyman, whom he encounters.

The tale provides O'Brien with an excellent opportunity for a satiric thrust at the clergy who were so generous in cursing anyone who interrupted their prayers (and who were a restrictive force in contemporary Dublin). He plays on the incongruity between Ronan's reputation as a "gentle generous friendly active man" (a literal translation of the *Buile Suibne*) and his desire to wreak vengeance on Sweeny. When angels inform him that Sweeny is returning to his senses, he prays to God with the result that the poor poet is besieged by terrible apparitions that ensure his relapse into madness.

In the original version Sweeny is gradually reconciled to Christ, and he accepts his sufferings as just penance for his crimes against Ronan. This is the theme, incidentally, of the lyric at Snah-da-den, which O'Brien did not choose to include. Paradoxically, for Sweeny, as for the unfortunate Lear, madness brings illumination, the development of a moral consciousness. Before his encounter with Ronan, Sweeny had little respect for human life; he was accustomed to inflicting his will on others in utter disregard for the consequences. In his painful exclusion from all human solace, Sweeny gradually comes to recognize inherent goodness in the created world and consequently to understand how he has violated the natural order. That revelation is expressed in a pure lyric voice, in hymns praising God and nature.

Moral consciousness, essential to the Joycean idea of the artist-priest, is alien to the new Sweeny. In O'Brien's version of the legend all references to spiritual redemption are eliminated; thus for example, in recounting Sweeny's final days with St. Moling, O'Brien emphasizes the poet's degradation. He includes the original description of a peasant woman digging her heel into cow dung and filling the hole with milk for the poet, but eliminates the significant fact that Sweeny does not die until he is brought within the door of Moling's chapel.

Sweeny, like "old Storybook" Finn, is both marvelous and

pathetic. His torments are made to seem weirdly comic, and his lyrics are insufferable to the motley band — cowboys, a good fairy, the pooka, Jem Casey, etc. — which rescues him. Like Finn, he has no audience, a radical departure from the Gaelic experience and a source of considerable damage to modern writers.

An essential feature of the old life style was the mutual dependence of story teller and community. The former was guardian of folklore and tradition, whose company was eagerly sought out. When increasing modernization and the loss of the Gaelic language displaced the old *seanachie*, he found that without an audience to prime him, his eloquence and memory deteriorated, and he could not always respond to folklorists who were trying to collect the old tales before they were lost forever.

O'Brien's version of the *Buile Suibne* takes another curious turn which also reflects a contemporary problem. Along with other characters in this novel within a novel within a novel, Sweeny eventually sits in judgment on Dermot Trellis. In the trial scene, which is vaguely reminiscent of that of H.C.E. in *Finnegans Wake*, Dermot is accused of various crimes against his craft. All the while, as I indicated earlier, he is being tormented with pains similar to those inflicted on Sweeny. The presence of both Finn and Sweeny among the judges seems to cast further doubt on the value of contemporary Irish writing. How do its merits compare with the literature of the past? On the other hand, who is to decide, since the judges themselves are a pack of drunken eccentrics?

Perhaps at this point I may be allowed a few observations based on *The Divided Self* by R. D. Laing. Laing characterizes the schizoid personality as one given to phantasy because he experiences the real world as "shrunken and impoverished." Such a personality, wishing to "remain always ungraspable, elusive, abhors action because it discloses and defines the self.[12] O'Brien's narrator, like Murphy, experiences a schizoid-like division between emotional and physical states of being. He views his own body with detachment, allowing it to deteriorate and become verminous. His sense of estrangement from an authentic self is reflected in the pattern of the novel which mirrors the writer's psyche in images which become progressively psychotic, while the body itself, alternately swelling to grotesque proportions in the person of Dermot and shrinking to emaciation in Sweeny, is subject to fantasies of self-multilation.

In O'Brien's satire, schizophrenia is endemic. The Irishman has become a victim of his own brilliant heritage. Enclosed in a myth of his own making in a pattern reminiscent of the Gaels of Corkadora, he cannot resist "doing the witty Celtic act," even though the gap between word and reality continues to enlarge. Personal motive, instinct, and the authentic self are obscured in a shower of rhetoric, if not already paralyzed by moribund institutions. Among the Plain People of Ireland, no one stops talking long enough to examine the meaning of a particular phrase, and so there is a perpetual exchange of moral, social, and literary clichés. For the artist the effects are even more traumatic. He becomes "elusive," disengages himself from a world that is at best eccentric, at worst, banal. As a result "the two way circuit between phantasy and reality"[13] begins to break down and he becomes imprisoned, as J. C. Mays has so ably demonstrated, in the "endlessly reflected world of art."[14]

Having completed his degree, the narrator achieves a brief reconciliation with his uncle, whom he now regards as "simple, well intentioned; pathetic in humility; responsible member of a large commercial concern." As a token of his esteem the uncle presents him with a second-hand watch which unfortunately proves inaccurate. That gift seems to symbolize for O'Brien, the tenuous nature of any linkage between the writer and contemporary Dublin. The writer is a dislocated person, a refugee trapped in a kind of time warp inhabited by ancient but spirited and lusty Gaels.

The art of Joyce, which O'Brien attacks so furiously and brilliantly, is an art rooted in reality, one which embraces the plain people of Dublin because its concerns are fundamental and life affirming. Its center is not Dedalus, the artist-intellectual, but Bloom, the ordinary-extraordinary man. A major theme in both *Ulysses* and *A Portrait* is that Dedalus' development as an artist hinges directly on his ability to experience the world of Bloom.

Much earlier W.B. Yeats had written of a similar division in such poems as "Fergus and the Druid," "The Lake Isle of Innisfree," and "The Hosting of the Sidhe." He presented the world of imagination as seductive, idealized, a refuge from the uncertainty and frustration he experienced as a young man. But it could also be sinister. Keats's La Belle Dame Sans Merci reemerges in Yeats's iconography as Niamah, the woman of the Sidhe, who entices the young poet, filling his head with beautiful dreams, while destroying his capacity to act.

Interestingly enough, considering his animus toward Synge,

certain elements in *The Shadow in the Glen* and *The Playboy* anticipate one of O'Brien's major themes in *At Swim-Two-Birds*. In the earlier works Patch Darcy and Old Mahon represent the possibility of madness that threatens the poet once he frees himself from the normal ties of community life. This concept is more fully developed in *The Playboy* where old Mahon as story teller cannot fully distinguish illusion from reality, and his grip fails him entirely once he succumbs to Christy's superior imagination. The image of Old Mahon "naked as an ash tree in the moon of May," prefigures O'Brien's own image of the isolated imagination: Sweeny trapped in the branches of a tree, speechless, his upturned eyes fixed on the moon.

This final view of Sweeny is linked to the short-lived reconciliation between the student-narrator and his uncle, a scene which parodies the episode between Bloom and Dedalus at Eccles Street. But while Dedalus's link to ordinary humanity has been confirmed by the night's ordeal, O'Brien's narrator is flung back into the labyrinth of the imagination; the "two way circuit between phantasy and reality" has fizzled out. Toying with the possibility of his own madness, the narrator compares the artist who, like Joyce, finds a universal meaning in the peculiar rhythms of Dublin to a man who thinks he has a glass bottom and will not sit for fear of breakage. The book ends in a flurry of self-mocking images of lunacy and suicide: art turned in upon itself, feeding upon itself, brought to a terrible impasse.

8. Patrick Kavanagh and Tarry Flynn

N *Collected Pruse* Patrick Kavanagh recalls that when he first went to Dublin "the Irish literary affair was still booming. It was the notion that Dublin was a literary metropolis and Ireland, as invented and patented by Yeats, Lady Gregory, and Synge, a spiritual entity."[1] Like Flann O'Brien and James Joyce before him, he felt that his own talent was unappreciated, while other writers achieved recognition by exploiting the new Irish mystique. The theme of estrangement between poet and people is central to *Tarry Flynn* as it is to *At Swim-Two-Birds* and *A Portrait of the Artist as a Young Man*. In Dublin, Kavanagh lashed out at the literary establishment, inviting and giving plenty of abuse in articles and reviews he wrote for the short-lived *Kavanagh's Weekly, The Irish Times, The Bell,* and *Envoy,* among others. One observer remarked that Kavanagh "shares with Mr. Frank Sinatra, Dylan Thomas, Picasso and the Marx Brothers the capacity for arousing the emotions to the screaming point for or against him."[2]

Although his work sometimes appears self-consciously "rustic" or naive (he wrote a column for the *Irish Press* under the name of "Piers Plowman"), he resented being labeled a "peasant poet" or a "poet of the plough." Such labeling smacked of stage Irishry and was a way of belittling and circumscribing his ability and achievement: "The metropolis is not interested in the imaginative reality of provincial society; it only asks the provincial to perform."[3] Like Flann O'Brien he complained that the public had come to expect Irish poets to be cast in the mold of Christy Mahon and that Synge had drawn attention away from the distinctive quality of ordinary speech in Ireland. In contrast to the heroic and extravagant playboy, Kavanagh presented the poet as a wise fool, a concept which has roots in Middle Irish literature. His special merit is his skill at catching the rhythms of country speech in both poetry and prose; his work is notable for its relatively plain style and its careful observation of the small details of everyday life.

Kavanagh has been compared to Wordsworth because of the unaffected lyrical strain in his poetry and prose, and his love of the commonplace, the weed as well as the hawthorne bush. But he is much more realistic about the day-to-day life of the farmer with dung on his boots. And far from supporting the notion that a life close to the soil enobles mankind, he shows us the poverty of life without tradition or intellectual stimulus. Much of the satiric humor of *Tarry Flynn*, which will be the focus of this chapter, stems from the disproportionate amount of fury and energy that is expended on trivial matters. The absurd jealousy over a small field. The eternal scheming to win a minor advantage or to deceive a neighbor. Kavanagh turns a critical eye on the manners and morals of the Irish people, but he is never as caustic as Joyce, O'Brien or Beckett. He had too much sympathy for his subject; having shared their experiences, he knew how bitterly circumscribed their lives were and how little they could do to escape.

Kavanagh's position was in other respects similar to that of his fellow Ulsterman, William Carleton. Like Carleton, whose work he admired, he was poor and largely self-taught; he attended local schools in County Monaghan until he was twelve. He also left home for a troubled career in Dublin, while his emotional and artistic center remained the rural world into which he was born. Unlike Carleton, he had little knowledge of Latin or Irish, and his work has little connection with the old Gaelic world. In "A Personal Problem" he admitted the limitation he felt in writing poetry which lacked the internal structure provided by myth: "what am I to do with the void/growing more awful every hour?"[4] Both his autobiography, *The Green Fool*, and his novel, *Tarry Flynn*, describe local legends and beliefs, including a story about Finn MacCool, but it is evident that much of the traditional culture has dwindled away with the Gaelic language. Neither the real village of Inniskeen nor the fictional Drumnay has the vital, intensely shared community life that one finds in Carleton's *Traits and Stories of the Irish Peasantry*. Instead one discovers that Drumnay, despite the political and cultural achievements of the revolutionary period, has many of the problems of the Mayo community satirized by Synge in *The Playboy*. It is a static, closed society in which little of any importance occurs, the height of excitement being a sermon on sexual sin. If anything, personal rancor has increased. The people still live in poverty and isolation as the enormous labor of maintaining even a small farm brings little recompense during the depression; the young are forced to emigrate or face long years of celibacy and dependence on their parents.

At one point Kavanagh talks about the minds of the people being formed by the landscape, "mostly cut-away bog, so that the only arable land was a thin stripe along the bottom of the hills and the hills themselves." Kavanagh mocks romantic conventions about rustic life. The "folk" are not open hearted, jolly, musical and extravagant; they are cautious, embittered, spiritually and mentally impoverished. Frustration erupts in violence and in petty quarrels; neighbors who were united against a common oppressor are now divided, suspicious of one another, resentful toward anyone who manages to lift himself above the ordinary. Despite the strong element of realism in *Tarry Flynn*, Kavanagh's basic mode is comic satire. Details are exaggerated, piled up on top of one another until the very excess is laughable. There are no ordinary people in Drumnay. Everyone is a grotesque:

> Between the three Flynn girls there was little to choose. They were all the same height, around five feet two — low-set, with dull clayey faces, each of them like a bag of chaff tied in the middle with a rope — breasts and buttocks that flapped in the wind. When they were unwashed and undressed in the morning a stranger passing seeing them would hardly be able to say who was who. They were all the daughters Mrs. Flynn ever had.[5]

The story never dissolves into pathos or the kind of deadly naturalism evident in the work of Brinsley MacNamara primarily because of the comic energy of the language with its pungent metaphors and needling tone:

> Tarry tested the tyres of his bicycle which stood outside the carthouse door. His mother followed him and began to speak very confidentially: "Petey Meegan sent word the day."
> "About what?" said Tarry
> "He has a notion of Mary. But don't breathe this to the face of clay. The Missioners must have shook him up."

Tarry was a little astonished. "He's a bit past himself," he said.

"Arra, nonsense. He's a good, sober, industrious boy with a damn good farm of land in Miskin. And an empty house. Oh, girls can't be too stiff these days. They're all hard pleased and easy fitted."

"But he must be well over the fifty mark," whispered Tarry devoutly.

"That's young enough for a healthy man. And mind you, Mary is no chicken. Only the day I was thinking that she's within a kick of the arse of thirty. Troth if she gets him she'll be lucky." (60–61)

Unlike the comic figures of the nineteenth century, Kavanagh's characters are fully in control of their English; their expressions have little of the purely rhetorical quality, the sheer playfulness evident in Synge, Carleton, Boucicault, and Lady Gregory. The broad humor generated by blunders and bulls has been replaced by a sharp and frequently scatological wit, which delights in the exposure of human folly. The people of Drumnay have little tendency to lose themselves in conversion or to become so emmeshed in fancy that they disconnect themselves altogether from the actual facts. For all their love of gossip and melodrama, they are firmly planted on the ground; it would take more than a "gallous story" to make them see beyond the immediate boundary of their little fields.

Very much at odds with the practical people of the village is the character of Tarry Flynn, who is both "seer" and fool, a dreamer with little ambition or shrewdness or skill in argument, who enjoys the hard manual labor of farming. Based on Kavanagh's own experiences growing up in rural Monaghan, Tarry Flynn offers an interesting contrast to Christy Mahon and even, though in a more subtle way, to Stephen Dedalus. For the poet Tarry Flynn, Drumnay is a "net of earthly intrigue" spread by an ambitious mother whose contemptuous treatment of him in many ways parallels old Mahon's treatment of Christy. She continually scolds him like a child, belittling him, stressing his foolishness, and in every way keeping him dependent upon her despite his twenty-six years. She represents the persisting grip of parental authority in rural areas where men often did not marry until middle age. The most telling signs of Tarry's emasculation at her hands are the patched trousers she forces him to wear, which look like "they had been torn by mad dogs and patched by mad women;" the crotch is distinguished by large buttons that he tries to conceal from young women by walking sideways.

In a culture that traditionally revered learning, Mrs. Flynn condemns Tarry's reading and writing of poetry as "lazeness lazeness lazeness." Her attitude suggests a loss comparable to that experienced by O'Casey's slum dwellers. With the breakdown of the old Gaelic tradition, the community is now held together by mutual fear and apathy; the old spirit of hospitality has eroded along with a shared memory of music and folk tales. The songs they sing are sentimental modern ballads. There are fewer social gatherings, less sharing of common tasks like harvesting and digging turf. In *The Green Fool* Kavanagh states bitterly: "There was no love of beauty. We were barbarians just emerged from the Penal days. The hunger had killed our poetry."[6]

Mrs. Flynn epitomizes some of the worst aspects of the Irish rural community in the thirties. Her sense of propriety and her rigid conformity to the local pattern of life are primarily determined by fear of the clergy and the neighbors rather than by any moral conviction. She does not wish to be ostracized or gossiped about or treated with contempt. She is ignorant, superstitious, hypocritical, and ruthless, but Kavanagh has made her comical in spite of all. Much of the earthy and satiric humor of the book is associated with her shortsighted, furious struggle to help Tarry get on in life. She has a biting tongue and is never at a loss for an appropriate metaphor to skewer the immediate object of her wrath. A local woman who has an eye on Tarry is dismissed, for example, as "that old pot walloper." And she has no qualms about expelling her own daughters from the household lest they "be stuck like a blind to me window all the days of me life."

Mrs. Flynn has little in common with traditional maternal figures like the heroine of *Juno and the Paycock* and Maire in *Riders to the Sea*. She is tough minded, suspicious, and shrewd, and so enjoys a quarrel that she continually stirs up trouble in her own household. Like so many Irish comic characters, she has a gift for drama, for making herself the center of a crisis by investing the minutiae of domestic and parish life with terrible significance. Like Sean O'Casey's Mrs. Gogan, she relishes the possibility of scandal or disaster, keeping an ear always tuned for gossip. Her downfall is precipitated by an unshakeable self-confidence. In the end she is trapped by her own schemes, foiled by the superior malice and conservatism of the community.

In a fertile world whose dominant image is the cow ringed to the bull, Drumnay is a "townland of death," peopled by bachelors and spinsters. Local men who have finally inherited a farm are extremely cautious about taking on the responsibility of a wife and family. Mrs. Flynn with three daughters despairs of "waiting for the bleddy geldings to make a move." In all the neighboring houses there are only four families with children. Young people marry for property, women taking much older men, rarely for love or affection. The rituals of courtship are entirely lacking in romantic passion; the language itself suggests the routine coupling of the barnyard: "me hand on yer drawers." Appropriately enough, would-be lovers meet in the cemetery to fondle one another among the grave stones.

Sexual frustration is a central theme in the novel. Tarry, himself, has had little experience of women, and this point is the basis of considerable self-mockery. Unfortunately his notion of impressing a woman is to lecture her on philosophy or canon law so that she won't suspect him of lewd intentions. He spends considerable energy planning a seduction but fails to act because, like his neighbors, he fears exposure and ridicule. In Drumnay, sex is acceptable only between marriage partners as the necessary means for producing children. Local women, such as the Dillons, who have borne illegitimate children are ostracized; no man concerned with his reputation would go near them in broad daylight.

Like Stephen Dedalus, Tarry Flynn is caught for a time by the classic opposition of madonna and whore. Mary Reilly seems unapproachable even as a prospective wife because she is too perfect, too far beyond him socially, and he succeeds in driving her away by the sheer force of his wounded vanity. On the other hand, once he manages to lure Molly Brady into the bushes, romantic idealist that he is, he bolts from her in horror, repelled by her physical appearance and disgusted with his own lechery. Tarry's reluctance toward women sets him apart, not only from the stage Irishman, but from the traditional hero of comedy, who represents above all else the revitalizing erotic principle. Although he is certainly potent and certainly drawn to women, he is restrained by the conservatism of post-famine Ireland, a conservatism reinforced by a celibate clergy and a set of social standards fashioned by Victorian England. Tarry's behavior is further complicated by the presence of a domineering, possessive mother, whom he must placate and toward whom he feels guilty. The tie between mother and son is a powerful dynamic where marriage is a purely practical arrangement and the survival of the family depends on the labor of the sons.

In "The Great Hunger," one of the most powerful of modern Irish poems, Kavanagh develops this theme further by exploring the sterile inner world of the small farmer, who has been so much the subject of myth and comedy and romance.

> Clay is the word and clay is the flesh
> Where the potato-gatherers like mechanical scarecrows move
> Along the side-fall of the hill — Maguire and his men.

Maguire has a much more comfortable standard of living than his forebears, but the years of famine and political oppression have bred a terrible sense of caution and a belief in hard physical labor as an end in itself. Maguire never marries, never ventures anything at all; instead he suffers continually from emotional and spiritual deprivation. Tied to his old mother long past maturity, he is obediently celibate.

> . . . the potato-seed
> Gives a bud and a root and rots
> In the good mother's way with her sons;
> The fledged bird is thrown
> From the nest — on its own.
> But the peasant in his little acres is tied
> To a mother's womb by the wind-toughened navel-cord
> Like a goat tethered to the stump of a tree —

In this poem Kavanagh repeatedly links the castration and death-in-life of Maguire to his unnatural dependence on his mother:

> His mother's voice grew thinner like a rust-worn knife
> But it cut venomously as it thinned,
> It cut him up the middle till he became more woman than man,
> And it cut through to his mind before the end.[7]

Later Kavanagh was to criticize the poem because he felt it wasn't "free," that is, it lacked detachment and the humor that balances much of his best work. But as Alan Warner concludes in *Clay is the Word*, the strength of the poem is in its cruel realism, its exposure of the "strangled impulse" and the crude ignorance that produced those "little lyrical fields" that delight the traveler.[8] Largely because of the explicit sexual references, copies of "The Great Hunger" were confiscated with they first appeared though it was eventually published without difficulty by Cuala Press.

In *Tarry Flynn*, which was also briefly suppressed, the stultifying quality of family life is reinforced by the absolute authority of the Church. The god who is worshipped in Drumnay has little in common with the "gay imaginative god, who made the grass and the trees and the flowers.[9] Piety is equated with chastity and ignorance, and any sign of independence or critical intelligence is discouraged.

In *The Playboy* the people have a certain skepticism about the regulations of the Church, and they ridicule Sean Keogh as a weakling for allowing himself to be so completely controlled by Father Reilly. In *Tarry Flynn* the clergy dominate both religious and social spheres, and as the two are everywhere connected, the priests wield great influence. It soon becomes apparent that poet and priest will collide on the issue of Tarry's role in the community. There is a growing suspicion in Drumnay that Tarry is a free thinker, and so he must be made to conform and to accept the authority of the priests. At first, interestingly enough, Tarry wants only to be recognized by them as a man of talent; in other words he looks to the Church to confer status. Instead he is rebuffed and publicly humiliated. Art is rightly regarded as revolutionary; he is warned against George Bernard Shaw and counseled to confine his reading to *The Messenger of the Sacred Heart*. Father Daly advises him that "a little learning is a dangerous thing," mistakenly, to Tarry's delight, attributing the line to Shakespeare. It is he who delivers the opinion that Tarry is a "perfect fool," urging his mother to "get him a wife" to anchor him firmly. Tarry is ridiculed as a dreamer with little common sense, but actually perceived as a threat to the narrowly circumscribed life of the village. The priest thinks of his parishioners as "child-like"; their naiveté and ignorance must be preserved for the sake of their souls. This attitude, while ensuring his own authority, reflects that of Irish bishops who forbade Catholics from entering secular universities once the doors were open to them.

In contrast to Tarry Flynn there is Eusebius Cassidy who also begins as a romantic, interested in the poetry of James Clarence Mangan, but is gradually submerged by the community. He learns how to "blend in," to flatter the clergy and to accept the humble life style of a small farmer. In a revealing scene he is pleased at being selected by the priest to carry a water bucket for the benefit of more affluent parishioners at a local dance. The social hierarchy is as inflexible as any other aspect of life in Drumnay; those who are poor and ignorant are expected to stay that way.

Although Tarry is regarded as a troublemaker, the great irony of all of this is that he is a timid soul and in many ways a conservative one. He is very conscious of his humble position and does not initially question the authority of church or parent, attending religious services mainly out of deference to his mother and the neighbors. He is also exceedingly conventional in his attitudes toward young women, all of whom he expects to be virgins "until such time as he'd meet them." Thus at least on the surface he is a fairly ordinary young man, if anything a little retarded in his emotional and intellectual development. A crisis finally develops as in Lady Gregory's "Spreading the News" because of the local capacity for developing a full scale drama out of the most trivial detail. Absurdly enough, Tarry is implicated in both a seduction and an attempted murder as rumor is fed by neighbors delighted at the prospect of a little diversion. No one is interested in the truth, including his own family; his mother merely denounces him for not keeping in with the priests.

In Kavanagh's novel the traditional theme of comedy is satirically inverted. Tarry is pursued by a possibly pregnant and, inany case, an undesirable woman; routed and hemmed in by authority and finally freed by an *alazon* figure — the tramp-uncle, who offers him revolutionary advice: "Do what pleases yourself." Expelled from the community circle, Tarry acquires perspective and a sense of humor, and he is able to come to terms with his mother. He finally leaves Drumnay in the company of his uncle, choosing, like Christy Mahon and Stephen Dedalus, the open road in search of a better life.

Despite his naiveté Tarry Flynn has little in common with the clowns of Boucicault or the stage Irish tradition. He is hardly cunning or articulate, and there is nothing in him whatsoever of the entertainer or the rogue. In his patched trousers, the crotch embellished with overcoat buttons, Tarry is clearly allied with the traditional Fool, mocked on all sides and particularly the butt of women. There is considerable disparity between Tarry's concept of himself as a lusty, eloquent man of character and the reality of local contempt. Because his innocence and poverty and fairly conventional attitudes make Tarry an easy mark for petty tyrants, Kavanagh's comedy has a painful edge to it. But Tarry is not simply "he who gets slapped," he is the visionary fool: the one who sees the beauty of the fields that others, including his mother, can only see in terms of economic profit.

The figure of the poet-fool appears as early as the ninth century in *Liadain and Curithir*, which refers to Comgan, a messenger for the two lovers, as Arch-poet and Fool of all Ireland. Comgan, like Sweeny, was the victim of a curse, in this instance that of a druid, after which he wasted away, losing his hair and finally much of his intellect. He had, however, the power of poetry, and his words were considered oracular. He is thus spoken of as Mac-de-Cherda, that is, the youth of two arts: folly and poetry. There are many references to him in medieval literature as, for example, in the twelfth century *The Vision of MacConglinne*, and there are quatrains attributed to him in *Cormac's Glossary*.[10]

The Vision has as its central character an even more fully delineated poet-fool, that is, MacConglinne, himself, who triumphs over a hostile clergy through divine inspiration as much as through art and cunning.[11] *The Vision* is a comic satire which ridicules church ritual and dogma, attesting to the fact that the conflict between artist and priest, a major theme in modern Irish literature, has very old and complex roots. This tale was written at a time when the bards apparently felt threatened by the centralization of church authority and the subsequent demand for tithes. MacConglinne, in fact, mocks these demands, while insisting on his own right to a generous reward. He not only insists on the traditional powers and privileges of the poet, but interestingly enough, usurps the supreme claim of the Church — that of divine inspiration and authority. MacConglinne's vision — a glutton's paradise — is brought by an angel of the Lord, but it is revealed only after it has been shaped by the poet's craft. MacConglinne is parodically associated with Christ in his suffering at the hands of the clergy and in his role as a redeemer who overcomes the hunger demon that has taken possession of the king. Like that of Christ, his real nature is for a time concealed. MacConglinne dons the coat of a jester or fool and gains the attention of the king, whose appetite is insatiable, by boldly interrupting his meal and demanding a share. Asserting the customary prerogative of the fool, he abuses the king in order to preserve him from a greater evil. Finally, the demon, tempted by MacConglinne's ludicrous tale of a land brimming with buttermilk and gravy, leaps out of the mouth of the unfortunate king and is banished.

The Vision strikes many other themes that will seem familiar to a student of modern Irish literature, but there is no evidence that Synge or Joyce or Kavanagh for that matter was familiar with this tale. What influenced Kavanagh, and probably Synge, was that the notion of the poet as a comical character, a playboy or fool survived in the oral tradition. Tales of such poets as Eoghan Ruadh Ó Súilleabháin (Owen Roe O'Sullivan) and Aodhagán Ó Rathaille (Egan O'Rahilly) emphasize the point that they dressed poorly and both looked and acted like fools in order to play tricks on the unsuspecting — particularly priests. ÓRathaille "wore a sugan (a straw rope) around his knees, around his belly and also one around his cap." Despite such an appearance the poet had a reputation of being "a terrible bad man as regards women.[12] While many of these tales are simply humorous, Daniel Corkery also detects a note of bitter irony, natural enough when an educated man is forced to play the buffoon:

> He goes into a bookshop in Cork — we are to picture him (Ó Rathaille) as the peasant in town. His gesture is uncouth, his garb outlandish, his English all brogue. He takes up a large and expensive classical work, and asks the price of it. The shopkeeper glances at the book, at the quaint figure, and indulgently informs him he can have it for nothing if only he can read it. The poet continues looking at the Greek or Latin, holding the book upside down. He contrives somehow to get the shopkeeper to ratify the off-hand promise — which done, he turns the book aright and reads with ease. . . .[13]

A similar note is sounded by Kavanagh, who maintains that the position of the poet has deteriorated even further despite a lingering belief in word-magic or satire: "In the country places of Ireland writing is held in certain awe: a writer was a dangerous man from whom they instinctively recoiled." That defensiveness might well be concealed by contempt; the man who was different was set apart, made into a kind of scapegoat. With self-mocking truculence he argues that "being made a fool is good for the soul. It produces a sensitivity of one kind or other; it makes a man into something unusual, a saint or a poet or an imbecile.[14]

The "foolishness" of Tarry Flynn conceals a deep core of sanity, and his understanding is increased by his role as adversary. Tarry keeps alive the love of the land, which has been a vital part of Irish history and poetry and so recovers a link with the larger reality from which the protagonists of *Murphy* and *At Swim-Two-Birds* sought to isolate themselves. In the imagination of Tarry Flynn there is harmony between intellectual and physical labor; the one nourishes and balances the other, both in turn depending on a profound sense of relation between man and nature. Through the poet's eyes Drumnay becomes a kind of Eden in which he can imagine himself as "green and chaste and foolish," within reach of God himself in "the constant point above time."

Given the circumstances in which he lives, there is no possibility of communicating this vision. The poet has become an outsider, powerless before an indifferent people and the strict orthodoxy of the priests. Defended by the mask of the fool, he is free to recreate what he loves best in Drumnay: the fertile land, the hawthorne hedge in front of his own door, the small hill in the distance covered with michaelmas daisies. The poetry he writes with increasing intensity as he is more and more excluded from community life has the smell and feel of the soil:

> The rattle of buckets, rolling of barrels under
> Down-spouts, the leading in of foals
> Were happenings caught in wonder
> The stones white with rain were living souls. (178)

It is poetry which stands in opposition to the romanticism inspired by the Celtic Revival, a way of looking at the world of ordinary experience which would leave a deep impression on the next generation of poets. The great discovery at the conclusion of the novel is that Tarry Flynn will not lose that world when he leaves Drumnay; his vision grows, if anything, more clear as he frees himself from the pressures and restrictions that have warped the lives of his neighbors. In this respect he is a harbinger of things to come: a new flowering of Irish poetry which absorbs what it can from Irish sources while freely exploring modern forms and ideas.

9. The Paycocks of Sean O'Casey

WHEN the Irish rebels finally surrendered in Easter week of 1916 and were being marched off to jail, they had to be protected by the British from angry mobs of Dubliners, who pelted them with garbage. Initially, there was little sympathy for the rebellion, which took the lives of three hundred civilians and burned rows of tenement houses at a time when many Irishmen were fighting with the British army on the battlefields of central Europe.[1] This sense of outrage in a people who had already endured quite enough was to find more lasting expression in the plays of Sean O'Casey.

The world of Sean O'Casey is the Dublin slums, crowded with people who had left their farms but found little or no employment in Ireland's capital city. At the turn of the century the Dublin poor lived in filthy, rotting tenements, riddled with typhoid and plagued by the highest infant mortality rate in Europe. O'Casey was himself the youngest of thirteen children, only five of whom survived into adult life. The family, even after the death of his father, might have lived fairly decently, but misfortune eventually reduced both his sister, who had been a teacher, and his sister-in-law to working as charwomen.[2] Out of his own harsh experience as well as his association with the labor movement, the Gaelic League and the Irish Citizen Army, O'Casey fashioned his best plays, *Juno and the Paycock* and *The Plough and the Stars*. Like Patrick Kavanagh he was a man of the people, largely self-taught, who spent long years as a laborer. He could not even afford a seat at the Abbey Theater before his first play was produced there when he was forty-three years of age. In *I Knock at the Door*, the first of the six-volume autobiography, his anguish as a lonely and vulnerable human be-

ing, partially blinded by eye disease, is very real. What is more difficult to discern is the development of that mordant sense of
humor, which was his best defense against the world and the most
vital aspect of his work.

Like Dion Boucicault, whose work he admired and with which
he was familiar from an early age,[3] O'Casey wrote plays that are
highly melodramatic and that are enlivened by music, song, and
dance; he even stages a hooley (a party) in *Juno and the Paycock.* He
makes brilliant and frequently satiric use of the pageantry, the
oratory, the parade of fierce national events. Despite its poverty,
O'Casey's world is charged with great physical exuberance, much of
it precipitated by the clowns: shrews, eccentrics, boozers, parasites,
a rag-tag assembly scraped from the very bottom of the refuse pits of
Dublin. The most memorable are Fluther Good in *The Plough and
the Stars* and Captain Jack Boyle in *Juno and the Paycock*, who
cavort around the perimeters of the central drama, shrewdly
resisting any effort to draw them into a major role.[4]

As Dubliners they are less naive and more self-assured than the
earlier rogues. As Boyle puts it: "We're Dublin men, an' not boyos
that's only afther comin' up from the bog o' Allen." Far from having
any respect for the "quality," they are abusive or indifferent toward
the occasional bourgeois who appears in their midst. They have shed
many of the values along with the language of their peasant
ancestors. Though the tenement community has some cohesion, and
there is still a marked respect for religion and the family, their lives
have a rootless quality. Limited employment brings little renumera-
tion or personal satisfaction, and alcohol is a chronic problem.
Although Fluther is always gallant toward the ladies, emnity between the sexes is inevitable in a culture where men go off to the
local pub to escape from domestic problems.

The suppressed energies, the hostility, the obsessions of the
Dubliners characteristically explode in verbal combat. Their
language bristles with aggressiveness; it has a needling, restless
quality, intended to prick, to deflate, to keep the listener slightly off
balance. The sheer love of invective is carried to far greater extremes by O'Casey than by any of the other modern writers we have
examined. It is a distinctly Irish quality, prominent in Swift and in
the satire of the bards, but scarcely to be heard in the Anglo-Irish
literature of the nineteenth century. The lyric strain is subdued in
O'Casey's best plays; the language tends to be epigrammatic in con-

trast to the sheer verbal extravagance of later plays such as *The Silver Tassie* and *Red Roses for Me*. Much of the dialogue has an eccentric, disjunctive quality, which suggests the speaker's obliviousness to anything outside of his or her own obsessions.

In *The Plough* anger is easily triggered and easily forgotten. Fluther is threatening the Covey with sudden death in one scene and playing cards with him in the next. Trapped in the static inferno of the tenements, like the damned souls in Sartre's *No Exit*, O'Casey's Dubliners can only turn on one another. Unlike the French bourgeoisie, however, they have immense resources of furious comic energy to keep them from despair.

O'Casey, who had learned from Boucicault, also exploited the tradition of the stage Irishman.[5] Fluther Good, his most ingratiating comic figure, is a boaster and a drinker who solemnly swears to remain sober — until the next glass of porter materializes. Though a bachelor, he is obviously fond of women and frequently intervenes as a peacemaker among them. In the company of men, he is as scrappy as a bantam rooster, and though he bears the scars of previous battles, including a broken nose, what he obviously relishes most is the preliminary argument, the duel of wit. He is a master of brinkmanship; in the course of the play he precipitates numerous quarrels with Peter and the Covey, but nimbly avoids an exchange of blows: "It's my rule never to lose me temper till it would be dethrimental to keep it." Though he is quick to defend his own self-esteem or that of any woman in his company, he views the weaknesses of his neighbors with a tolerant eye. Despite his ignorance and his misuse of words, which are, typically, made to seem comic, there is something of the philosopher about old Fluther. He is capable of real insight, particularly regarding the relation between men and women:

> *Mrs. Gogan*. . . . She dresses herself to keep him with her, but it's no
> use — afther a month or two, th' wondher of a woman wears off.
> *Fluther*. I dunno, I dunno. Not wishin' to say anything derogatory,
> I think it's all a question of location; when a man finds th'
> wondher of one woman beginnin' to die, it's usually beginnin'
> to live in another.
> (Act 1)

Despite his love of argument, Fluther avoids any commitment

to political ideology. He enjoys the rhetoric and the excitement, the opportunity to get drunk. When the insurrection boils up in the streets around the tenement, Fluther joins a band of looters and eventually comes home lugging a barrel of whiskey. The scene is reminiscent of the Harlem riot in Ralph Ellison's *Invisible Man* where the tenement dwellers, finding the boundaries of their lives have suddenly collapsed, explode in a whirl of reckless action.

Without a family to support, Fluther is detached from the usual domestic concerns. He lives from day to day with little money and little ambition, but a great deal of buoyant humor, an excellent defense against a poverty ridden world. He is in the play to provide comic relief, but he also represents a type of Dublin survivor who floats to the top of the maelstrom while others, like Jack and Nora Clitheroe, are destroyed by the powerful currents of revolution.

As a man who likes to boast of his prowess as a fighter, a patriot and a militant workingman, Fluther is clearly related to the *miles gloriosus* of Roman comedy. Unlike Captain Boyle, however, he is capable of a certain courage. He goes with Nora to the barricades looking for Jack, and he goes out again under a dangerous crossfire to make funeral arrangements for Mollser. In the final scene he has the boldness of the Shaughraun, playing a cool hand of cards to cover the presence of one of the rebels while the British are search-ing the household. Prodded by them, he answers testily enough:

> Sergeant Tinley (*roughly*). Gow on, git aht, you blighter.
> Fluther. Who are you callin' a blighter to, eh? I'm a Dublin man, born an' bred in th' city, see?
> Sergeant Tinley. I down't care if you were Broin Buroo; git aht, git aht.
> Fluther (*halting as he is going out*). Jasus, you an' your guns! Leave them down, an' I'd beat th' two o' yous without sweatin'! (Act 4)

Though Fluther wins an occasional round with Fortune, at heart he is an evader of real issues and real problems. He survives by insulating himself with words and whiskey, but woe to anyone who depends on him for long. It is a trait he shares with Captain Jack Boyle and with all the other male characters in *The Plough*.[6] At the critical moment in Act 3 when a doctor is needed for Nora Clitheroe, Fluther staggers in drunkenly, crowned with the flamboyant cap of the Fool. His roared defiance, "Th' whole city can topple home to hell," is answered by Nora's scream as she quite literally does topple into hell.

The story of the Clitheroes is sheer pathos. Jack is a naive, egotistic young man who dies unnecessarily, leaving his wife in a state of despair. Their child also dies after Nora goes into labor prematurely, and she never recovers from the multiple emotional shocks. Unfortunately, their story weakens the play because neither character is sufficiently well developed to carry the dramatic impact which the author intended. Furthermore, by making Jack and his timorous, self-protecting buddies representative of the Irish insurgents, O'Casey forfeited a marvelous dramatic opportunity. The leadership alone were among the most oddly assorted and unlikely personalities ever to plot a revolution.[7]

The best of O'Casey is in the second act of *The Plough and the Stars*, whose theme and absurdly comic tone recall the Cyclops chapter in *Ulysses*. Here there is no attempt to deal with the larger problems or the complex personalities of history. What we get is a narrow but brilliant perspective: the visionary Padraic Pearse erecting the platform upon which he will be quite literally martyred, viewed purely as theatre by the tenement dwellers of Dublin. Pearse was a poet and playwright and one of the most fanatically determined of the rebel leaders. His play *The Singer* vividly foreshadows the sacrificial role he, himself, played in the Rising. The theme is explicit in the speech which we hear through the window of the pub in Act 2. An excellent example of the kind of rhetoric that inflamed Irish audiences in the last century, it is an ardent plea for blood sacrifice.[8] The Irish patriot is transformed into the Irish martyr; his death becomes holy, Christ-like, because his blood is spilled for the "redemption" of Ireland. the iconography of religion becomes again the iconography of war.

Pearse's impassioned call to arms is juxtaposed against a series of farcical collisions between Bessie Burgess and Mrs. Gogan, the Covey and Peter, the Covey and Fluther. the result is black Irish comedy; Yeats's "terrible beauty" becomes a terrible brawl as the Dubliners respond to the potent mixture of whiskey and revolution. The heroics of the Irish Citizen Army are deflated by the mock heroics of Fluther, whipping off his coat and preparing to do battle with the Covey:

> *Fluther.* Now, you're temptin' Providence when you're temptin' Fluther! . . .
> *The Covey.* . . . One minute with him is all I ask; one minute alone with him, while you're runnin' for th' priest an' th' doctor.

Fluther. Let him go, let him go, Tom! let him open th' door to
sudden death if he wants to! (Act 2)

The flow of invective inside the pub provides a grotesquely
comic counterpoint to the rhetoric of Pearse.

People in Ireland dread war because they do not know it. Ireland
has not known the exhilaration of war for over a hundred years.
When war comes to Ireland she must welcome it as she would the
Angel of God. . . .

His voice gives way to a furious exchange between Bessie Burgess
and Mrs. Gogan:

Mrs. Gogan. Y' oul' rip of a blasted liar, me weddin' ring's been
well earned be twenty years be th' side o' me husband, now
takin' his rest in heaven . . . an' any kid, livin' or dead, that
Jinnie Gogan's had since, was got between the borders of th'
Ten Commandments! . . .
Bessie. Liar to you, too, ma'am, y' oul' hardened threspasser on other
people's good nature, wizenin' up your soul in th' arts o'
dodgeries, till every dhrop of respectability in a female is dhried
up in her, lookin' at your ready-made manoeuverin' with th'
menkind! (Act 2)

The most striking irony is embodied in the prostitute Rosie
Redmond, who is soliciting clients all the while Pearse is addressing
the crowd. The equation is obvious. Each is a seducer of men, and
in the context of the scene, Rosie is the more sympathetic figure
because she is more honest and direct: she gives full value for money
received.[9] Through Rosie Redmond, O'Casey manages to strike at
both sides of the opposing political factions. Redmond is the name
of the Irish leader who preached moderation and parliamentary
reform, while Rose, "Dark Rose, Rose of all my days," is a traditional name for Ireland. It is little wonder that Dublin audiences
were enraged and that some of them climbed up on the stage of the
Abbey Theatre to get their hands on Fluther. This scene
underscores the fact that Irishmen were drawn to the nationalist
movement by the sheer spectacle, the sheer self-indulgence of the
parades, the music, speeches, the sense of importance they

generated. Peter Flynn's most coveted possession is his glorious green uniform, complete with plume and sword, but the closest he'll ever come to militant action is his annual pilgrimage to the grave of Wolfe Tone. Even more infuriating is the fact that in this scene Fluther's boasting and posturing directly parodies the actions of the Irish rebels, thereby reducing their tragic sacrifice to the foolishness of clowns. The solemn moment in which the Volunteers, fired by the words of Pearse, pledge themselves to Ireland is undercut by Fluther's comical defense of Rosie. Clitheroe and his companions are willing to die for an ideal that has become — according to O'Casey — debased and false, that offers no salvation to ordinary people whose problems are primarily economic rather than political. Fluther leaves the pub triumphantly with Rosie in his possession. Unlike Jack Clitheroe, he is getting exactly what he bargained for — no more, no less.

For all the comic energy in O'Casey's plays, they seldom provoke sustained laughter; one is always conscious of the defensive quality of the clowns, the bottled up ferocity that comes out of continual frustration. While Fluther can occasionally match the word to the deed, "Captain" Jack Boyle is a complete imposter, a man, who despite his blather about the high seas, is obviously more at home in a pub. His posturing fails to dupe anyone for long, and his shifting opinions eventually reveal an appalling ignorance and intolerance. In the early scenes, however, his comic reversals and his efforts to outwit his wife, Juno, generate considerable farce. He is so obviously irresponsible and self-indulgent in his maneuvers to avoid work. For all his talk of mastery and adventure, he is the universal guilty husband trying to cope with a strong minded wife. His attempts to outwit her are utterly transparent, but as quickly as she corners him, he slips away under cover of an even more preposterous story: "Nobody but meself knows the sufferin' I'm goin' through with the pains in these legs o' mine!" Boyle's avowals, denials, pleas, alibis are delivered with an irritable air of self-importance. Like the comic figures before him, he is a grand talker, but he puts his gift to a new purpose, pitting imagination against the grim reality of the tenements. Boyle promises to reform, to get a job, to avoid Joxer, to stop drinking, but of course he never will; that would mean admitting that he is simply an ordinary working man.

While earlier writers like Boucicault exploited drunkenness for comic potential, O'Casey, whose own brothers were alcoholics, offers a different perspective. Many of his drinking scenes are hilarious; indeed, as noted earlier, the very best scene he ever wrote, Act 2 in *The Plough*, takes place in a pub. In contrast to the crowded tenement apartment in Act 1, it is the real locus of Dublin life, but during the crises in both plays, key male figures are too hopelessly drunk to act, and the women must salvage what they can. The gay, improvident Celt, whom Boucicault personified as the Shaughraun, becomes a hopeless burden in *Juno and the Paycock*, a cantankerous drunk. He is unable or unwilling to take practical measures even to ward off starvation. Captain Jack with a shovel in his hand becomes a more fantastic notion than Captain Jack on the high seas.

During the initial scenes in *Juno and the Paycock*, Boyle's folly invites laughter because he so stubbornly refuses to see himself as he is. He is a "humourous" figure, bound to a particular pattern of behavior, without any flexibility whatsoever. Although he is quite conventional in his habits and prejudices, he likes to think of himself as a man of unusual depth and experience. His grandiose projection of himself as a philosopher is undercut by the real and obviously banal:

> *Boyle.* An', as it blowed an' blowed, I ofen looked up at the sky
>   an' asses meself the question — what is the stars, what is the stars?
> *Voice of Coal Vendor.* Any blocks, coal-blocks; blocks, coal-blocks!
> *Joxer.* Ah, that's the question, that's the question — what is the stars?
> *Boyle.* An' then, I'd have another look, an' I'd ass meself — what is
>   the moon?
> *Joxer.* Ah, that's the question — what is the moon, what is the moon?
> *The Coal Vendor.* D'yez want any blocks? (Act 1)

This is excellent comedy, reminiscent of Flaubert's classic scene in which Madame Bovary's romantic exchange with a new lover is interrupted by the cries of a cattle auction.

The more serious Boyle's problems become, the more reckless and self-indulgent he is and the more determined to ignore the consequences. He struts like the fabled "paycock,"[10] but exploits Juno instead of protecting her, allowing her to become the sole support of the family. He is, himself, exploited by Joxer, "past Chief Ranger of the Dear Little Shamrock Branch of the Irish National Foresters," who flatters him with an inexhaustible string of clichés and keeps him company in return for free drinks. The pair are obviously related to the *miles gloriosus* and the parasite-slave of New Roman comedy.

While Boyle is full of gaiety slipping off to his favorite pub with Joxer, he perpetually complains at home. Much of his defensive, self-pitying protest is quite comical, however, particularly when he is posing as an irate father before Mary's suitors. He is shrewd enough in sizing up Bentham, the stage Englishman, who eventually seduces and abandons his daughter. Unfortunately, he has so discredited himself that when he speaks with some wisdom, having recognized another imposter, no one listens.

In this play Sean O'Casey draws an even sharper distinction between the male imposters and the women who keep the home together regardless of the cost to themselves. Juno is an excellent, strong, patient and loving woman who, in spite of the public opinion that intimidates Boyle, determines to support Mary.[11] She admonishes her daughter, who is anxious about her unborn child:

Mary. My poor little child that'll have no father!
Mrs. Boyle. It'll have what's far betther — it'll have two mothers.

There is indeed not one "whole man" on the scene; Captain Boyle, Bentham, and Johnny Boyle all betray those who love or depend on them. Johnny Boyle finally pays with his life for his role in the death of Tancred, another "diehard" Republican. He is even weaker and more impotent than Jack Clitheroe and his patriotism is treated as a mindless reflex. His death is a kind of mercy killing as he is so afraid of life, having been crippled emotionally as well as physically by his part in the Irish revolution. Boyle, who likes to fantasize about his military exploits, has little patience with his son. The contrast between romance and reality is underscored, but O'Casey's point is weakened because the advocates of war in this play are mere phantoms.

The second act of *Juno and the Paycock* begins on a convivial note as the Boyles, on the strength of their expected inheritance, borrow all the money thay can and furnish their apartment in a fairly vulgar way. Irish ignorance is again made to seem comic, but O'Casey is offering a fair assessment of the culture of the tenement dwellers, whom he presents in the round. In Dublin at the turn of the century there was very little left of the old Gaelic life style. One thinks of Synge's description of the very simple, beautiful objects in the homes of the Aran Islanders; in comparison, the Boyles have only cheap, factory-made objects. Boyle doesn't speak Irish and has a very muddled understanding of the history of his country.[12] The Revival has had little impact on the people in the slums, who frequent the pubs or the music halls, but not the Abbey Theatre.

The hooley begins with the Boyles and their guests singing some of the old ballads; the captain even recites a "poem" of his own creation, but the songs quickly peter out. In place of the traditional Irish fiddler, they turn to the gramaphone, which pipes out a music hall ditty, "If you're Irish, Come into the Parlor." O'Casey is apparently stressing the cultural impoverishment of the Dublin poor, cut off from the ancient traditions of which he had direct knowledge through his study of the Irish language. The position of the Boyles is all the more tenuous because they haven't mastered English, and they are still at the very bottom of the social structure, lacking the skill and the opportunity to better their lives. Despite their limitations, O'Casey's Dubliners, unlike those of Joyce's middle class, have a dynamic quality, an exuberance of spirit, which can explode in a brawl or a jest into which they plunge themselves with contagious intensity.

In this play their gaiety is short lived as the Boyles discover that Bentham has managed to bungle the will upon which they had depended, and their inheritance is lost. As the family situation deteriorates, with both Mary and Johnny visibly ailing and in need of strong support, Boyle becomes increasingly waspish. He is now an utterly desperate man, whose precarious self-esteem would not survive a serious look at reality. He blames various members of the household, turning with particular vehemence on his daughter, whose unfortunate pregnancy will embarrass him. Critics, notably David Krause, tend to view Boyle as consistently amusing, as someone whom we can laugh with as well as at because he represents a "universal frailty."[13] For my own part, I fail to see anything amusing in his threats to strike his daughter and to drive her out of the house. At this point in the play, the fool turns knave, as Boyle reveals the mean-tempered old bigot lurking behind the mask of the buffoon.

Self-delusion is endemic in the Boyle household, but neither Mary nor Johnny has their father's ability to survive. Both become painfully trapped and exploited because of their romantic inclinations, their utter failure to understand the man or the cause to which they give themselves. The result is death for Johnny and an impoverished life for Mary.

While Juno determines to survive the wreckage by leaving Boyle, the good captain floats off in a fog of alcohol, spinning a final fantasy about himself as a rebel hero. The world is in a "state of chassis" all right, but at this point Captain Boyle can't even feel the falling debris.

In *Beyond Laughter* Martin Grotjohn discusses the clown's role as a debased father figure. Through the clown, the all-powerful father is rendered foolish, his antics invite mockery; we laugh at his helplessness. Grotjohn points out that the cap and bells, the donkey ears, the drooping tassels of the medieval fool are symbols of castration and impotence. Such symbols tend to be disguised in modern times, but the enormous tie of the circus clown, his baggy pants or tiny walking stick, all represent the father who was once big and powerful, but is now impotent. The great clown, like Charlie Chaplin or W. C. Fields, remains loveable. He depreciates himself but, because of his skillful disguise, he doesn't make the audience feel guilty. They are free to enjoy the catharsis of comedy, the open expression of antagonism toward the father.[14]

Some of the uneasiness we feel in the presence of Boyle probably stems from the fact that he is so thoroughly depreciated: his impotence is so obvious, so painfully exposed. O'Casey's anger is too much in evidence here, as it is in his treatment of the Irish insurgents. Thus there is a kind of relief in the final scene when Boyle manages to reassemble his disguise. Having spent the last of his money on a few pints to bolster his courage, he returns to his deserted apartment, which has just been emptied of furniture by the creditors:

> *Boyle.* The counthry'll have to steady itself . . . it's goin' . . . to
> hell . . . Where'r all . . . the chairs . . . gone to . . . steady
> itself, Joxer . . . Chairs'll . . . have to . . . steady themselves . . .
> No matther . . . what any one may . . . say . . . Irelan' sober
> . . . is Irelan' . . . free. . . . If th' worst comes . . . to th'
> worse . . . I can join a . . . flyin' . . . column. . . . I done . . .
> me bit . . . in Easther Week . . . had no business . . . to . . . be . . .
> there . . . but Captain Boyle's Captain Boyle!
> (Act 3)

The play ends with a brilliant scene of blackest comedy. The fool, once again securely enmeshed in his illusions, is unaware that his son is dead; it is the sober, realistic Juno who will have to bear the brunt of this new disaster. Boyle will probably be more uncomfortable and more needy than before, but he has managed to escape the harsh tragedy that has overtaken the rest of his family. In his drunken raving, he imagines Commandant Kelly dying in his arms, his romantic vision of heroism brutally undercut by the fact that Johnny, who actually took part in the Rising, has been executed as a traitor by the I.R.A. The current of macabre humor is reminiscent of the final scene in *The Plough and the Stars* in which the British soldiers sip their tea and sing a chorus of "Keep the Home Fires Burning," while the Dublin tenements are literally going up in smoke. In such scenes O'Casey moves away from the conventions of melodrama; Boyle's final performance approaches the outermost limits of the absurd. His reaction to the family crisis is so utterly inappropriate, it is laughable in the same way Estragon is laughable in *Waiting for Godot* when he observes that, if he hanged himself, he might at least achieve an erection. Boyle's impotence is more farreaching, for while Estragon knows that he only talks to pass the time, to cover up the void of inaction, Boyle has no self-awareness whatsoever. He does not dare to face the truth because he could not survive its implications. He must continue the dance, the posturing, the self-protecting fantasies.

10. A Borstal Boy

"God help the poor Irish, if it was raining soup, we'd be out with forks." Like much of Brendan Behan's humor, this remark has personal relevance. Approximately seven years of his life were spent in prison for bungled attempts to carry out the revolutionary aims of the IRA. Those years had a profound effect on his emotional and intellectual development and provided him with material for his best work, *The Quare Fellow*, *The Hostage*, and *Borstal Boy*. Neither *The Quare Fellow* nor *The Hostage* has a well defined central comic character; however, I would like to briefly discuss these plays to illustrate Behan's major concerns as a writer as well as the nature of his comic talent.

The Quare Fellow takes place inside a Dublin prison, focusing on events leading up to the execution of a nameless criminal, the "quare fellow," who never actually appears on stage. The play strongly sympathizes with the prisoners, with their isolation and physical and emotional deprivation. Their suffering comes to represent the human condition while in the final scene the condemned man emerges as a kind of Christ figure, despite the fact that he brutally murdered his own brother.

Behan's unorthodox theme is developed through realistic detail. One sees the grim round of prison life from the inside as the convicts move back and forth between their cells and the prison yard, where a grave is being dug for the quare fellow. As they joke and quarrel among themselves, they seem much like ordinary men in their beliefs, prejudices, and fears. One significant difference is that the great majority are from working class backgrounds; the prison reflects a class system that protects and supports those with wealth and status, while the man at the bottom of the heap suffers, not only economic and social discrimination, but the full penalty of the law. Like O'Casey, Behan writes out of strong socialist and humanist sympathies, and he falters in the creation of middle-class characters who tend to be stereotypes like the convicted rapist, a religious hypocrite who quotes Carlyle. Beyond that, he has a distinctly Irish sense of death in the midst of life, a presence at once alluring and terrifying and therefore treated with barbed humor.

As the cold, monotonous, brutal quality of prison life is revealed, the crimes of the inmates are gradually outweighed by the calculated cruelty of the state which subjects them to a system which is wholly degrading and which, despite the profession of Christian principle, continues to execute men by hanging. The guards are not sadistic, but they also have been degraded by the prison system, and they routinely inform on one another and mete out punishment in hope of advancement. There are two remarkable exceptions. One is Crimmins, a romantic embodiment of Irish Ireland who has a natural purity and goodness (also characteristic of the Irish speaking prisoner C). The other is Regan, a blunt, compassionate, deeply religious man who, with Crimmins, offers emotional support to the quare fellow during his last few hours of life.

Although he has complete contempt for the social order which the prison system supports, as a moralist, Regan operates within that system to ameliorate its brutality. Outspoken in his opposition to capital punishment, he proposes that the quare fellow is a scapegoat figure, being executed by a "crowd of bigger bloody ruffians than himself. . . ." He believes that those in power, particularly the judges, are more guilty of vice than the prisoners, whom he regards as condemned to do penance for the rest of mankind. Thus Regan fuses Marxist and Catholic ideology, the ideology, in effect, of the left wing IRA, which had a strong influence on Brendan Behan.

The humor which permeates *The Quare Fellow* has the quality of an old fashioned Irish wake in its blend of mirth and melancholy. While the ritual knocking and screaming of the prisoners immediately preceding the execution suggest the keen, there is also a good deal of the burlesque, ranging from the con games played by the old alcoholics, Dunlavin and Neighbor, to the posturing of the guards. Even the hangman is a figure of fun — a British bartender who sings a sentimental ballad, "The Rose of Tralee," unintentionally punning on the "pure crystal fountain" ("poor Christian fountain"). Dialect is used as a source of humor and vitality; it is characteristically needling, aggressive, epigramatic, although Dunlavin, for one, can lapse into a maudlin stage Irish brogue when he's trying to wheedle a favor: "old and bet, sir, that's us. And the old pains is very bad with us these times, sir" (shades of Captain Boyle!). In the second act prisoners gamble on the possibility of the last minute reprieve, a grim game to disguise their fear of death as well as to break up the monotony. Here the focal point is the grave which the prisoners are forced to dig and around which they cavort and threaten one another. One old man scoffs: "We'll be eating the cabbages off that one in a month or two," and is himself tossed into the grave.

Death by hanging is grimly described by Warder Regan, who emphasizes the fact that it can be slow and torturous. His attitude cuts ironically through the orthodox Catholic position:

> *Healey.* Ah yes, you're helping the Canon at the execution
>   tomorrow morning, I understand.
> *Warder Regan.* Well, I shall be with the condemned man sir,
>   seeing that he doesn't do away with himself during the night and
>   that he goes down the hole with his neck properly broken in the
>   morning without making too much fuss about it. (Act 1)

Regan later suggests that the whole ritual should take place in Croke Park, a popular center for Gaelic sports, so that the taxpayers can get their money's worth. His outrage has a peculiar ironic and historic resonance because so many Irish political prisoners suffered death by hanging under an English penal code.

The theme of the condemned man is fundamental to the work of modern writers such as Kafka, Pinter, Ionesco, and Sartre, for whom man is the victim of powerful and deadly forces which he can neither understand nor resist. The institutions which formerly gave him a sense of identity and value — family, nationality, religion — have broken down in the face of continual war and genocide. Individual acts of heroism have come to seem futile against a technology capable of obliterating the entire human race. Until recently Irish writers, with the important exceptions of Samuel Beckett and Flann O'Brien, have not expressed any comparable sense of pessimism. In *Juno and the Paycock* and *The Plough and the Stars*, only the weak despair; Sean O'Casey, like Brendan Behan, believed that there were definable and hence remediable causes of human misery[1]: The penal system can be reformed, the poor can be offered decent wages, the Irish and the English can learn to live with one another. This pronounced difference in attitude probably stems from the fact that, despite a history of oppression, the Irish people have retained Christian values and can still identify England as a cause of some of their internal problems. For all his irreverence and nonconformity Behan was a moralist, who believed in social and political reform and used an exuberant comic genius to gain sympathy for his point of view.

The Hostage also deals with the theme of the condemned man; it is allegedly based on an episode in which a British soldier captured by the IRA during the Suez crisis in 1955 was accidentally suffocated. The play was written originally in Irish for Gael Linn, an organization founded to promote Irish language and culture. In discussing his decision to use Irish, Behan indicated that he believed he could express certain moods in that language which he could not express in English, explaining that "Irish is more direct than English, more bitter."[2] That bitterness is, however, charged with comic energy as melancholy and mirth again "flash together." The rapidly paced events that lead to the death of the hostage are interlaced with witty dialogue and the wildly burlesque antics of the characters. This might be termed gallows humor because of the centrifugal force of death, but it is not the *humour noir* of Beckett's *Watt*, the laugh that laughs at "that which is unhappy." It is too spirited a response, too alive to the pleasures of resistance.

After *An Giall*, as the original version of the play was called, received favorable notice, Joan Littlewood, the director of an avante garde theatre in London, offered to produce it if Behan would undertake the translation. As this proceeded rather slowly, Littlewood and her cast, who had staged *The Quare Fellow* in 1956, filled in some of the gaps themselves. Behan evidently gave them considerable freedom, and so topical allusions as well as camp humor were added, which were updated in later productions. The result was a free wheeling extravaganza and a smash hit.

Like *The Quare Fellow*, *The Hostage* is iconoclastic in temper, frequently and unabashedly outrageous in its ridicule of national pieties, a point which was immediately picked up by London critics.

In this play Behan provides us with the "buck lepper" version of the stage Irishman, a mad patriot who parades around in kilts, playing the bagpipes, believing he is in the thick of a revolution.

"Monsewer" had been content with life as an English gentleman until, discovering his Irish heritage, he began to cultivate Irishness
with a passion, learning the language at Oxford and ultimately
fighting for the IRA during the Civil War. The peace treaty unhing-
ed what remained of his wits; he clings to the romantic past ready to
make the supreme sacrifice for the Republican cause. For the mad
Monsewer, it would be "great happiness" to die for Ireland.
Through Monsewer, Behan satirizes the Anglo-Irish who allied
themselves with the Republican cause and became more Irish than
the Irish in behalf of the cultural revival.[3] Monsewer is so devoted to
the concept of *fine Gael* that he has to be accompanied by a
translator to get about in Dublin.

Sean O'Casey infuriated Dublin by bringing the Plough and the
Stars, the flag of the Irish Citizen Army, into a pub where a prostitute is soliciting customers. Brendan Behan went a step further:
the rooming house which Monsewer owns and which is run by a loyal
subordinate from the old days, has been turned into a brothel, sym-
bolizing the degradation of the old Republican ideal.

Held captive in the brothel is Leslie Williams, a young
Englishman, who becomes a pawn in the continuing struggle of Irish
nationalists to expel the English from Northern Ireland. He is taken
hostage for another young man in Belfast, condemned to death for
shooting a policeman. (It is worth noting that Behan himself served
four years of a fourteen year sentence for firing at the Dublin police
during an IRA memorial service.)

Most of the other characters in *The Hostage* are social outcasts
of one kind or another, a scruffy, belligerent lot, the most outspoken
of whom is Pat, an old IRA man. Witty and cynical, he ridicules
the younger militants as mechanical fools, completely devoid of
humor or common sense. Nonetheless, when the crisis comes he acts
instinctively according to the revolutionary code, with tragic results
for Leslie.

The central theme of the play is that nationalism is destructive,
outdated, at the very least foolish because the world is changing too
rapidly and is far too dangerous to accommodate cultural isola-
tionism. Behan's sympathies are with the proletariat; like O'Casey's
tenement dwellers, they have borne the heaviest losses in the internal
warfare that continues in Ireland.

Leslie, the hostage, and Theresa, the country girl who reaches
out to him in a brief interlude of affection, are both orphans, sym-

bolically placed outside the mainstream of English and Irish culture and thus a potential source of a new generation conceived without the blight of race hatred. What further distinguishes them, particularly in the Irish version, is their innocence in contrast to the world around them in which love of God, country, or fellow human being has been thoroughly debased. Their relationship is unfortunately short-lived like most such love relationships — when they exist at all — in modern Irish comedy. Their world is still in a "state of chassis." There is no immediate promise of peace or resolution; thus any commitment between lovers must be tenuous.

Behan's purpose, as in *The Quare Fellow*, is a humanitarian one. Underneath the joking is a serious statement about the futility of modern warfare and a conciliatory gesture from an old IRA man. Ulick O'Connor maintains, however, that Behan was uneasy with the Littlewood production, which was so emphatically an "entertainment" and so insistent in its ridicule of Irish types. With the exception of Leslie and Theresa, the characters are made ludicrous in their allegiance to a cause whose time has passed. The laughter is cathartic, but in a sense one has the spectacle of Handy Andy all over again. Everything that speaks of a peculiarly Irish mode of life — language, patriotism, religious beliefs — is being held up to laughter, and there is no balancing sense of cultural richness as there is in *Ulysses*. In the stage Irish tradition Behan's characters are boisterous drinkers and talkers, who sing and joke and dance to provide comic relief until the nightmarish scene in which Leslie is killed. At the final curtain he springs to life, a sentimental gesture tacked on to the English version.[4]

Borstal Boy, an autobiographical account of Behan's own experience as a political prisoner in England, provides a real cultural context. The book also confirms the widely observed fact that the most compelling character he ever created was Brendan Behan. Long before the publication of *Borstal Boy*, Behan had attracted public attention because of his witty and rambunctious behavior. Within a month the autobiography sold twenty thousand copies and not only brought him literary fame but "helped to fix his public image": a boy from the slums who liked to thumb his nose at the establishment, who had spent years in prison, but who finally won international acclaim because of his innate and untutored genius.[5]

At the age of sixteen Behan was arrested in Liverpool with his

"Sinn Fein conjuror's outfit" — explosives intended for the British shipyards. His arrest and internment are described in *Borstal Boy* through scenes which vividly express the fear, degradation, loneliness, and oddly humorous encounters of prison life. Behan provides a very open and frank account of the everyday routine, the threats of the guards, the complete lack of privacy, the physical attraction of other men, which it make clear how rooted in personal experience were the two major plays. He is adept at quickly and memorably characterizing a wide range of personalities as, for example, in this impression of the owner of the boardinghouse where he was captured:

> This landlady was mean and as barren as a bog. Her broken
> windows would be a judgement on her for the cheap sausages and
> margarine she poisoned her table with, for she was only generous
> with things that cost little in cash, locking hall doors at nighttime
> and kneeling down to say the Rosary with the lodger and her
> sister, who always added three Hail Marys for holy purity and the
> protection of her person and modesty, so that you would think half
> the men in Liverpool were running after her, panting for a lick of
> her big buck teeth.[6]

And the chief administrator at Walton Jail where he was held for sentencing:

> The governor was a desiccated-looking man, in tweed clothes and
> wearing a cap, as befitted his rank of Englishman, and looking as if
> he would ride a horse if he had one. He spoke with some effort,
> and if you did not hear what he was saying you'd have thought
> from his tone, and the sympathetic, loving, and adoring looks of the
> screw, P.O., and Chief, that he was stating some new philosophical
> truth to save the suffering world from error.
> (51)

Much of the dramatic tension in Part I of *Borstal Boy* derives from Behan's consciousness of being an Irish Revolutionary in an English jail. When first captured, he is determined to live up to the memory of men like Tom Clarke who, after fifteen years of penal servitude for planting explosives, took a leading role in the Easter Rising for which he was finally executed. In court he declares:

> My name is Brenden Behan, I came over here to fight for the Irish

> Workers and Small Farmers' Republic, for a full and free life, for
> my countrymen, North and South, and for the removal of the baneful
> influence of British Imperialism from Irish affairs. God save
> Ireland.
> (7)

But under the conditions at Walton, he realizes that he could not
withstand the punishment endured by earlier patriots.

To begin with he is excommunicated by an English priest when
he refuses to repudiate the IRA. Although he remains a fundamentally religious person, this experience makes him skeptical of the institution of the Church. And when he is invited later on to serve
Mass despite the fact that he may not receive the sacraments, he
does so only in

> . . . memory of my ancestors standing around a rock, in a lonely
> glen, for fear of the landlords and their yesmen or sneaking
> through a back-land in Dublin, and giving the password, to hear
> Mass in a slum public house, when a priest's head was worth five
> pounds and an Irish Catholic had no existence in law.
> (333)

Behan seems as much outraged by the priest's insistence on his ignorance as a working class boy as by his use of religion as a political
weapon. The autobiography may, in fact, be read as a rebuttal,
demonstrating the rich heritage of history, legend, music, and conversation available to the ordinary Dubliner if, like Behan, he has
the wit or the leisure to appreciate it. Unfortunately, his ferociously
articulate response at this point precipitates a beating from the
guards. Thereafter he is locked up in isolation, condemned to what
he terms *"unaigneas gan cuineas,"* loneliness without peace. He
acknowledges his fear and determines to survive despite the hostility
of many of the other prisoners and the guards who abuse him as an
"Irish pig."

What is particularly strong and moving in Behan's memoir is
his willingness to put aside the mask and speak openly of the difference between the "gallous story" and the "dirty deed," between
songs and processions in memory of Irish heroes and the reality of an
English jail: "I thought it better to survive my sentence and come
out and strike a blow in vengeance for them, than be kicked to death
or insanity here. And even that was not the truth. I only wanted to

survive the night." The critical test comes with the approaching execution of two Irishmen condemned for the alleged murder of British civilians. Behan makes a devastating comedy out of his reaction to another Irishman, Callan, in jail for stealing an overcoat, but determined to prove his courage by staging a demonstration on the eve of the execution. As Callan roars out, "Up the Republic" to Behan's timid response, the latter comments: ". . . all honour to him, of course, I'll never deny it to him, but tell them at home how all alone he stood and shouted for the cause all on his own. If only he leaves me out of it."

Once he is remanded to the Borstal at Hollesley Bay, a detention center for juveniles, Behan is drawn into a new role, that of "Paddy," the comic Irishman. Relieved to find himself in a relatively humane institution, he becomes a genial performer sought after by the other prisoners whom he regales with Irish songs and obscene limericks and jokes. His memoir amply attests to his craving for companionship and his use of comedy to break out of isolation and surround himself with an admiring throng of friends. He warms to applause, enjoying the tone of friendly approval that he hears in the nickname "Paddy." Behan admits his willingness to stretch the truth and to suppress his own feelings in order to be accommodating, to avoid friction. In a curious way his career parallels the historical experience of the Irish in the nineteenth century, abused and ridiculed because of cultural differences and then applauded when those differences began to seem amusing, perceived through the distorting prism of a stereotype and often conforming to that stereotype.

In this section of the book there are many fine, dramatic scenes of life in the Borstal as well as splendid prose passages describing the natural landscape:

> The autumn got weaker and beaten, and the leaves all fell, and a
> bloody awful east wind that was up before us and we on our way
> to work in the morning, sweeping down off the top of the North Sea,
> which in the distance looked like a bitter band of deadly blue
> steel out along the length of the horizon, around the freezing
> marshes, the dirty grey shore, the gunmetal sea, and over us the sky,
> lead-colored for a few hours, till the dark fell and the wind rose,
> and we went down the road from work at five o'clock in the
> perishing night.
> (345-346)

The dialogue, including Cockney, Welsh, rural English, and Northern Irish, attests to Behan's excellent ear for the nuances of the spoken word. It also demonstrates that he was becoming more tolerant of people regardless of racial, national, or religious background. He discovers that he has more in common with the English working class than with some of the Irish he encounters in prison: ". . . in Ireland, down the country anyway, if a girl got put up the pole she might as well leave the country or drown herself and have done with it — the people are so Christian and so easily shocked." He remains defensive toward the upper classes and the formally educated, presenting himself as a tough, blunt, street-wise Dubliner, as condescending in his way as Captain Boyle: "I was no country Paddy from the middle of the Bog of Allen."

Nonetheless Sections II and III of *Borstal Boy* are inferior to the opening portion; they rarely attain the same level of intelligent introspection and one grows weary of Behan as a loveable character. The best part of the book remains his fine description of the loneliness and fear he experienced in Walton Jail, the racy dialogue and lyric prose passages and certain first-rate dramatic scenes like that of his capture in Liverpool. There are also many witty comments to liven up an otherwise ordinary page ("It's a queer world, God knows, but the best we have to be going on with.") For those interested in Irish culture, *Borstal Boy* remains a fascinating portrait of a quintessential Dubliner.

Brendan Behan's public career as a "broth of a bhoy" has been well chronicled. After the generally conservative mood of the fifties, his performance as "wild Irish" delighted a vast audience, particularly in England and America, where newsmen followed him around waiting for samples of the famous Irish wit. Ulick O'Connor emphasizes Behan's shrewdness at public relations; he was evidently quick to seize opportunities to bring himself to the attention of the media, frequently turning mischance — a drunken brawl or a night in jail — into a comic interlude.[7] He created a legend by his escapades and by his superb gift as a story teller and mime, able to captivate listeners for hours at a time. He had a fine tenor voice and an excellent repertoire as well as a talent for parody and for composing limericks extemporaneously. Before he was well known he obviously relished the role of provocateur, of defeating the expectations of the intelligentsia and the middle class when he revealed his considerable knowledge and skill as a speaker in both English and Irish.

Behan became familiar with Irish through the help of his fellow IRA men during internment in Dublin and first attracted attention as a poet writing in this ancient tongue. He spoke of himself disparagingly as a *rannaire*, that is, a rimer, rather than a *fili*; but translations of his work, as for example "A Jackeen cries at the loss of the Blaskets," suggest that he had talent as a poet. This particular poem confirms his affiliation with the stark simplicity of the old, vanished culture. It reveals an ascetic element in Behan's nature, linking him temperamentally to the islanders and further back in time to the solitary monks who wrote the first lyric poems in Irish. As a *jackeen* (a countryman's contemptuous term for a Dubliner), however, he would have been doubly removed, in culture as well as time, from the world of the Blaskets. By writing in Irish, Behan was apparently attempting to establish continuity with that remote world. After 1950 he wrote no further poetry; it is believed that he lost faith in his own ability and in the future of Gaelic literature.[8]

Reading through the work of contemporary poets, Thomas Kinsella, John Montague, Seamus Heaney, Seán Ó Tuama, and observing how they have burrowed into the substrata of history toward the sources of Irish culture, one cannot help thinking that Behan's career took a fatal turn in the fifties. This is not to say that his gifts were those of a poet rather than a dramatist, merely that he sacrificed the private to the public man. This conclusion is also suggested by Colbert Kearney who, in his analysis of Behan's work, argues that "the persona of the Irish poems would seem to be the closest approximation to his basic personality."[9]

In "North" Seamus Heaney speaks of composing like the *fili* in "darkness," of "keeping your eye clear, as the bleb of the icicle." History then becomes a source of renewal and strength, ensuring the writer a measure of perspective, not simply the makings of a good anecdote. Working at his craft in silence and darkness, keeping himself aloof, he sees with the inner eye of vision. The result is a distinctive voice and a new sense of authority in Irish literature.

The dramatist is necessarily a more public figure and his relation with his audience is a more precarious one. The success of Behan's work depended in no small measure on the fact that he was often in the spotlight himself.

Onto the figure of the stage Irish bard, which infuriated Patrick Kavanagh and Flann O'Brien, he grafted that of the rebel,[10] that is, the rebel as comedian, a bit of a turnabout for the defender of the Workers and Small Farmers' Republic, a bit of a throwback to the Shaughraun. By ridiculing Irish nationalism and turning his political past into grist for the publicity mill, he must have felt, at some level, that he was betraying his deepest roots.[11]

It is hardly a new discovery that Behan was a stage Irishman, and it is a point that I do not wish to belabor considering his tragic early death from the combined ravages of diabetes and alcoholism. The general consensus is that he first created and then was trapped by his public image, by the expectations of the crowd. Toward the end of his life, the amiable witty surface cracked open under the pressure of what must have been extraordinary inner violence. He wrote less and less as his fame increased and he deteriorated physically, collapsing into drunken diabetic comas. His biographer has provided a sympathetic account of the contradictory elements of his personality with its shifting moods of savagery and kindness, of asceticism and drunken excess. What is germane to this study is the magnetism of the public mask, the appeal of the comic Irishman.

Conclusion

I N *The Performing Self* Richard Poirier talks about "a violent and unsuccessful magnification of the self through language in the effort to meet and overwhelm the phenomenon of death."[1] It seems to me that something of this urgency characterizes the comic Irishman. He comes after all from a culture that was under sentence of death for hundreds of years. In order to survive he stepped into a role which was created for him, but which he gradually charged with the force of his own temperament. He refused to accept boundaries, particularly as they were defined historically and socially, or to believe that this world contains all there is. Like Denis O'Shaughnessy he understood that "plain words" are the words of a man without imagination.

In Gaelic Ireland the "three indications of dignity" were: "a fine figure, a free bearing, eloquence."[2] The archetypal hero had great verbal power as well as military skill. In more recent times the poet and novelist James Stephens observed that "it is conversation that keeps away death." Good conversation was prized among the country people, and real virtuosity was expected of poets, schoolmasters, and storytellers. The first two engaged in extemporaneous battles of wit in which their powers of rhetoric and composition were publicly displayed and publicly judged. Storytelling was a performance in itself, structured by simple but specific rituals. A session began and ended with a traditional formula, but details were improvised and so could last for two hours, punctuated by verbal response which might take the form of encouragement or a brief commentary or jest. The best storytellers were also practiced in the art of rhetoric, their style distinguished by a perceptible rhythm as well as by the use of assonance and alliteration, a richly interwoven pattern of sound and stress.

In the traditional wake, performance and gaiety of every kind
— courtship rites, music, mime, dance, storytelling — were intended specifically as an antidote to grief. This ritual is apparently of ancient origin; historical records exist from the tenth century when it
was customary throughout western Europe. Wakes probably continued much longer in Ireland because of that country's relative
isolation and the oral tradition. They served a central social and
cathartic function, evidently helping to relieve many of the tensions
of everyday life. Fighting was not uncommon, and anger was often
discharged upon a scapegoat through ridicule or physical abuse.
Mock marriages were another prominent feature, and accounts of
games such as Making the Ship and The Bull and the Cow have a
strong phallic element, suggesting that the wake originally included
fertility rites.[3] This idea apparently appealed to James Joyce when
he began to chronicle the adventures of Tim Finnegan, and it is
humorously parodied by Samuel Beckett in *Murphy*. As protodrama
which expresses that characteristically Irish blend of mirth and
melancholy, it has found its way into the work of many other
writers, including Lover, Carleton, Boucicault, Synge, O'Casey,
and Beckett.

The connection between festival and funeral ("funferall") was
observed in an uncomprehending way by many nineteenth century
writers who liked to assume that the Irishman was a cheerful,
reckless fellow who willingly risked life and limb at the slightest opportunity. In *Rural Life in Ireland*, first published in 1821, for example, we are told that "a real Irishman should despise life under
any circumstances" and that he "enters on a fray for sport and never
thinks of the consequences."[4] Bayle Bernard, the biographer of
Samuel Lover, comments that "an air of burlesque romance runs
through half of this people's history. They seem to turn life into a
carnival in which the only occupation is the concoction of a good
joke or the pursuit of a mad adventure. . . . Even misfortune does
not sadden them."[5]

In *Handy Andy* the humor frequently turns on precisely this
conception of Irish character. One is invited to laugh freely at
Andy's misfortunes because he invariably recovers and he suffers no
emotional injury. In most of the other work we have discussed there
is also a heightening of comic tension with the threat of death or
disaster, but there is an important difference. Laughter is provoked
by the intensity of the comic performance, the deliberate heightening of illusion by one who consciously resists defeat. Thus the

playboy becomes most eloquent and most forceful when old Mahon appears on the scene, threatening to spoil his romance with Pegeen. When Captain Boyle's household finally disintegrates around him, he prepares to "join a flying column," adopting the romantic posture of "the man on the run," an ironic metaphor for his true predicament. Even in the case of the more complex Buck Mulligan, one may detect a similar tendency. He is at his most amusing in the opening chapter of *Ulysses*, attempting to tease Stephen Dedalus out of his brooding melancholy.

It seems to me that much of the appeal of the comic Irishman rests on just this ability to laugh at death or disaster, not because he is indifferent, but because his culture provided precisely this defense. His genius may lie not in the magnification of the self, but in its protean quality, his willingness to improvise — to "join a flying column" — and thus resist. Like the druid he is a shape changer, an idea which is reflected even in the simpler clowns like Handy Andy and the Shaughraun, both of whom at critical moments assume a disguise. In his negative aspect the comic character presents a mask that is wholly false like the seemingly benign narrator of *At Swim-Two-Birds*, who turns his real fury inward through progressively distorted, wildly mocking self-images. As the hero or poet, Denis O'Shaughnessy, Christy Mahon, and Tarry Flynn, he has the power to ennoble both self and community by sheer imaginative force. In contrast, the wholly inflexible Murphy is doomed to extinction.

There is, as we have seen, among modern writers a reaction against the easy eloquence associated with "playing the Irishman." Talking is regarded as a way of avoiding serious issues or solving real problems close at hand. Thus while Buck Mulligan is at first a welcome foil to young Dedalus, his mockery eventually wears thin, and one is conscious of the anxiety and hostility underneath. The elaborate linguistic patterns and narrative structures developed by Joyce are, among other things, a means of resolving this dilemma by imposing strict forms to contain the "spontaneous flow of language." Flann O'Brien tries the reverse technique, parodying a wide range of linguistic styles to produce a work that is almost hermetically sealed (like Murphy's mind) against the "filthy modern tide." Tarry Flynn, in a voice befitting his role as "wise fool," uses very simple language to reaffirm the love of place characteristic of Irish literature from earliest times when the *dinnshenchus* (place lore) was composed. Beckett, even more suspicious of the richness of his native tongue, explores the implications of silence, which in plays such as *Waiting for Godot* and *Endgame* takes on an uncanny resonance.

As both O'Casey and Behan exploited the stage Irish tradition, their comic characters prefer to talk rather than to act to ward off disaster. O'Casey is, however, ironic in his treatment of this stratagem; its limitation, particularly in the case of Captain Boyle, meditating on the stars while his wife goes out to scrub floors, is quite clear. O'Casey enjoyed a good scrap and wasn't disappointed when Dublin audiences found his two best plays infuriating. Behan, much more vulnerable, tended to woo his audience by playing to their expectations — unless they were conspicuously intellectual or middle-class. In an article aptly entitled "Last Playboy of the Western World," Kevin Sullivan remarks that "the writer in Behan was continually in danger of being shouted down by the talker, the playwright upstaged by the vaudevillian. . . ."[6] Too much of his energy evaporated in talk until finally he lacked the necessary will to write. His last book, *Confessions of an Irish Rebel*, is a rambling series of anecdotes collected by tape recorder.

There has been only one authentic hero in this study, a feature which has been only briefly explored because I am interested primarily in character rather than in structure or theme. The fact that Irish comedy is more concerned with anti-heroes or clowns is probably related to the unhappy course of history. From the sixteenth through the nineteenth century there was little opportunity for the pleasant intricacies of romance, which provide the traditional pattern of comedy. Irish heroes were tragic figures who gave their lives for Cathleen ni Houlihan. It is not surprising that in comedy the emphasis is on survival.

The role of the comic Irishman is complicated by the fact that death, often represented in Irish iconography as a beautiful woman, has a certain seductive appeal. Clearly not all of the characters we have discussed have this kind of sensibility. It is usually expressed through the macabre, which is little in evidence in nineteenth century literature (aside from Carleton), but is integral to the work of Synge, Joyce, O'Casey, Behan, O'Brien, and Beckett. This kind of humor may dwell on mortality and pain, reflecting not only anxiety but ambivalence, a halfhearted willingness to submit to the inevitable, the "three legged tree" or the "wooden suspender." More typically there is bravado, an aggressive teasing of fate, a willful show of strength, as though by grappling with it, one might overthrow the spectre of death. This was vividly impressed upon me by a Dublin production (1977) of *Measure for Measure* in which the part of Bernardine was played by a stage Irishman, whose appearance — half naked in a shambles of red hair and beard — was purely comic: ". . . I have been drinking hard all night, and I will have more time to prepare me. . . . I will not consent to die this day. That's certain."

In Irish literature and folklore the hangman — and indeed the devil, himself — appears as a clown, while the idea of gaming or sporting with death is often worked out very graphically. In "The Battle of the Factions" by William Carleton, when the narrator slyly tells us that the "bones of contention were numerous," his statement has a literal as well as symbolic content. In the course of the epic battle being described, numerous bones were in fact secured from a graveyard and put to use by the fighters gleefully maiming and murdering one another. A similar sense of the macabre operates in *The Playboy* where Philly Cullen recalls amusing himself as a youngster by fitting together, like so many pieces in a crossword puzzle, bones uncovered in a nearby field. Folklore offers innumerable accounts of tricks played with a corpse which is being waked. In a typical example the ropes binding the rigid limbs are cut so that the corpse suddenly appears to sit up. In other tales someone pretends to be dead or is led to believe he has died, a trick which worked its way into *Handy Andy*, *The Shaughraun*, *The Shadow and the Glen*, and *The Tailor and Antsy*. In the latter work by Eric Cross a wake is staged for the benefit of visitors who are completely taken in until the "corpse" discovers he's not been given his share of the whiskey. A potent restorative in *Finnegans Wake*, *usique beatha* (literally "water of life") performs a similar function in many humorous tales.

Indeed, the Irish sense of the macabre seems directly linked to their acute consciousness of death, "the stone in the midst of all." That stone is literally present, for their landscape is visibly marked by cairns, monoliths, great stone monuments to the dead of prehistoric times. With the coming of Christianity there was naturally an emphasis on the brevity of this life, but in Ireland that emphasis was intensified by the tragic effects of war and colonization. After centuries marked by continuing failure to expel the British despite open rebellion and widespread social upheaval, political martyrdom became a way of keeping the cause of independence alive.

As we have seen, Joyce, O'Casey, and Behan turned their

keenest satire against Irish nationalists who embraced the "myth of sacrifice." In all cases we find the specific use of the macabre to expose a truth too often disguised by a flamboyant posture and rhetoric. Thus in *The Plough and the Stars* Mrs. Gogan taunts Peter who likes to parade in a ceremonial green uniform complete with sabre and plume:

> . . . Th' loveliest part of th' dress, I think, is th' ostrichess plume . . . When yous are goin' along, an' I see them wavin' an' noddin' an waggin', I seem to be lookin' at each of you hangin' at th' end of a rope, your eyes bulgin' an' your legs twistin' and jerkin', gaspin' for breath while yous are tryin' to die for Ireland!
> (Act 2)

In *The Hostage* when the mad Monsewer declares his readiness to be martyred, the response is characteristic:

> *Pat.* Let's hope it would be a fine day for you.
> *Meg.* Or you wouldn't get the crowd.
> (Act 1)

The spectacle is both comical and horrible as the "hero" is reduced to a buffoon willing to forfeit his life to win applause.

It might be useful at this point to discuss the difference between macabre humor and black humor, which is often used to denote a quality that is mordant, pessimistic, verging on the absurd. Max Schultz uses the term specifically to refer to American literature of the sixties in which black humor is the response to a world devoid of intrinsic values. In such a world there is "a shift in perspective from the self and its ability to create a moral ambience to emphasis on all the moving forces of life which converge collectively upon the individual." In the face of a bewildering series of ultimately meaningless choices, the self becomes "chimerical," cause and effect break down, as does the consanguinity of relationship and the consecutiveness of history. He goes on to say that in black humor there is no individual release or social reconciliation as there is in traditional comedy, that man is instead condemned to a pointless journey with death as the only true destination.[7]

In the literature we have discussed, traditional values are, if anything, confirmed by circumstances, and while the comic figure may avoid moral responsibilities, there is always someone else, a Juno or a Stephen Dedalus, to accept them. The protagonist of *At Swim-Two-Birds* does experience modern Dublin as a diminished world in which family, religion, art, education have little vitality, but his personal estrangement takes on significance because of his relation to Gaelic culture. It seems to me, however, that Shultz's definition might well apply to *Murphy*, a novel in which the hectic circuit of mechanical action is altogether meaningless, and our solipsistic philosopher is resigned to a "long slide back to the womb." Unlike the other comic characters, Murphy does not resist fate; he is indifferent to the world of "the nothing new." Here there is not so much a "bewildering" range of "trackless choices," as a precise numerical set in which one route is very much like the other, tedious rather than frightening.

The macabre laugh is sounded at Murphy's wake, where the birthmark on his bare burnt buttock is viewed by "17 eyes" and later when "body, mind and soul" are scattered over a barroom floor. Death in the macabre tends to be ludicrous, it is never undercut by sentimentality or pathos as in *Lolita*, *Something Happened*, or *Slaughterhouse-Five*. In *Murphy*, as in *The Plough and the Stars* and *The Hostage*, there is, moreover, a double perspective: that of the character who courts death, whether out of malaise or romantic idealism, and the observers who view him as a comical object. The cutting edge of the macabre is the latter prespective. It is a quality that is becoming rare in contemporary Irish literature.

Much of the finest writing — fiction, drama, poetry — in Ireland today is Northern in theme and inspiration, and the dominant tone is tragic. There have been too many victims, too many brutal injuries on both sides. And whatever one's political perspective, it is not humanly possible to think of the H Block prisoners starving themselves in the old Republican style as "comical objects."

This shift in sensibility is clearly expressed in "Proxopera," a superb story by Benedict Kiely in which the clown has put on the faceless mask of a modern gunman. In the course of the narrative, which continually weaves together the past and present, myth and history of a divided people, the clown like the devil is recognized by his feet. For Binchey, a retired schoolmaster who is being forced to drive a car full of explosives into the streets of his town, images of gaiety and innocence are perverted. A laughing boy has become a madman. The Black Pig has reemerged as a prophecy of terror and destruction. A humorous song about a drunken adventure becomes a grotesque counterpoint to real acts of violence.

The comic sense depends on change; it is dynamic, open-ended, expressing "the felt rhythm of life."[8] A historic conflict that appears to be working its way to a bitter, fated conclusion is the essence of tragedy. "Proxopera" is not wholly tragic, however, for the very reason that the rhythm of life does reestablish itself in the rich, unifying memory of Binchey, who chooses finally to resist the gunmen. As a result his son is injured and his home is burned, but it is not entirely destroyed. The story closes with a resonant image of the beloved home first perceived by Binchey as a young boy. That image reflects an optimism that has survived centuries of oppression because of an ability to reach beyond the limits of time and place. Not the "stone," but the "living stream" is remembered:

> . . . through a gap in the reeds he looks, as he waits for the perch, across the water at the white house. Reeds make one frame for the picture. Beech trees, set back from the avenue that leads up to the house, make another. . . . And the most beautiful thing of all, cutting across a corner of the lawn, a small brook tumbling down to join the lake. To have your own stream on your own lawn is the height of everything.[9]

Notes

Part 1 — Introduction

1. The terms "Hiberno-English" and "Anglo-Irish" are also used. For additional information, see Diarmaid Ó Muirithe, ed., *The English Language in Ireland* (Dublin: Mercier, 1977), P.W. Joyce, *English As We Speak It in Ireland* (Dublin: Gill, 1910), and Seán De Fréine, *The Great Silence* (Mercier: Dublin, 1978).

2. *Gaelic* also includes Scottish Gaelic and Manx. The terms *Gaelic* and *Irish* are often used interchangeably, particularly to emphasize the older native culture.

3. For an excellent account of this period, see David Beers Quinn, *The Elizabethans and the Irish* (New York: Cornell Univ. Press, 1966).

4. "Metre and Movement in Anglo-Irish Verse," *Irish University Review*, 8 (Autumn 1978), 158–160.

5. Desmond Fennell, "The Irish Language Movement: Its Achievements and Its Failures," *20th Century Studies* (Nov. 1970), 75.

6. Introduction, *Tales of Ireland* (Dublin: Curry, 1834), x.

7. See Northrop Frye, "The Argument of Comedy," *Theories of Comedy*, ed. Paul Lauter (New York: Anchor, 1964), 450–460.

1. The Rustic Clown or Fool

1. "Laughter in Ireland," 1916, Ms., Columbia University, New York, 6.

2. Ibid., 7. When the novel was republished in 1945, Sean O'Faolain called it a "classic of Irish humour," noting that it had helped to establish the picture of the "light hearted, devil-may-care, hot tempered, amiable Irishman." See *Adventures of Handy Andy*, ed. and foreword by Sean O'Faolain (Dublin: Parkside Press, 1945).

3. Lover published a collection of folk tales, *Legends and Stories of Ireland*, in 1831.

4. As quoted by Bayle Bernard, *The Life of Samuel Lover* (New York: Appleton, 1874), 201.

5. An analysis of ethnocentric theories regarding the Irish may be found in Lewis Curtis, *Anglo-Saxons and Celts* (Bridgeport, Conn.: Univ. of Bridgeport, 1968). See, in particular, "The Importance of Being Paddy," 49–65.

6. An excellent source on this subject is Thomas Flanagan, *The Irish Novelists, 1800-1850* (New York: Columbia Univ. Press, 1959).

7. *The Fool* (New York: Farrar and Rinehart, 1935), 317.

8. W. J. Lawrence, *Speeding Up Shakespeare* (London: Argonaut, 1937), 144 158.

9. Michael MacDonagh, *Irish Life and Character* (London: Hodder and Stoughton, 1898), 88.

10. A study on Victorian caricatures of the Irish may be found in Lewis Curtis, *Apes and Angels* (Washington: Smithsonian Institute, 1971).

11. *Language and Literature in Society* (Chicago: Univ. of Chicago Press, 1953), 183-186.

12. *Handy Andy* (London: Dent, 1910), 358.

13. Patrick Kennedy, *Irish Fireside Folktales*, ed. Schulenburg (Dublin: Mercier, 1976), 116-124. See also "Fool Tom and His Brother Jack, 175-176, "The Farmer and His Servant," 178-180, and "Donald and His Neighbors," 184-186 in *Béaloideas*, Vol. 10 (1940). These Royal Hibernian Tales are among the most widely circulated tales about fools.

14. *Visions and Beliefs* (New York: Putnam, 1920), 196.

15. Ibid., 199.

16. *Some Experiences of an Irish R.M.* (London: Longmans, Green, 1899); *Further Experiences of an Irish R.M.* (London: Longmans, Green, 1908); *In Mr. Knox's Country* (London: Longmans, Green, 1915). The latter is much inferior to the first two collections.

17. The term *Celt* is properly indicative of language rather than race and refers to Scottish Gaelic, Breton, Manx, Welsh and Irish. Arnold's racial theories were persistently associated with the Irish, however.

18. In *Lectures and Essays in Criticism*, ed. R.H. Super. (Michigan: Univ. of Michigan, 1962), pp. 291-395. This view was echoed by the prominent Celtic scholar, Kuno Meyer: "I look on them . . . precisely as we Germans regard the Poles, a people only fit for poetry, rhetoric and sedition." As quoted in the *Irish Times*, Jan. 10, 1940, 4. Rept. Jan. 10, 1915.

19. *The Irish Cousins* (London: Heinemann, 1970), 92-96.

20. *Experiences of an Irish R.M.* (London: Dent, 1970), 51.

21. Ibid., 316.

22. "Matthew Arnold and the Celtic Revival," in *Perspectives of Criticism*, Vol. 20, ed. Harry Levin (Cambridge: Harvard Univ. Press, 1950), 197-221.

23. *Some Experiences of an Irish R.M.*, 68.

24. *The Irish Cousins*, 92-96.

25. *Some Experiences of an Irish R.M.*, 313-314.

26. Ibid., 212.

27. Ibid., 136.

28. *Our Irish Theatre* (Hertfordshire: Colin Smythe, 1972), 20.

29. Ibid., 52-53.

30. *Lady Gregory* (New York: Harcourt, Brace, 1961), 74.

31. *Our Irish Theatre*, 53.

32. "Laughter in Ireland," 1.

33. *The Irish Comic Tradition* (Oxford: Oxford Univ. Press. 1969), 182-209.

34. "Conversation in Ireland," Ms. No. 65B2294, n.d., N.Y. Public Library, 1.

35. *Seven Short Plays* (New York: Putnam, 1909), 207.

36. Ibid., 160.

37. Attributed to the poet and novelist, James Stephens.

38. The Irish clown also has a long history in American fiction and drama, but that is outside the realm of this study.

2. The Rogue

1. The full title is *A Genuine History of the Most Notorious Irish Highwaymen, Tories and Rapparees* (Wilmington: Borsal and Niles, 1799). I have also consulted John J. Marshall, *Irish Tories, Rapparees and Robbers* (Dungannon, 1927); the Windele Papers, Vol. 2, National Library, Dublin; J. P. Prendergast, *Ireland from the Restoration to the Revolution*; William Lecky, *A History of Ireland in the Eighteenth Century*, Vol. 1; and Sean O'Sullivan, *Legends from Ireland* (London: Batsford, 1977).

2. *A History of Ireland in the Eighteenth Century*, Vol. 1 (London, 1892; rpt. New York: AMS, 1969), 355.

3. Ibid., 358-359.

4. O'Hanlon was originally called a "tory;" the term *rapparee* did not come into general use until after the revolution and the rise of the English political party designated "tories." *Rapparee* refers literally to a "half pike" or broken beam carried as a weapon.

5. *Rogues and Rapparees*, 7-35.

6. Ibid., 38.

7. Ibid., 41.

8. In *Miscellanies*, II (Boston: Fields, Osgood, 1869), 370-380. For the original version, see JRSAI, 4 (1856) 53-60.

9. "The Irish Hero," *Nineteenth Century Fiction*, 21 (Sept. 1966), 109-130.

10. That is, Fion MacCumhaill. The text offers the most common English spelling.

11. "The Rageous Ossean," *Modern Drama*, 4 (Dec. 1961), 268-291. See also, *The Irish Comic Tradition*, 32-33.

12. For an excellent survey of this material, see James John MacKillop, "The Myth of Finn MacCool in English," Diss., Syracuse

University, 1975. I am particularly indebted to Chapter 4, 233-312. See also *Bealoideas*, 34 (1966), 106-133 and *The Irish Comic Tradition*, 19-23.

13. In *Tales and Sketches of the Irish Peasantry* (Dublin: Duffy, 1854), 97-112.

14. James MacKillop takes this position in "Finn MacCool: The Hero and the Anti-Hero in Irish Folk Tradition," *Views of the Irish Peasantry 1800-1916*, ed. Casey and Rhodes (Conn.: Archon, 1977), 86-106.

15. In Samuel Lover, *Legends and Stories of Ireland* (Dublin: Wakeman, 1831). This is a literary version of the folktale commonly known as "Hudden and Dudden."

16. In William B. Yeats, *Irish Fairy and Folk Tales* (New York: Mod. Lib., n.d.), 285-299.

17. *The Works of William Carleton*, III (New York: Collier, 1882), 1045. All quotations are from this source. Phelim's trick of feigned idiocy is one found in many folktales. Of particular interest are those having to do with poets or "playboys" who take advantage of the assumption that a poorly dressed Irish speaker lacks intelligence.

18. The term "blarney" may derive from the following incident described by John J. Marshall in *Popular Rhymes and Sayings of Ireland*, 2nd series (Dungannon: Tyrone, 1926). In 1602 Cormac MacCarthy was accused of treasonable practices which he denied. When asked to yield his castle at Blarney to show good faith, he kept putting it off until "blarney talk" became a local proverb. Marshall attributes its widespread usage to the Cork wits of the early nineteenth century, notably Prout, Maginn, and Croker.

19. In this respect one might say that Phelim is related to the *gean-canach*, that is, a *love talker*, in folklore a leprechaun who personifies love and idleness. He was reputed to lurk around hedges on the lookout for innocent milk maids. Those whose lives and fortunes were ruined through love were said to have met the *gean-canach*. See William B. Yeats, *Irish Fairy and Folk Tales*, 348.

3. The Stage Irishman

1. Maurice Bourgeois, *John Millington Synge and the Irish Theatre* (London: Constable, 1913), 109-110.

2. *The Stage Irishman* (London: Longmans, Green, 1937), 142-154. See also J.O. Bartley, *Teague, Shenkin and Sawney* (Cork: Cork Univ. Press, 1954). Bartley has noted that the Irish constitute by far the largest number of nationalized characters in English drama and are usually intended to be humorous.

3. James Malcolm Nelson comes to a similar conclusion in "From

Rory and Paddy to Boucicault's Myles, Shaun and Conn: The Irishman on the London Stage, 1830-1860," *Éire-Ireland* 13 (Fall, 1978), 79-105.

4. See, for example, Ned Lebow, "British Images of Poverty in Pre-Famine Ireland," in *Views of the Irish Peasantry*, ed. Daniel Casey and Robert Rhodes, 57-85.

5. A point made by David Krause, "The Theatre of Dion Boucicault," in *The Dolmen Boucicault* (Dublin, 1964). This essay contains an excellent account of Boucicault's life and influence to which I am indebted. See also *The Profane Book of Irish Comedy* (Ithaca: Cornell Univ. Press, 1982), 181-195. Krause argues that Boucicault's "rogue-hero" is the "combined braggart-warrior and parasite-slave of Greek and Roman comedy."

6. As quoted by David Krause, "The Theatre of Dion Boucicault," 32.

7. Of *The Shaughraun* Joseph Holloway made the following evaluation, which reveals much about the Irish audience at the turn of the century: "It is a perfectly constructed work of its kind, and not a line of the dialogue seems superfluous, or out of place, perhaps the 'wake scene' jars a trifle, but all else could not be improved upon — the blending of humour, pathos, villainy, love-making and exciting situations is done with such a practiced hand as to glide impreceptibly into one another, and form a complete and most entertaining whole." Ms. 4434, p. 13. National Library, Dublin.

8. It is possible that Myles's name and some of his traits derive ultimately from Cahier Na Capul, the legendary horsethief. There is a character of the same name in *The Collegians* by Gerald Griffin. I would also like to point out that there are some similarities between *The Shaughraun* and Carleton's "Three Wishes." Both deal with rogues, both contain the song "Brian O'Lynn", and Billy Dawson also speaks of being "on the shaughraun." William Carleton did actually accuse Boucicault of plagiarizing the title of his popular novel *Willie Reilly and his Dear Cooleen Bawn*.

9. Shaun the Post appears in *Finnegans Wake* delivering the famous letter, which he is unable to read.

10. *The American Language*, 1st ed., (New York: Knopf, 1919), 93.

11. "For a time, to call somebody Harvey Duff was like calling him a traitor. . . ." The name "survived as synonymous with policeman in the street rhymes of Dublin children." Brendan Behan used to shout: "Harvey Duff, don't catch me/catch the fellow behind the tree." From a note by Georges-Denis Zimmermann in *Songs of Irish Rebellion* (Dublin: Figgis, 1967), 274.

12. People in the West again come close to starvation after widespread crop failure in 1879. The terrible privation suffered by the very

young and very old was described as "barbarous" by public health officials.
From the *Proceedings of the Dublin Mansion House*, 1880.

13. "British Images of Poverty in Pre-Famine Ireland."

14. Ms. 4434, p. 9. National Library, Dublin.

4. The Comic Hero

1. New York: Viking, 1972, 189.

2. *The Works of William Carleton*, III (New York: P.F. Collier, 1882), 649.

3. Ibid., 645.

4. A secret society organized primarily to inflict damage on landlords and bailiffs.

5. *The Works of William Carleton*, *III*, 653.

6. Some of Carleton's work probably contributed to the unfortunate reputation of the Irish poor during the nineteenth century. However, the problem is too complex to treat adequately here.

7. *The Works of William Carleton*, *III*, 641.

8. Ibid., 645.

9. Ibid., 977–1033. All subsequent references to this story are to this edition, with one exception noted below.

10. David O'Donoghue, *The Life of William Carleton*, *I* (London: Downey, 1896), 96.

11. For an account of the bardic schools and the courts of poetry, see Daniel Corkery, *The Hidden Ireland* (1924; rpt. Dublin: Gill, 1967). See also Louis Cullen, "The Hidden Ireland: Re-assessment of a Concept," *Studia Hibernica* (1967) 1–47.

12. *The Irish Comic Tradition* See in particular, "Fantasy in Irish Humour and Ribaldry," 11–46.

13. Robert Wolff, *William Carleton: Irish Peasant Novelist* (New York: Garland, 1980), 50. This tale does not appear in the original version, but in version 2; it was excised from version 3 as anti-Protestant. The Garland edition, now unfortunately out of print, provides textual variations. See also, the 1973 Mercier Press edition, 9–16. A study of Carleton's revisions of *Traits and Stories* would provide valuable insights.

14. "The Hedge School" in *The Works of William Carleton*, *III*, 834. See also Patrick Dowling, *The Hedge Schools of Ireland* (London: Longmans Green, 1935).

15. *William Carleton: Irish Peasant Novelist*, 49–52.

16. *The Irish Novelists 1800–1850*, 289.

17. After seeing *The Shaughraun* in 1904, John Synge observed that the Abbey Theatre could learn a lesson or two from Boucicault. He saw vitality in Boucicault's work and "good acting comedy." As quoted by

David Krause, "The Theatre of Dion Boucicault," 60. I can find no evidence that Synge knew Carleton's work, though Yeats did.

18. *The Complete Works* (New York: Random House, 1935), 494.

19. See, for example, Norman Podhoretz, "Synge's Playboy: Morality and the Hero," in *Twentieth Century Interpretations*, ed. Thomas Whitaker (New Jersey: Prentice-Hall, 1969), 68-74.

20. See Seán Ó Súilleabháin, *Irish Wake Amusements* (Dublin: Mercier, 1976), 92-98.

21. "The Rageous Ossean," *Modern Drama*, 4 (Dec. 1961) 268-291. See also *The Profane Book of Irish Comedy*, Chapter 2.

22. In Yeats's sense of the mask: "All joyous or creative life is a rebirth as something not oneself, something which has no memory and is created in a moment and perpetually renewed." For an analysis of Yeats's concept, see Richard Ellmann, *Yeats: The Man and the Masks*, in particular, 171-176.

23. "The Aran Islands," *The Complete Works*, 370.

24. Preface to *The Playboy of the Western World*.

25. Alan Bliss, "The Language of Synge", *J.M. Synge Centenary Papers* (Dublin: Dolmen, 1972, 51.

26. John Garvin, "The Anglo-Irish Idiom in the Works of Major Irish Writers," *The English Language in Ireland*, ed. Diarmaid Ó Muirithe (Dublin: Mercier, 1977), 101.

27. "In West Kerry," *The Complete Works*, 511.

28. Wylie Sypher, *Comedy* (New York: Doubleday, 1956), 217.

29. *John Millington Synge and the Irish Theatre* (London: Constable, 1913), 204.

Part 2 — Introduction

1. "Satirists and Enchanters in Early Irish Literature" in *Studies in the History of Religions* ed. David Lyon and George Moore (New York: Macmillan 1912), 98-99.

2. *The Irish Comic Tradition*, 114-115. Mercier bases his translation partly on Kuno Meyer's *Bruchstücke der älteren Lyrik Irlands*.

3. *The Siege of Howth*, trans. Whitley Stokes, *RC* VIII (1887), 49. Quoted by Robert Elliott, *The Power of Satire* (Princeton: Princeton Univ. Press, 1960), 30. The latter contains a valuable discussion of early Irish satire, 18-48.

4. "Satirists and Enchanters in Early Irish Literature," 106.

5. *The Táin*, trans. Thomas Kinsella (London: Oxford Univ. Press, 1977), 126.

6. *Tromdámh Guaire*, ed. Owen Connellan, *Transactions of the Ossianic Society* V (Dublin: O'Daly, 1860).

7. A point Robin Flower emphasizes in *The Irish Tradition* (Oxford: Clarendon, 1966), 24-66.

8. "Satirists and Enchanters in Early Irish Literature," 110.

9. *The Hidden Ireland* (Dublin: Gill and Macmillan), 83.

10. David Beers Quinn, *The Elizabethans and the Irish* (New York: Cornell Univ. Press, 1966), 126.

11. Seán Ó Súilleabháin, *Diarmuid na Bolgaighe agus a Chómhursain* (Dublin an Gúm, 1937), 10-11. Trans. Dáithi Ó hÓgáin, " The Visionary Voice," *Irish University Review* 9 (Spring 1979), 45.

12. *Poets and Dreamers* (New York: Oxford, 1974), 16-17.

13. See, for example, Thomas Kinsella, "The Irish Writer" in *Davis, Mangan, Ferguson?* (Dublin: Dolmen, 1970) 57-58.

14. *The Irish Comic Tradition*, 105-127.

15. Ibid., 178.

16. As quoted by Alan Warner, *Clay is the Word* (Dublin: Dolmen, 1973), 67.

17. *The Best of Myles*, ed. Kevin O Nolan (New York: Walker, 1968), 235.

18. Darcy O'Brien, *Patrick Kavanagh* (Lewisburg: Bucknell Univ. Press, 1975), 64.

19. "Patrick Kavanagh," in *Irish Poets in English*, ed. Sean Lucy (Dublin: Mercier, 1973), 164.

5. James Joyce and Buck Mulligan

1. "James Clarence Mangan," in *The Critical Writings of James Joyce*, eds. Ellsworth Mason and Richard Ellmann (New York: Viking, 1959), 184-185.

2. "The Day of the Rabblement, *The Critical Writings of James Joyce*, eds. Mason and Ellmann. 71.

3. *Ulysses* (Middlesex, Eng.: Penguin, 1960), 292. All references are to this edition.

4. Martin Grotjahn, *Beyond Laughter* (New York: McGraw-Hill, 1970), 45. The term refers to someone who uses language as a weapon and who displays "a strong erotization of word and language."

5. Edward MacLysaght, *Irish Families* (Dublin: Hodges, Figgis, 1957), 233.

6. E. L. Murphy, "The Hell Fire" The Walsh Ms. 11664, National Library, Dublin. See also Joseph Hammond, *"The Hellfire Club* (Dublin: Duffey, n.d.) and Max Caulfield, *The Irish Mystique* (New Jersey: Prentice-Hall, 1973), 57-76. Maurice Craig claims that there is no solid evidence that the club even met in Montpelier. See *Dublin 1660-1860* (Dublin: Hodges, Figgis, 1952), 101.

7. James H. Maddox has made some of these connections in *Joyce's "Ulysses" and the Assault Upon Character* (New Jersey: Rutgers, 1978).

8. Ellen Moers, *The Dandy* (New York: Viking, 1960), 297.

9. "Oscar Wilde: The Poet of 'Salome,' " in *The Critical Writings of James Joyce*, eds. Mason and Ellmann, 202.

10. St. Stephen's Day in Ireland was traditionally when mummers made their appearance carrying a wren. For a more specific account, see Alan Gailey, *Irish Folk Drama* (Cork: Mercier, 1969).

11. For a good general analysis of this chapter see Bernard Benstock, "Telemachus" in *James Joyce's "Ulysses,"* eds. Clive Hart and David Hayman, 1-16.

12. *Joyce's "Ulysses" and the Assault Upon Character*, 24.

13. "Laughter," in *Comedy*, intro. Wylie Sypher (New York: Doubleday, 1956), 156.

14. For an excellent discussion of the fundamental concepts in this chapter, see Robert Kellogg, "Scylla and Charybdis" in *James Joyce's "Ulysses,"* eds. Clive Hart and David Hayman, 147-180.

15. S. L. Goldberg explores this idea in *The Classical Temper* (London: Chatto and Windus, 1961), 115-116.

16. *Swift* (London: Nonesuch, 1949), 437.

17. Phyllis Greenacre, "Jonathan Swift," in *Art and Psychoanalysis*, ed. William Philips (Cleveland: World Publishing, 1963), 128.

18. As Joyce intended. See Frank Budgen, *James Joyce and the Making of "Ulysses"* (Indiana: Indiana Univ. Press, 1967). 116.

19. "Nestor" in *James Joyce's "Ulysses,"* eds. Clive Hart and David Hayman, 17-28.

20. *Common Sense and Beyond* (New York: Random House, 1968), 160.

21. *James Joyce* (New York: Oxford Univ. Press, 1959), 102-133. For a dissenting opinion, see Bonnie K. Scott, "John Eglinton: A Model for Joyce's Individualism," *Éire-Ireland*, 12 (Summer 1975), 347-357.

22. James MacKillop estimates that there are approximately two-hundred Irishisms (lone words, puns, place names, and direct translations) in *Ulysses* and 5,500 in *Finnegans Wake*. " 'Beurla on It': Yeats, Joyce and the Irish Language" in *Eire-Ireland*, 15 (Spring 1980), 145.

6. Samuel Beckett's *Murphy*

1. Lady Gregory should also be given credit for this statement, see *Our Irish Theatre*, 20.

2. "The Geography of Irish Fiction" in *The Irish Novel of Our Time*, ed. Patrick Rafroidi and Maurice Harmon (Pub. De L'Universite De Lille, III, 1975-76), 89-92.

3. "Beckett's *Murphy*: a Cartesian Novel," *Perspective*, 2 (Autumn 1959), 156-165. See also, Hugh Kenner, *Samuel Beckett* (Berkeley: Univ. of California, 1968), 83-91.

4. For a discussion of the "Joycean Shadows" on *Murphy*, see Barbara Gluck, *Beckett and Joyce* (Lewisburg, Bucknell Univ. Press, 1979). For an analysis of some of the intellectual and psychological problems being worked out through the structure and characterization, see J.C.C. Mays, "Mythologized Presences: *Murphy* in its Time," in *Myth and Reality in Irish Literature*, ed. Joseph Ronsley (Ontario: Wilfrid Laurier Univ. Press, 1977), 197-218.

5. For an interesting analysis of Beckett's use of astronomy, see Sighle Kennedy, *Murphy's Bed* (Lewisburg: Bucknell Univ. Press, 1971).

6. *Murphy* (New York: Grove, 1957), 252-253. All references are to this edition.

7. "The Beckett Hero" in *Samuel Beckett*, ed. Martin Esslin (New York: Prentice Hall 1965), 37-51.

8. Vivian Mercier has noted that Beckett rarely uses Irish dialect, and then it is usually relegated to working-class characters. See *Beckett/Beckett* (New York: Oxford, 1977), 42. For a more extensive study of the characters, see Robert Harrison, *Samuel Beckett's "Murphy"* (Athens: Univ. of Georgia, 1968).

9. Ruby Cohn provides a useful analysis in *Samuel Beckett: The Comic Gambit* (New Jersey: Rutgers Univ. Press, 1962), 45-64.

10. *The Irish Comic Tradition*, 53-56.

11. *Samuel Beckett*, 57.

12. For a discussion of the poetry, see Lawrence Harvey, *Samuel Beckett: Poet and Critic* (New Jersey: Princeton Univ. Press, 1970), 183-220. For a general account of Beckett's life and character see Deirdre Bair, *Samuel Beckett* (New York: Harcourt Bruce, 1978).

13. *Samuel Beckett: Poet and Critic*, 196.

14. As quoted in *Samuel Beckett: Poet and Critic*, 249.

7. Flann O'Brien and Mad Sweeney

1. Anne Clissmann's *Flann O'Brien* (New York: Barnes and Noble, 1975) contains an account of his publishing history as well as a general account of his life to which I am indebted.

2. For a discussion of O'Brien's relation to Joyce see *Flann O'Brien*, 76-150 and J.C.C. Mays, "Brian O'Nolan and Joyce On Art and on Life," *James Joyce Quarterly*, 11 (Spring 1974), 238-256.

3. Breandan O'Conaire discusses this point in "Flann O'Brien, *An Beál Bocht* and other Irish Matters," *Irish University Review*, 3 (August 1973), 121-140.

4. Cited by Anne Clissmann, *Flann O'Brien*, 238.

5. Jack White, "Myles, Flann and Brian," in *Portraits of Brian O'Nolan*, ed. Timothy O'Keefe (London: Martin Brian and O'Keefe, 1973), 73.

6. *The Best of Myles*, 234.

7. At its most acerbic in "A Bash in the Tunnel' where Joyce is pictured as a meanspirited, fugitive drunk. "See *A Bash in the Tunnel*, ed. John Ryan (Brighton: Clifton, 1970), 15–20.

8. *Flann O'Brien*, 115.

9. For an analysis of the structure as well as a radically different interpretation of the tone, see Rugh apRoberts, "*At Swim-Two-Birds* and the Novel as Self-Evident Sham," *Éire-Ireland*, 6 (Summer 1971), 76–96.

10. *At Swim-Two-Birds* (New York: Viking, 1968), 253. All references are to this edition.

11. *Buile Suibne*, trans. J. O'Keeffe, *Irish Texts Society*, 12 (London: Nutt, 1913). For a discussion of the Merlin theme, see James Carney, *Studies in Irish Literature and History* (Dublin Institute for Advanced Studies, 1955) 129–164.

12. *The Divided Self* (Middlesex: Pelican, 1966) 85–88.

13. Ibid., 85.

14. "Brian O'Nolan and Joyce on Art and on Life," 242.

8. Patrick Kavanagh and Tarry Flynn

1. "Self Portrait" in *Collected Pruse* (London: MacGibbon and Kee, 1967), 14–15.

2. As quoted by Darcy O'Brien, *Patrick Kavanagh* (Lewisburg: Bucknell Univ. Press, 1975), 52.

3. *Kavanagh's Weekly*, 24 May 1952, 7.

4. Brendan Kennelly, "Patrick Kavanagh," in *Irish Poets in English*, 181–182.

5. *Tarry Flynn* (Middlesex: Penguin, 1978), 62. All subsequent references are to this edition.

6. *The Green Fool* (Middlesex: Penguin, 1977), 63.

7. *The Great Hunger* (Dublin: Cuala, 1942).

8. *Clay is the Word*, 54.

9. "The Irish Tradition" in *Collected Pruse*, 233.

10. Enid Welsford, *The Fool*, 100–103.

11. *Aislinge Meic Conglinne*, trans. and ed. Kuno Meyer (London: Nutt, 1892).

12. See, for example, Ms. 635, pp. 113–115 and pp. 84–90, Folklore Collection, University College, Dublin.

13. *The Hidden Ireland*, 163.

14. *The Green Fool*, 246, 10.

9. The Paycocks of Sean O'Casey

1. For the historic background, see Desmond Ryan, *The Rising* (Dublin, 1949).

2. C. Desmond Greaves questions some of these generally accepted facts in *Sean O'Casey: Politics and Art* (New Jersey: Humanities Press, 1979), 13-34.

3. O'Casey played the role of Fr. Dolan in *The Shaughraun* at the Mechanics Theatre. See *Inishfallen Fare Thee Well* (New York: Macmillan, 1949), 251.

4. In *The Profane Book of Irish Comedy* David Krause offers an illuminating discussion of how the structural inversion of Irish comedy is related to its central themes.

5. In fact, he was severely criticized for "exploiting" the Dublin poor in the "Anglo-Irish tradition" by offering "diversions" and "Handy Andy incidents." *Inishfallen Fare Thee Well*, 246-248.

6. Raymond Williams explores the use of rhetoric as a mode of evasion. "Sean O'Casey," in *Sean O'Casey*, ed. Thomas Kilroy (New Jersey: Prentice-Hall, 1975), 53-60.

7. C. Desmond Greaves suggests that O'Casey's treatment of the insurgents was at least partly motivated by a need to justify the fact that he had not taken part in the revolution. See *Sean O'Casey: Politics and Art*, 65-109.

8. That O'Casey was much more sympathetic to Pearse than this scene suggests is discussed by Raymond Porter, "O'Casey and Pearse," *The O'Casey Review* 2 (Spring 1976), 104-114.

9. Saros Cowasjee considers Rosie an O'Casey heroine because of her boldness and realism. *Sean O'Casey* (London: Oliver and Boyd, 1963), 71.

10. Bernard Benstock sees the "paycock" as a "totem of spiritual paralysis," who tries to imitate his betters, the "bonvivants of the aristocracy." *Paycocks and Others: Sean O'Casey's World* (Dublin: Gill and Macmillan, 1976), 10-11.

11. David Krause speaks of the "native vigour and shrewdness" of such characters, who prevent the plays from lapsing into melancholy and pessimism. For a sound discussion of the overall structure and themes of these two major plays, see *O'Casey: The Man and His Work* (London: MacGibbon and Kee, 1960), 47-93. See also *The Profane Book of Irish Comedy*, chapters 3 and 5 in which Krause emphasizes O'Casey's comic assault on the "national pieties."

12. Ronald Ayling discusses how O'Casey enriched the texture of his

plays with a "diverse selection of quotations, references and clichés drawn from both popular and learned sources," often for satiric and ironic effect. "Sean O'Casey's Dublin Trilogy" in *Sean O'Casey*, ed. Thomas Kilroy, 77-89.

13. *Sean O'Casey: The Man and His Work*, 77-78.

14. *Beyond Laughter* (New York: McGraw-Hill, 1970), 92-97.

10. A Borstal Boy

1. Some critics, however, do argue that Behan's position is abrusdist. See, for example, Ted Boyle, *Brendan Behan* (New York: Twayne, 1969).

2. As quoted by Ulick O'Connor, *Brendan Behan* (New York: Grove, 1973), 193. For an account of the Irish version as well as a description of the original Littlewood production, see 192-207. See also Colbert Kearney, *The Writings of Brendan Behan* (New York: St. Martin's, 1977), 117-134.

3. Benedict Kiely offers the amusing observation that Monsewer is "one of Behan's visions of God." "That Old Triangle" in *The World of Brendan Behan*, ed. Sean McCann (New York: Twayne, 1966), 107.

4. For another perspective on the function of humor in these plays, see *The Profane Book of Irish Comedy*, 153-170.

5. Ulick O'Connor, *Brendan Behan*, 210.

6. *Borstal Boy* (New York: Knopf, 1959), 6. All references are to this edition.

7. *Brendan Behan*, 225-230.

8. *The Writings of Brendan Behan*, 46-61. Behan was the youngest writer represented in *Naubheársaiócht*, a collection of Irish poetry edited by Seán Ó Tuama in 1950.

9. Ibid., 51. Kearney also discusses the fact that *death* is a pervasive theme in Behan's poetry.

10. For a sympathetic view of this aspect of Behan's career, see Anthony Butler, "The Rebel" in *The World of Brendan Behan*, 44-58.

11. Ulick O'Connor comes to a similar conclusion. See *Brendan Behan*, 207.

Conclusion

1. *The Performing Self* (New York: Oxford Univ. Press, 1971), 102.

2. *The Instructions of King Cormac Mac Airt*, trans. Kuno Meyer (Dublin: Hodges, Figgis, 1909), 254.

3. *The Irish Comic Tradition*, 49-53. For a more comprehensive account, see Seán Ó Súillebháin, *Irish Wake Amusements*.

4. *Rural Life in Ireland* (London: Methuen, 1904), 115.

5. *The Life of Samuel Lover*, Vol. 1 (London: King, 1874), 75.

6. "The Last Playboy of the Western World," in *The World of Brendan Behan*, 93.

7. *Black Humor Fiction of The Sixties* (Ohio: Ohio Univ. Press, 1973), 7-8.

8. See Susanne Langer, "The Great Dramatic Forms: The Comic Rhythm," in *Theories of Comedy*, ed. Paul Lauter (New York: Doubleday, 1964), 497-522.

9. "Proxopera," in *The State of Ireland* (Boston: Godine, 1980), 389.

Selected Bibliography

Literature

Beckett, Samuel. *Murphy*. New York: Grove, 1957.

Behan, Brendan. *Borstal Boy*. New York: Knopf, 1959.

———. *The Quare Fellow and The Hostage*. New York: Grove, 1964.

Carleton, William. *Tales and Sketches of the Irish Peasantry*. Dublin: Duffy, 1854.

———. *The Works of William Carleton*. 4 Vols. New York: Collier, 1882.

Connellan, Owen, ed. *Tromdámh Guaire*. *Transactions of the Ossianic Society*, Vol 5. Dublin: O'Daly, 1860.

Cosgrave, John. *A Genuine History of the Most Notorious Irish Highwaymen, Tories and Rapparees*. Wilmington: Borsal and Niles, 1799.

Gregory, Lady Augusta. *Seven Short Plays*. New York: Putnam, 1909.

———. *Our Irish Theatre*. Hertfordshire: Colin Smythe, 1972.

———. *Poets and Dreamers*. New York: Oxford, 1974.

———. *Visions and Beliefs in the West of Ireland*. New York: Putnam, 1920.

Joyce, James. *Ulysses*. Middlesex: Penguin, 1976.

———. *A Portrait of the Artist as a Young Man*. New York: Viking, 1972.

Kavanagh, Patrick. *Collected Pruse*. London: MacGibbon and Kee, 1967.

———. *The Great Hunger*. Dublin: Cuala, 1942.

———. *The Green Fool*. Middlesex: Penguin, 1977.

———. *Tarry Flynn*. Middlesex: Penguin, 1978.

Kiely, Benedict. "Proxopera". In *The State of Ireland*. Boston: Godine, 1980.

Kinsella, Thomas, trans. *The Táin*. London: Oxford, 1977.

Krause, David, ed. *The Dolmen Boucicault*. Dublin: Dolmen, 1964.

Lover, Samuel. *Handy Andy*. 1842; rpt. London: Dent, 1910.

———. *Legends and Stories of Ireland*. Dublin: Wakeman, 1831.

———. *Rory O'More*. New York: Turner and Fisher, n.d.

Meyer, Kuno, trans. and ed. *Aislinge Meic Conglinne*. London: Nutt, 1892.

O'Brien, Flann. *At Swim-Two-Birds*. New York: Viking, 1968.

———. *The Poor Mouth*, trans. Patrick Power. London: Picador, 1978.

O'Casey, Sean. *Three Plays*. New York: St. Martin's Press, 1970.

O'Donoghue, David, ed. *The Life of William Carleton*, 2 Vols. Dublin: Downey, 1896.

O'Keeffe, J., trans. *Buile Suibne. Irish Texts Society*, Vol. 12. London: Nutt, 1913.

O'Nolan, Kevin, ed. *The Best of Myles*. New York: Walker, 1968.

Somerville and Ross. *Experiences of an Irish R. M.* London: Dent, 1970.

Synge, John M. *The Complete Works*. New York: Random House, c. 1935.

Cultural History and Criticism

Adams, Robert. *Common Sense and Beyond*. New York: Random House, 1968.

apRoberts, Ruth. "*At Swim-Two-Birds* and the Novel as Self-Evident Sham." *Éire-Ireland*, 6 (Summer 1971), 76-96.

Arnold, Matthew. *Lectures and Essays in Criticism*, ed. R. H. Super. Ann Arbor: Univ. of Michigan Press, 1962.

Arensberg, C. M. *The Irish Countryman*. New York: Smith, 1950.

Barnard, G.C. *Samuel Beckett: A New Approach*. New York: Dodd, Mead, 1970.

Bartley, J. O. *Teague, Shenkin and Sawney*. Cork: Cork Univ. Press, 1954.

Benstock, Bernard. "The Three Faces of Brian O'Nolan". *Éire-Ireland*, 3 (Autumn 1968), 51-65.

————. *Paycocks and Others: Sean O'Casey's World*. Dublin: Gill and Macmillan, 1976.

Bernard, Bayle. *The Life of Samuel Lover*. New York: Appleton, 1874.

Bourgeois, Maurice. *John Millington Synge and the Irish Theatre*. London: Constable, 1913.

Brown, Malcolm. *The Politics of Irish Literature*. Seattle: Univ. of Washington, 1973.

Budgen, Frank. *James Joyce and the Making of "Ulysses"*. Bloomington: Indiana University Press, 1960.

Bushrui, S.B., ed. *A Centenary Tribute to John M. Synge, 1871-1909*. New York: Barnes and Noble, 1972.

Casey, Daniel and Robert Rhodes, eds. *Views of the Irish Peasantry, 1800-1916*. Conn.: Archon, 1977.

Chandler, Frank. *The Literature of Roguery*, 2 Vols. Boston: Houghton, Mifflin, 1907.

Clissmann, Anne. *Flann O'Brien*. New York: Barnes and Noble, 1975.

Cohn, Ruby. *The Comic Gambit*. New Jersey: Rutgers, 1962.

Colby, Robert. "The Irish Hero." *Nineteenth Century Fiction*, 21 (Sept. 1966), 109-130.

Collis, Maurice. *Somerville and Ross*. London: Faber and Faber, 1968.

Corkery, Daniel. *The Hidden Ireland.* 1924; rpt. Dublin: Gill, 1967.

Cowasjie, Saros. *Sean O'Casey.* London: Oliver and Boyd, 1963.

Coxhead, Elizabeth. *Lady Gregory.* New York: Harcourt, Brace, 1961.

Cronin, John. *Somerville and Ross.* Lewisburg: Bucknell Univ. Press, 1972.

Cullen, L.M. "The Hidden Ireland: Re-Assessment of a Concept." *Studia Hibernia,* 9 (1969), 1-47.

Curtis, Lewis. *Apes and Angels.* Washington: Smithsonian, 1971.

———. *Anglo-Saxons and Celts.* Connecticut: Univ. of Bridgeport Press, 1968.

De Fréine, Seán. The Great Silence. Dublin: Mercier, 1965.

Donovan, Kathleen. "Good Old Pat: An Irish-American Stereotype in Decline." *Éire-Ireland,* 15 (Fall 1980), 6-14.

Dowling, Patrick. *The Hedge Schools of Ireland.* London: Longmans, Green, 1935.

Duggan, George. *The Stage Irishman.* London: Longmans, Green, 1937.

Duncan, Hugh. *Language and Literature in Society.* Chicago: Univ. of Chicago Press, 1953.

Ellis-Fermor, Una. *The Irish Dramatic Movement.* London: Methuen, 1964.

Ellmann, Richard and Ellsworth Mason eds., *The Critical Writings of James Joyce.* New York: Viking, 1959.

Esslin, Martin, ed. *Samuel Beckett.* New York: Prentice Hall, 1965.

Evans, Emyr Estyn. *Irish Folkways.* New York: Devin-Adair, 1957.

Fallis, Richard. *The Irish Renaissance.* New York: Syracuse, 1957.

Federman, Raymond. *Journey to Chaos.* California: Univ. of California Press, 1965.

Fennell, Desmond. "The Irish Language Movement." *20th Century Studies.* (Nov. 1970), 64-87.

Flanagan, Thomas. *The Irish Novelists, 1800-1850.* New York: Columbia Univ. Press, 1959.

Flower, Robin. *The Irish Tradition.* Oxford: Clarendon, 1966.

Gailey, Alan. *Irish Folk Drama.* Cork: Mercier, 1969.

Gluck, Barbara. *Beckett and Joyce.* Lewisberg: Bucknell Univ. Press, 1979.

Goldberg, S.L. *The Classical Temper.* London: Chatto and Windus, 1961.

Gorman, Herbert. *James Joyce.* New York: Rinehart, 1948.

Greaves, C. Desmond. *Sean O'Casey: Politics and Art.* New Jersey: Humanities, 1979.

Harmon, Maurice. "Cobwebs Before the Wind." In *Views of the Irish Peasantry, 1800-1916,* eds. Daniel Casey and Robert Rhodes, 129-159.

————, ed. *J. M. Synge Centenary Papers, 1971*. Dublin: Dolmen, 1972.

————. *Modern Irish Literature, 1800-1967*. Dublin: Dolmen, 1967.

Harrison, Robert. *Samuel Beckett's "Murphy."* Athens: Univ. of Georgia Press, 1968.

Hart, Clive and David Hayman, eds. *James Joyce's "Ulysses."* Berkeley: Univ. of California Press, 1974.

Harvey, Lawrence. *Samuel Beckett: Poet and Critic*. New Jersey: Princeton, 1970.

Hogan, Robert. *The Experiments of Sean O'Casey*. New York: St. Martin's, 1960.

———— and Michael O'Neill, eds. *Joseph Holloway's Abbey Theatre*. Carbondale: So. Illinois Univ. Press, 1967.

Jordan, John. "A World of Chassis." *University Review*, 1 (Spring 1955), 21-28.

Joyce, P. W. *English As We Speak It In Ireland*. Dublin: Gill, 1910.

Kearney, Colbert. *The Writings of Brendan Behan*. New York: St. Martin's, 1977.

Kelleher, John V. "Matthew Arnold and the Celtic Revival." In *Perspectives of Criticism*, Vol. 20, ed. Harry Levin. Boston: Harvard Univ. Press, 1950, 197-221.

Kennedy, Sighle. *Murphy's Bed*. Lewisburg: Bucknell Univ. Press, 1971.

Kennelly, Brendan. "Patrick Kavanagh." In *Irish Poets in English*, ed. Seán Lucy. Dublin: Mercier, 1973, 159-184.

Kenner, Hugh. *Dublin's Joyce*. Boston: Beacon, 1962.

————. *Samuel Beckett*. Berkeley: Univ. of California Press, 1968.

Kiely, Benedict. *Poor Scholar*. New York: Sheed and Ward, 1948.

Kilroy, Thomas, ed. *Sean O'Casey*. New Jersey: Prentice-Hall, 1975.

Kinsella, Thomas. "The Irish Writer." In *Davis, Mangan, Ferguson?* Dublin: Dolmen, 1970, 57-70.

Klein, A.M. "The Black Panther." *Accent*, 10 (Spring 1950), 139-155.

Knott, Eleanor and Gerard Murphy. *Early Irish Literature*. New York: Barnes and Noble, 1966.

Krans, Horatio. *Irish Life in Irish Fiction*. New York: Columbia Univ. Press, 1903.

Krause, David. *The Profane Book of Irish Comedy*. New York: Cornell, 1982.

————. "The Rageous Ossean." *Modern Drama*, 4 (Dec. 1961), 268-291.

————. *Sean O'Casey: The Man and His Work*. London: MacGibbon and Kee, 1960.

Lawrence, W.J. *Speeding Up Shakespeare*. London: Argonaut, 1937.

Lebow, Ned. "British Images of Poverty in Pre-Famine Ireland." In *Views of the Irish Peasantry*, eds. Daniel Casey and Robert Rhodes, pp. 57-85.

Le Fanu, W.R. *Seventy Years of Irish Life.* London: Arnold, 1907.

Leventhal, A.J. "The Beckett Hero." In *Samuel Beckett*, ed. Martin Esslin. New York: Prentice Hall, 1965, 37-51.

Lucy, Seán. *Irish Poets in English.* Dublin: Mercier, 1973.

————. "Metre and Movement in Anglo-Irish Verse." *Irish University Review*, 8 (Autumn 1978), 151-177.

Lyons, F.S.L. *Ireland Since the Famine.* New York: Scribners, 1971.

McCann, Sean. *The World of Brendan Behan.* New York: Twayne, 1966.

MacDonagh, Thomas. *Literature in Ireland.* Dublin: Talbot, 1916.

MacKillop, James. " 'Beurla on It': Yeats, Joyce, and the Irish Language." *Éire-Ireland*, 15 (Spring 1980), 138-148.

————. "Finn MacCool: The Hero and the Anti-Hero in Irish Folk Tradition." In *Views of the Irish Peasantry*, eds. Daniel Casey and Robert Rhodes, 86-106.

————. "The Myth of Finn MacCool in English" Diss. Syracuse University 1975.

Maddox, James H. *Joyce's "Ulysses" and the Assault Upon Character.* New Jersey: Rutgers, 1978.

Maxwell, Constantia. *Country and Town in Ireland Under the Georges.* Dundalk: Dundalgan, 1949.

Mays, J. C. C. "Brian O'Nolan and Joyce on Art and on Life." *James Joyce Quarterly*, 11 (Spring 1974), 238-256.

Mercier, Vivian. *Beckett/Beckett.* New York: Oxford, 1977.

————. *The Irish Comic Tradition.* Oxford: Oxford Univ. Press, 1969.

Mintz, Samuel. "Beckett's *Murphy*: A Cartesian Novel." *Perspective*, 11 (Autumn 1959), 156-165.

Nelson, James Malcolm. "From Rory and Paddy to Boucicault's Myles, Shaun and Conn: The Irishman on the London Stage, 1830-1860." *Éire-Ireland*, 13 (Fall 1978), 79-105.

O'Brien, Darcy. *Patrick Kavanagh.* Lewisburg: Bucknell Univ. Press, 1975.

O'Conaire, Brendan. "Flann O'Brien, *An Béal Bocht* and Other Irish Matters." *Irish University Review*, 3 (August 1973), 121-140.

O'Connor, Frank. *A Short History of Irish Literature.* New York: Capricorn, 1967.

O'Connor, Ulick. *Brendan Behan.* New York: Grove, 1973.

O'Driscoll, Robert, ed. *Theatre and Nationalism in Twentieth Century Ireland.* Toronto: Univ. of Toronto Press, 1971.

————ed. *The Celtic Consciousness.* New York: Braziller, 1982.

O'Faolain, Sean. *The Irish.* New York: Devin-Adair, 1956.

Ó hÓgáin, Dáithi. "The Visionary Voice." *Irish University Review*, 9 (Spring 1979), 44-61.

O'Keefe, Timothy. *Portraits of Brian O'Nolan*. London: Martin Brian and O'Keefe, 1973.

Ó Muirithe, Diarmaid, ed. *The English Language in Ireland*. Dublin: Mercier, 1977.

Ó Súilleabháin, Seán. *Irish Wake Amusements*. Dublin: Mercier, 1976.

Porter, Raymond. "O'Casey and Pearse." *The O'Casey Review*, 2 (Spring 1976), 104-114.

Powell, Violet. *The Irish Cousins*. London: Heinemann, 1970.

Quinn, David Beers. *The Elizabethans and the Irish*. New York: Cornell Univ. Press, 1966.

Rafroidi, Patrick and Maurice Harmon, eds. *The Irish Novel of Our Time*. Lille: L'Universite De Lille, III, 1975-76.

Robinson, Fred Norris. "Satirists and Enchanters in Early Irish Satire." In *Studies in the History of Religions*, ed. Lyon and Moore. New York: Macmillan, 1912.

Robinson, Hilary. *Somerville and Ross*. New York: St. Martin's, 1980.

Ronsley, Joseph, ed. *Myth and Reality in Irish Literature*. Ontario: Wilfrid Laurier Univ. Press, 1977.

Rural Life in Ireland. London: Methuen, 1904.

Ryan, John. *A Bash in the Tunnel*. Brighton: Clifton, 1970.

Scott, Bonnie K. "John Eglinton: A Model for Joyce's Individualism." *Éire-Ireland*, 12 (Summer 1975), 347-357.

Spenser, Edmund. *A View of the Present State of Ireland*, ed. W.L. Renwick. London: Eric Partridge, 1934.

Stockwell, La Tourette. *Dublin Theatres and Theatre Customs*. Tennesse: Kingsport, 1938.

Warner, Alan. *Clay is the Word*. Dublin: Dolmen, 1973.

Watters, Eugene and Matthew Murtagh. *Infinite Variety: Dan Lowrey's Music Hall, 1879-97*. Dublin: Gill and Macmillan, 1975.

Comic Theory

Corrigan, Robert W. ed. *Comedy: Meaning and Form*. California: Chandler, 1965.

Elliott, Robert. *The Power of Satire*. Princeton: Princeton Univ. Press, 1960.

Feibleman, James. *In Praise of Comedy*. New York: Russell and Russell, 1962.

Freud, Sigmund. *Jokes and Their Relation to the Unconscious*, ed. and trans. James Strachey. New York: Norton, 1963.

Frye, Northrop. "The Argument of Comedy." In *Theories of Comedy*, ed. Paul Lauter. New York: Anchor, 1964, 450-460.

Grotjohn, Martin. *Beyond Laughter*. New York: McGraw-Hill, 1970.

Pearce, Richard. *Stages of the Clown.* Carbondale: So. Illinois Univ. Press, 1970.

Torrance, Robert. *The Comic Hero.* Boston: Harvard Univ. Press, 1978.

Schulz, Max. *Black Humor Fiction of the Sixties.* Athens: Ohio Univ. Press, 1973.

Styan, J. L. *The Dark Comedy.* Cambridge: Cambridge Univ. Press, 1968.

Sypher, Wylie, ed. *Comedy.* New York: Doubleday, 1956.

Welsford, Enid. *The Fool.* New York: Farrar and Rinehart, 1935.

Index

Abbey Theatre, 22, 96; and Beckett, 90–91, 120; and Gregory, 22, 24; and Joyce, 106; and O'Casey, 149, 158; and Synge, 73, 79; and Yeats, 22, 110.

A.E. (pseud. of George Russell), 105, 107,119.

Aislinge Meic Conglinne (The Vision of MacConglinne), 72, 86, 146–147.

Arnold, Matthew, 15–16, 19–20, 22, 39, 80.

Beckett, Samuel, 47, 68, 110–122, 138, 163–164, 175–176; and Joyce, 120; macabre humor, 71, 113, 115–116, 118–121, 176, 179; Works: *Molloy*, 116–117, 121; *More Pricks than Kicks*, 116–117; *Murphy*, 110–122, 148, 174–175; *Waiting for Godot*, 27, 116, 121.

Behan, Brendan, 30, 47, 93, 161–172, 176; macabre humor, 162–164, 176, 178; and O'Casey, 92–93, 162–163, 165; Works: *Borstal Boy*, 93, 166–170; *The Hostage*, 50, 93, 164–166; *The Quare Fellow*, 161–164, 166.

Bergson, Henri, 104.

Boucicault, Dion, 8, 28, 35, 40, 69, 75, 77, 145; humor, 35, 80, 174; language, 53, 74, 79, 140; and O'Casey, 47, 50, 150–152, 155–156; Works: *Arrah-na-Pogue*, 53–54; *The Colleen Bawn*, 48–50, 54, 56; *The Shaughraun*, 50–54, 177.

Bourgeois, Maurice, 41–43, 79.

Boyle, Capt. Jack, 150, 152, 155–160, 163, 170, 175, 176.

brogue, 1, 3, 6, 11, 41, 43, 45, 52, 104–105. *See also*, dialect, Irish English.

Buile Suibne (The Frenzy of Sweeny), 78, 131–136, 146

bulls and blunders, 11–12, 36–37, 41–42, 45, 52, 80, 140.

Carens, James, 109.

Carleton, William, 13, 23, 28, 53, 58–69, 72–73, 77, 79–80, 136, 174; Gaelic culture, 5, 13, 23; and Kavanagh, 138–140; macabre humor, 40, 71, 176–177; Works: *The Black Prophet*, 10, 59–60; "Denis O'Shaughnessy Going to Maynooth," 59–67; *The Emigrants of Ahadarra*, 59; "A Legend of Knockmany," 33–34; "Phelim O'Toole's Courtship," 35–39, 61; "Phil Purcel, the Pig Driver," 12; *Red Count O'Hanlon*, 32; "The Three Wishes," 34.

Clarke, Austin, 90, 120.

comic hero, 6–7, 13, 44–45, 48–50, 54–56, 58–79, 176.

Corkery, Daniel, 3, 71, 86–87.

Cormac's Glossary, 86, 146.

Cúchulainn, 33, 85, 91, 121.

Dedalus, Stephen, 28, 66, 90, 102–108, 128, 175; and Flann O'Brien, 135–136; and Murphy, 113–114; and Tarry Flynn, 140, 142, 145.

dialect, Irish English, 1, 21, 23, 25, 36–37, 52–53, 60, 72–74. *See also*, brogue.

Dickens, Charles, 9.

Duggan, George, 42.

Emmet, Robert, 53–54, 98–99.

Finn MacCool, 33–34, 53–54, 97–98, 110, 127, 131, 133–134, 138.

Flanagan, Thomas, 53, 64, 67.

Flynn, Tarry (character), 72, 92, 139–142, 144–148, 175.

Gogarty, Oliver St. John, 100, 108-109.
Gregory, Lady, 5, 14, 22-27, 37, 79-80, 137; dialect, 21, 72, 140; humor, 9, 35; and Joyce, 95-97; and Yeats, 22-23; Works: *Cuchulain of Muirthemne*, 73; *Hyacinth Halvey*, 23-25; *The Full Moon*, 14, 23; *The Jackdaw*, 23; *Poets and Dreamers*, 87-88; *Spreading the News*, 23-25, 145; *Visions and Beliefs*, 14; *The Workhouse Ward*, 23-24, 26
Good, Fluther, 150-155.

Handy Andy (Andy Rooney), 1, 4-7, 9-14, 24, 46-47, 72, 79, 166, 175.
Hellfire Club, 101.
Holloway, Joseph, 55-56.
Hyde, Douglas, 4, 72-73, 98.

Irish Revival, 19, 22, 24, 57, 90, 96-98, 104, 106-107, 120, 123, 148, 158.
Irish Wake, 70, 116, 162, 174, 177.

Joyce, James, 28, 88-90, 94-109, 138; and Beckett, 120, 122; and Carleton, 59, 61; and Flann O'Brien, 91, 123, 126-131, 133, 135; and Kavanagh, 147; and O'Casey, 158; macabre humor, 71, 98-99, 176; Works: *The Dubliners*, 89; *Finnegans Wake*, 33, 102, 128, 134, 174, 177; "Gas from a Burner," 89-90; "The Holy Office," 96-97; *A Portrait*, 58, 100, 103, 124, 137, 138; *Ulysses*, 53, 90, 97-109, 128, 153, 166.

Kavanagh, Patrick, 89, 91-93, 147, 172; and Carleton, 138, 140; and Joyce, 147; Works: "The Great Hunger," 143-144; *The Green Fool*, 138-141; "The Paddiad," 91; *Tarry Flynn*, 87, 138-148.
Kelleher, John V., 19.
Kiely, Benedict, 64-65, 179-180.
Krause, David, 33, 52, 71, 158.

Laing, R.D., 134-136.

Lecky, W.E.H., 3, 28-29.
Liadain and Curithir, 146.
Lover, Samuel, 9-10, 14, 23, 28, 40, 69, 74, 91; humor, 9, 35-36, 42, 174, 177; Works: *Handy Andy*, 4-5, 9-14, 23, 25, 31-32; *Rory O'More*, 44-46.

macabre humor, 5, 30-31, 34, 40, 50, 59-60, 62, 70, 89, 177-179. See *also*, Beckett, Samuel; Behan, Brendan; Carleton, William; O'Brien, Flann; Joyce, James; O'Casey, Sean and Synge, John M.
Martin, Violet. See, Somerville and Ross.
Mercier, Vivian, 24, 62, 88-89, 120.
Mangan, James Clarence, 95-96, 144.
Myles Na gCopaleen, See, O'Brien, Flann.
Moore, George, 107-109.
Mulligan, Buck, 90, 95-109, 114, 175.
Murphy (character), 90, 110-119.
Myles-na-Coppaleen (character), 6, 48-50, 56, 127.

O'Brien, Flann, 71, 90-91, 137-138, 163, 172; as Myles Na gCopaleen, 126, 130; Works: *An Béal Bocht*, 123-125; *At Swim-Two-Birds*, 89-91, 123, 127-137, 148. See *also*, Joyce, James.
O'Casey, Sean, 11, 22, 32, 92, 125, 141, 149-160, 174-176; humor, 36, 53, 71, 160, 176, 178; Works: *Juno and the Paycock*, 50, 149-150, 156-160; *The Plough and the Stars*, 149-156, 178. See *also*, Behan, Brendan and Boucicault, Dion.
O'Connor, Ulick, 166, 170, 172.
O'Keefe, John, 42.
omadhawn (clown or fool), 1, 4-5, 9-15, 22-27, 36, 39, 45, 78, 124.
O'More, Rory (character), 44-48, 50, 55.
O'Nolan, Brian. See, O'Brien, Flann.
oral tradition, 3, 23, 28, 30, 80, 97.
O'Shaughnessy, Denis, 6-7, 61-68, 72, 78, 80, 173, 175.
O'Toole, Phelim, 5-6, 35-39, 44, 47, 51.

Otway, Caesar, 60, 65.

Pearse, Padraic, 153-155.
playboy (character), 1, 6, 8, 32, 65, 68-79, 93, 145, 175; type, 91-92, 147.

Raftery, Anthony, 87-88.
rapparee, 28-30, 32, 53.
Robinson, Fred Norris, 83-85.
rogue, 5-6, 28-40, 45, 47-57, 67-81, 150.
Rogues and Rapparees, 29-30.
Russell, George. *See* A.E.

satire, characteristics of, 9, 24, 26, 29, 62, 64-65, 71-72, 80-81, 83-94, 106-108, 129, 131, 147, 150.
Shaw, George Bernard, 47, 52, 61, 102, 144.
Seanachie (storyteller), 23, 61, 80, 134.
the Shaughraun (character), 56, 156, 172, 175.
Somerville and Ross (Edith Somerville and Violet Martin), 5, 15, 19-20, 22-23, 27; *Some Experiences of an Irish R.M.*, 15-22.
Spenser, Edmund, 45.
stage Irishman, 6, 11-12, 22, 41-46, 90-92, 142, 177; and Behan, 164-165, 172; and Boucicault, 46-57; and O'Casey, 151, 154.
stage Irish tradition, 22, 52, 101, 109-110, 137, 145, 163, 166, 176.
Stephens, James, 173.
Swift, Jonathan, 21, 24; and Beckett, 111, 114, 118-120; and Flann O'Brien, 126; and Joyce, 96-97, 104-106; and O'Casey, 150.
Synge, John M., 21-22, 28, 40, 51, 57, 61, 92, 174; and Beckett, 120; and Flann O'Brien, 91-92, 135-136; and Joyce, 94, 104-105; and Kavanagh, 137-138, 140, 147; and O'Casey, 158; Works: "The Aran Islands," 73-74; *Deirdre of the Sorrows*, 73; *The Playboy of the Western World*, 1, 6, 8, 13, 68-79, 89-92, 135-136, 140, 144; *The Shadow in the Glen*, 51, 69, 78, 135-136; "The Vagrants of Wicklow," 67.

Thackeray, William, 31-32, 39.
Tromdámh Guaire (*The Burdensome Bardic Company*), 85-86.

Welsford, Enid, 11.
Wilde, Oscar, 101-102, 105, 114.

Yeats, William Butler, 14, 22-23, 53, 59, 73-74, 76, 88, 110, 112, 137, 153; and Joyce, 95-97, 105, 110.